Telling it Slant

Critical Approaches to Helen Oyeyemi

For human Jon and cylon John

Telling it Slant

Critical Approaches to Helen Oyeyemi

Edited by Chloé Buckley and Sarah Ilott

sussex
ACADEMIC
PRESS
Brighton • Chicago • Toronto

2 4 6 8 10 9 7 5 3

First published in hardcover 2017, reprinted in paperback 2020, by
SUSSEX ACADEMIC PRESS
PO Box 139
Eastbourne BN24 9BP

Distributed in North America by
SUSSEX ACADEMIC PRESS
Independent Publishers Group
814 N. Franklin Street
Chicago, IL 60610

British Library Cataloguing in Publication Data
A CIP catalogue record for this book is available from the British Library.

Library of Congress Cataloging-in-Publication Data
Names: Buckley, Chloé, editor. | Ilott, Sarah, 1987– editor.
Title: Telling it slant : critical approaches to Helen Oyeyemi / edited by Chloé Buckley and Sarah Ilott.
Description: Brighton : Sussex Academic Press, 2016. | Includes bibliographical references and index.
Identifiers: LCCN 2016032685 | ISBN 9781845197902 (hardback)
| ISBN 9781789760743 (paperback)
Subjects: LCSH: Oyeyemi, Helen—Criticism and interpretation. | BISAC: LITERARY CRITICISM / European / English, Irish, Scottish, Welsh. | LITERARY COLLECTIONS / Caribbean & Latin American.
Classification: LCC PR6115.Y49 Z88 2016 | DDC 823/.92—dc23
LC record available at https://lccn.loc.gov/2016032685

Contents

Acknowledgements

The editors have made all efforts to obtain the permission of all rights holders in all territories of any work referenced herein from which substantial quotations have been taken. In particular, we would like to acknowledge the following rights holders:

Quotations from *The Opposite House* by Helen Oyeyemi, copyright © 2007 Helen Oyeyemi. Used by permission of Bloomsbury Publishing PLC.
Quotations from *White Is for Witching* by Helen Oyeyemi, copyright © 2009 Helen Oyeyemi. Used by permission of Pan Macmillan.
Quotations from *Mr Fox* by Helen Oyeyemi, copyright © 2011 Helen Oyeyemi. Used by permission of Riverhead, an imprint of Penguin Publishing Group. A division of Penguin Random House LLC. Also by permission of Pan Macmillan.
Quotations from *Boy, Snow, Bird* by Helen Oyeyemi, copyright © 2014 Helen Oyeyemi. Used by permission of Riverhead, an imprint of Penguin Publishing Group, a division of Penguin Random House LLC. Also by permission of Pan Macmillan.
Quotations from *what is not yours is not yours* by Helen Oyeyemi, copyright © 2016 Helen Oyeyemi. Used by permission of Riverhead, an imprint of Penguin Publishing Group, a division of Penguin Random House LLC. Also by permission of Pan Macmillan.

The publishers apologize for any errors or omissions in the above list and would be grateful to be notified of any corrections that should be incorporated in the next edition or reprint of this book.

We would like to thank all contributors for their enthusiasm and cooperation in bringing this collection together. Our special thanks go to Vicky Ilott for the original artwork that she created for the cover, which sums up the themes and styles of Oyeyemi's work beautifully. We are grateful to Teesside University for sponsoring a symposium on

Helen Oyeyemi in February 2015, and to the staff and students who attended the event and facilitated a lively discussion. We owe further thanks to Teesside University and to Manchester Metropolitan University for financial support. Thanks are due to Sussex Academic Press for their support in publishing this book.

Chloé Buckley would like to acknowledge the support of colleagues at Lancaster University who helped her to complete this book whilst she was finishing her PhD and to Manchester Metropolitan University for underwriting some of the costs. She is grateful to Dr Catherine Spooner and the Contemporary Gothic Reading Group at Lancaster University for their enthusiastic discussion of Oyeyemi's *White Is for Witching*, which provided the original spark for this project. She would also like to thank Sarah Ilott for suggesting this collaboration and for her continued expertise and energy. Finally, she thanks Jon and Lucas for their love and support throughout the endeavour.

Sarah Ilott would like to acknowledge the support of her colleagues at Teesside University. She would also like to acknowledge the support of the English Section in underwriting some of the costs associated with this publication. She is grateful to Chloé Buckley for her enthusiasm, organisation and determination in seeing this project through to completion. Her family, friends, and husband John deserve thanks for their love and support throughout.

Cover Artist's Statement

The cover image responds to the 'desiccated bodies' described in Helen Oyeyemi's *White is for Witching*. Constituted from a combination of scanned flesh and found images, the woman's form is ruptured and folded in such a way as to literalise Oyeyemi's description of corsetted bodies becoming 'like parchment scrolls'.

V. ILOTT

Introduction

Chloé Buckley and Sarah Ilott

The title of this collection of essays – 'Telling it slant' – is taken from Helen Oyeyemi's second novel, *The Opposite House*, which begins by positioning readers outside of dominant and normative cultural and narrative spaces and within the titular 'Opposite House' (2008: 1). *The Opposite House* explores the trauma of cultural and bodily displacement, opening out into an imaginative space somewhere betwixt and between a real, historical London and a fantastical spiritual plain constructed out of syncretic Santeriá religious mythology. This deliberately defamiliarising opening typifies the style of Oyeyemi's work, which is positioned at the margins of histories, locations and genres. Claims of marginality are often made of authors considered within a body of postcolonial writing, and whilst this is one way of interpreting Oyeyemi's work it does not wholly account for her 'slant' perspective. Her novels require their readers to occupy a liminal space, unable to anchor themselves firmly either in the 'real' historical world or in a purely imaginative realm. Often, readers are positioned in that moment of hesitation that Todorov argues characterises the 'fantastic', unable to discern whether the events and effects of the story are supernatural or purely psychological (Todorov 1973: 33). Her work defamiliarises the mundane through richly symbolic, intertextual and haunting narratives that work to undermine rather than to confirm accepted ways of knowing or being. 'Telling it slant' is a rich metaphor for Oyeyemi's literary practices, summing up a body of work that mixes literary genres, divorces cultural traditions from linear notions of origin, and disrupts modes of identification that persist in seeing the individual as discrete or complete, regardless of a postmodern worldview that has sought to tell us otherwise for decades. Oyeyemi's brand of postmodern, postcolonial writing, however, does not celebrate the fragment or the incomplete. It is not an affirmation of a postmodern identity negotiated at the margins, but a troubling whisper that highlights the trauma that seeps into histories, nations and bodies that have become broken.

Oyeyemi's oeuvre is attracting a growing body of criticism, but no reading of her work to date attempts to account for more than one or two individual novels from a particular theoretical perspective. The chapters in this collection represent an extensive exploration of Oyeyemi's work, drawing on a variety of critical perspectives and literary theories. Her work demands a wide-ranging approach that can articulate the diverse polyphony of the novels. Thus, though there is not one dominant critical perspective that can assert a comprehensive and totalizing reading of Oyeyemi's fiction, the readings in this collection all recognise the importance of intertextuality as both a critical tool and as a way of conceiving of the literary work. For Roland Barthes, the text is a network, rather than a closed, monumental object emanating from one source, a particular author, or a single culture. Oyeyemi's work exemplifies Barthes's image of the text as 'a multidimensional space in which a variety of writings, none of them original, blend and clash' (1977: 146). In different ways, each of Oyeyemi's novels blend, mix and clash myths, narratives, fragments, tropes, and images from a breath-taking range of literary and cultural sources. Often, this intertextuality is overt and metafictional, but in a more fundamental sense Oyeyemi's novels are informed and constituted by voices and texts from multiple sources.

In part, this is because Oyeyemi is a voracious reader: 'There are so many books in the world I haven't read,' she complains, 'sometimes I feel as if they're all piled on top of my head weighing me down and saying, "Hurry up"' (Oyeyemi in Sethi 2005: n.p.). Here, Oyeyemi classes herself as 'more of a reader than a writer' in her insatiable desire to consume fiction. However, Oyeyemi's identification as a reader buckling under the weight of literature belies the complex role allotted to readers in her work. Her reading manifests in her works in their playful intertextuality, of course, but these works also constitute what Barthes terms the 'writerly' text' (1974: 4). Barthes's notion of the 'writerly' text is defined against the 'readerly' text, the latter of which is a traditional literary work such as the classical realist novel. Whilst the 'readerly' text locates the reader as the receiver of a fixed, predetermined, reading, the 'writerly' text 'is *ourselves writing*, before the infinite play of the world (the world as function) is traversed, intersected, stopped, plasticized by some singular system' (Barthes 1974: 5). Oyeyemi's works proliferate meanings but disregard narrative structure and closure, prompting instead readings that do not give texts meaning per se, but that appreciate their plurality. Following Barthes's concept of the writerly, Oyeyemi's works locate their readers inside the network of the text and require them to produce meanings that are not final or totalizing. In this collection, we therefore place

Oyeyemi in conversation with other authors, theorists and mythologies. Oyeyemi is variously considered in the context of women's writing alongside feminist writers such as Barbara Comyns, Hélène Cixous, Angela Carter and Margaret Atwood, as working in the fairy tale tradition, rewriting traditional European fairy tales like 'Fitcher's Bird' and 'Bluebeard' as well as making reference to traditional storytelling from China and the Indian Subcontinent, and in relation to the twentieth-century cinema of Alfred Hitchcock. Oyeyemi's novels are also read in dialogue with gothic literature of the eighteenth and nineteenth centuries, and in particular with the legacy of Mary Shelley's *Frankenstein* (1818), with Yoruba mythology, and with Caribbean folklore, indicating some of the myriad ways in which Oyeyemi engages with and transforms literary traditions.

The metaphor of the text as a network, or woven fabric made up of numerous threads, suggests a model of reading that travels outwards towards other texts, rather than inwards towards a central, definitive meaning. Through their intertextuality, Oyeyemi's works also offer a rhizomatic structure suggestive of that described by Gilles Deleuze and Félix Guattari in *A Thousand Plateaus* (1987: 7–15). Like this rhizomatic model of the book, Oyeyemi's works make multiple heterogeneous connections, with any thread connecting to any other (Deleuze and Guattari 1987: 7–8). Oyeyemi's rewriting of a multiplicity of texts and literary traditions often results in what Deleuze and Guattari describe as a rupturing of unified structures or narratives, shattering a seemingly familiar story only to start it up again along new lines (Deleuze and Guattari 1987: 9). Oyeyemi's works do not offer a neat image of the world, but constitute an attempt to deterritorialise their readers, leading outward to destabilizing new locations. Reading Oyeyemi's works as intertextual and rhizomatic assures that they remain open. Though their multiple codes and threads cannot be reconstituted into a coherent and definitive totality, this should not lead the reader or the critic into the aporia of deconstructive criticism. Meaning can be drawn from Oyeyemi's works, though it is only possible to make sense of these writerly novels in provisional and dynamic ways. Conceiving of Oyeyemi's novels as intertextual thus necessitates considering their cultural and social contexts, acknowledging that the imaginative spaces Oyeyemi constructs intersect with lived contemporary and historical, social and political realities.

This intersection with the socio-political realities of her day – alongside her biographical status as a Nigerian immigrant in a country that prizes whiteness and marginalises migrants – means that it is possible to read Oyeyemi's work as constituting what Deleuze and Guattari have termed 'minor literature.' Oyeyemi's English language and settings are 'deterritorialised' and her works are relentlessly and unapologetically political, with the fates of individual characters always connected to the social circumstances in which they are subjugated (as women, non-whites, or homosexuals, for example) (Deleuze and Guattari 1983: 16). As Deleuze and Guattari state with reference to Kafka as an example of an author of minor literature: 'the question of the individual becomes even more necessary, indispensible [sic], magnified microscopically, because an entirely different story stirs within it' (1983: 16). Deleuze and Guattari's work does tend to place an undue representative burden on the 'minor' author by creating a binary with 'great' literatures that they do not deem to be so necessarily political, which we would wish to resist (it is problematic to assume that writing that represents a normative or majority position is not also deeply imbricated in political power structures). However, it is undoubtable that Oyeyemi's work does indeed function to 'express another, potential community, to force the means for another consciousness, and another sensibility' (Deleuze and Guattari 1983: 17). The readings of Oyeyemi's work included here are thus located in the specific politics of the places and spaces they engage, whilst individual characters are considered as social and political beings that whilst not being representative of any totalising position, are often symbolic of the negotiation of intersecting traumas.

Oyeyemi's first three novels are set in contemporary Britain and engage with its multiculturalism. Growing up in London in the nineties and noughties, Oyeyemi would have been party to the dominant narrative of multiculturalism's ascent and decline, as the official party-line of multiculturalism introduced with Tony Blair's Labour government in 1997 soured following race riots in northern cities and increasing Islamophobia following the 9/11 attack on the Twin Towers and Britain's subsequent involvement in the 'War on Terror.' The idea of multiculturalism as a failed ideal largely centred on the purported failure of communities due to the 'parallel lives' lived by those in the towns affected by the riots (CCRT 2001: 10). Yet Oyeyemi undermines this dominant narrative of British multiculturalism, neither celebrating its diversity nor bemoaning it as a failure located in individual communities that have not done the work of assimilation. Oyeyemi's representation of Britain is one that foregrounds its colonial history and highlights the power dynamics that have consistently worked to construct non-white communities as Other to a British self that is located in whiteness. Hers are tales of the alienation, atomisation and overt racism experienced by black and minority ethnic communities in contemporary Britain.

In Oyeyemi's British novels (*The Icarus Girl, The Opposite House, and White Is for Witching*) there are three marked sites of Britishness that point towards particular socio-political contexts, each of which prioritise different criteria in the construction of a national identity. Oyeyemi situates her first two novels in London, a city often celebrated for its multicultural diversity in contemporary fiction and criticism, as well as political discourse. In contemporary British literature, novels such as Hanif Kureishi's *The Buddha of Suburbia* (1990), Zadie Smith's *White Teeth* (2000), and even Monica Ali's *Brick Lane* (2003) have depicted London as the backdrop for playful experiments with and performances of identity, ending with a sense of optimism about the future. Critical readings of the metropolis have often followed suit, and John McLeod's *Postcolonial London: Rewriting the metropolis* depicts 'The postcolonial writing of London as a utopian space of cultural and social transformation [that] is often engaged with a transfigurative politics', engaging with authors who 'daringly imagine an alternative city in which divisive tensions are effectively resisted, and progressive, transformative kinds of social and cultural relationships are glimpsed' (2004: 16). Oyeyemi's depiction of London counters this utopian image of multiculturalism, by making it into an uncomfortable space for her characters. Jess, in *The Icarus Girl*, is bullied at school and dislikes leaving the safety of her understairs cupboard, never mind venturing out into the London streets. Maya, in *The Opposite House*, yearns to return to Cuba, even though she has lived in London since she was very young. Her London flat becomes a haunted space as the novel progresses, and its proximity to the bleak and decaying spiritual realm of the Opposite House becomes increasingly apparent.

In *White Is for Witching*, the protagonists live in Dover, an important border town both in that it serves as a port and houses a detention centre for asylum seekers entering the UK, and because its white cliffs have long stood as a metonym for England, connoting an idea of Englishness predicated on imperial ideology. In Oyeyemi's novel, Dover becomes a liminal space, its borders – both imaginative and real – are porous and unstable, and the image of Englishness offered by the white cliffs is transposed into a source of anxiety. Oyeyemi's use of the Dover setting reflects Vron Ware's sentiment, that:

> The politics of the border represents one of the most important issues of our epoch, one that calls for constant vigilance and intervention by those who are opposed to fortresses of wealth and privilege surrounded by the dispossessed, the starving, and the desperate, whose temporary services are required as labor but who have no right as citizens. (2010: 106)

The Kentish setting of *White Is for Witching* is used to reflect a broader cultural malaise associated with xenophobic fears of a threat to the national body politic in terms of intrusion of the racial Other. It allows for the exploration of the interconnected political and theoretical questions of hospitality, the foreigner and the border that are central to constructions of Britishness. Katie Burton's chapter in this collection considers the importance of borders in Oyeyemi's work, reading the construction and deconstruction of bodily borders as symbolic of a wider process of the negotiation of a British identity.

Finally, Oyeyemi revisits Cambridge, where she attended university, recasting it in *White Is for Witching* as an exclusive community in which neither black British Ore nor Kosovan refugee Titiana ever feel at home. A seat of learning and English upper-class education, Cambridge is recast as a gothic 'tomb' in which gloomy portraits of former masters glare down at outsiders and the bedrooms unnervingly feel as though they have 'more than four corners' (Oyeyemi 2009: 145, 147). On the surface, student life seems inclusive in its diversity, but Ore's invitation to join the Nigerian society only upsets her as it reinscribes her difference and marks her as Other. London (as emblematic of a multicultural diversity whose utopian image is at odds with lived reality), Dover (as representative of the xenophobic nationalism that focuses on borders and exclusion), and Cambridge, (in which ideas of a meritocracy reinforce a classist snobbery by refusing to acknowledge differences in opportunity), are juxtaposed productively in Oyeyemi's early work, in which her characters' sense of belonging and national identity is constantly negotiated yet never complete.

Many of Oyeyemi's cultural influences are drawn from a Yoruba mythology aligned with the author's Nigerian heritage. Oyeyemi's first novel is set partly in Nigeria, whilst her second and third both make reference to Nigerian characters and gods. Yet these cultural references – to abiku, aje, and juju, for example – are often divorced from sites of origin and affiliated with spaces and peoples that have no explicit link to Nigeria. In an article on *White Is for Witching*, Helen Cousins suggests that the 'fraternization between colonizer and colonized has led to a hybridization, collapsing or blurring of the opposition by affiliating the Yoruba elements with the white characters in the novel', effecting what she terms a 'Yoruba Gothic' (2012: 50). This dislocation coincides with Oyeyemi's own sense of being at a remove from Nigeria 'and thus not particularly Nigerian' (Martin 2007: n.p.). Such a collapsing of times and spaces works to foreground Britain's colonial ties and thereby rehistoricise contemporary understandings of race and racism in Britain. Oyeyemi's second and third novels also make reference to Caribbean influences with characters – worldly and otherworldly – that derive from there, including the mythical souçouyant and Orisha drawn from the syncretic Afro-Caribbean Santeriá religion. The confluence of Britain, Nigeria, and the Caribbean in these works calls to mind the slave trade that saw enslaved Africans transported to the Caribbean in order to produce the cash crops that supported Britain's growth into a capitalist and imperialist power. As well as re-centring Britain's imperial history by calling to mind these former ties, the Yoruba legacy in Oyeyemi's works also links to an epistemological shift, in which new ways of knowing and experiencing the world are foregrounded. Nicola Abram's chapter in this collection follows up the Yoruba connection in Oyeyemi's dramatic works *Juniper's Whitening* and *Victimese*, exploring how they draw on West African myth to pose an alternative mode of reading. Abram suggests that a specifically Yoruba epistemology is required to make sense of the different modes of knowledge enabled by the experience of watching Oyeyemi's plays performed onstage.

Oyeyemi's fourth and fifth novels introduce another context to her oeuvre as their plots are situated in New England. Oyeyemi moved to New York for a short period in 2007 in order to attend a creative writing graduate programme at Columbia University, and with her move so readers are introduced to cultural influences drawn from New York and New England, as Hawthornes, Whitmans and Novaks begin to litter her texts. However, Oyeyemi's own sojourn in New York was short lived, and she left for Prague after one semester, describing New York as a 'confrontational city' and the workshop model of teaching as 'stressful' (Nazaryan 2014a: n.p.). Unlike the British locations of Oyeyemi's fiction that are distinguishable and specific, the locations of Oyeyemi's North American plots lose some of that specificity. The Flax Hill location of Oyeyemi's fifth novel is identified as being in Massachusetts, however it appears to be a fictional amalgamation of small-town New England locales, and is described in imprecise terms by the bus driver as simply being in 'New England' (Oyeyemi 2014: 11). This location functions as a space of reinvention for her characters, reflecting the lived experience of multiple waves of migrants – from the confederate south and from Eastern Europe, in particular – who have found a new space to call home. The heroine of *Boy, Snow, Bird,* Boy Novak, recalls this history of American migration through the allusion to the actress Kim Novak, star of Hitchcock's *Vertigo* (1958), who was born in Chicago to Czech parents. New England serves in Oyeyemi's fiction as a heterotopic space in which ideas of Englishness are reconfigured and made 'new.' As with all 'real' locations in Oyeyemi's fiction, the New England and New York locations of *Boy, Snow, Bird* and *Mr Fox* are heterotopic in the sense suggested by Michel Foucault since they offer a space in which multiple places exist at once, spaces which both reflect and distort reality, in which past and present and reality and fantasy blur (1987: 46–49). Oyeyemi's lingering concern with ideas of Englishness can be detected in *Mr Fox,* which takes its title from Joseph Jacob's *English Fairy Tales* (1890) and offers rewritings of traditional European fairy tales by a New York City novelist and his muse.

As well as ranging widely across locations and bringing them together in ways that highlight multiple waves of migration and interconnected histories and cultures, Oyeyemi's work makes important new interventions in contemporary gothic, postcolonial writing and feminist literature. First, Oyeyemi's work constitutes an innovative engagement with gothic literature as tropes from a two-hundred year-old western gothic tradition are re-contextualised in order to examine the fraught process of establishing identity in a postcolonial, postmodern context. *White Is for Witching,* for example, uses the model of gothic narrative identified by Robert Kiely as aiming at the breakdown and disintegration of character and narrative coherence (1972: 193, 153). *White Is for Witching* asks its readers to untangle the threads of a narrative that at its outset offers a number of possible endings. Elsewhere, Sarah Ilott argues that the novel strategically employs gothic to explore how English identity remains haunted by the colonial past, reflecting 'the contemporary manifestations of fear and trauma associated with the "unhomely" experience of migration and the psychological and material traumas of alienation and racism that cause ethnic minority characters to experience themselves as Other' (2015: 54). Oyeyemi recontextualises the figure of the vampire as it appears in Bram Stoker's *Dracula* as a figure embodying racist fears of 'reverse colonisation' to explore how white Miranda's fetishistic desire for black British Ore constitutes a kind of vampirism that threatens to eradicate Ore completely. Oyeyemi's use of gothic to explore the trauma of postcolonial and postmodern identity formation in turn offers new ways to read gothic and prompts readers to reconsider its tropes. Most pertinently, Oyeyemi reconfigures the discourse of monstrosity, offering characters that initially seem monstrous, but as the narrative twists and skews, seem equally heroic. Jo Ormond explores this aspect of Oyeyemi's narratives in her chapter on victims and villains in Oyeyemi's fairy tale rewritings *Boy, Snow, Bird* and *Mr Fox*, and Chloé Buckley explores the shifting configuration of the gothic child as simultaneously innocent and disturbing in *The Icarus Girl* and *The Opposite House.*

Oyeyemi is also a trouble-making feminist voice in the landscape of contemporary fiction, employing feminist strategies in the way that she rewrites genres, parodies other texts, and critiques the characterisation of 'woman' in literature. In particular, Oyeyemi revisits what Kate Ferguson Ellis designates the 'feminine' gothic of Anne Radcliffe and the Brontë sisters (1989: xiii). Oyeyemi borrows the gothic tropes of incarceration and victimisation in the depiction of ambiguous heroines such as Miranda Silver in *White Is for Witching* and Mary Foxe in *Mr Fox*. However, these characters also shift through a multiplicity of narrative positions traditionally associated with 'woman' – including victimised gothic heroine, femme fatale and witch – refusing to settle into one role. Thus, Oyeyemi suggests her female characters are nomadic subjects, echoing Rosi Braidotti's affirmative feminist philosophy. In Braidotti's writing, the nomadic subject is the self in progress, a dynamic being who is located at the intersection of power and social relations, but who is able to occupy an affirmatory rather than oppressed position within those relations. In Braidotti's words, the feminist nomadic subject is 'a non-unitary and multi-layered vision [. . .] a dynamic and changing entity' (2011: 5). Oyeyemi also revisits the gothic birth myth of *Frankenstein,* explored in Ellen Moers's study of 'female gothic' (1985: 93). Throughout her oeuvre, but particularly in *The Opposite House* and *Boy, Snow, Bird,* Oyeyemi explores the complexities of relationships between mothers and children, which are sometimes antagonistic and painful and other times nurturing and affirming. Oyeyemi's fictions disrupt a binaristic construction of the mother as either nurturing or monstrous. Oyeyemi also revisits the work of second wave feminists, notably Hélène Cixous, bringing their radical and affirmatory writing into dialogue with the concerns of women often written out of Western histories of feminism. As Sarah Ilott suggests in her chapter on 'Female Monstrosity, Appetite and Voice', Oyeyemi combines the political and psychological frameworks of second-wave feminism with an intersectional approach that recognises differences in female experience (particularly with regards to race, class, and sexuality). In so doing, she is able to repurpose the powerful symbolism and sense of possibility of an alternative existence embodied by authors like Cixous for black and minority women, nevertheless retaining a realistic perspective on patriarchal and imperial systems that intervene and resist the transformative potential suggested by writing, thinking, or being otherwise.

Finally, Oyeyemi's oeuvre marks a new direction in postcolonial studies. Writing from and largely locating her work within the former colonial centre, the binarising model of writing back famously advocated in Bill Ashcroft, Gareth Griffiths and Helen Tiffin's seminal study – *The Empire Writes Back* (1989) – does not hold for Oyeyemi's work. Neither does Oyeyemi's work celebrate the utopian potential of what Homi Bhabha terms 'Third Spaces' in multicultural societies in which boundaries between cultures are productively collapsed (1994: 56). Instead, Oyeyemi's work foregrounds enduring colonial legacies referenced through the physical and psychological trauma associated with migration, displacement, racism and contested national identities. This turn to the legacies and negotiation of trauma reflects a recent turn in postcolonial studies, evidenced in the considerable volume of work on postcolonial trauma published in the last decade (see for example Najita 2006; Craps 2012; Ifowodo 2013; Ward 2015; Brett 2016). Oyeyemi's articulation of trauma resonates with Marianne Hirsch's concept of 'postmemory', as 'a *structure* of inter- and trans-generational transmission of traumatic knowledge and experience. It is a *consequence* of traumatic recall but (unlike post-traumatic stress disorder) at a generational remove' (2008: 106). Oyeyemi's literature engages with the legacies of historical traumas of enslavement, colonisation and displacement as experienced at a generational remove in the contemporary world, thereby articulating the enduring legacies of historical traumas for a new generation and exploring (often unsuccessful) attempts at healing and reconciliation. Her fiction articulates these historical traumas through the monsters, hauntings and doubles familiar to a gothic canon, following in the footsteps of authors such as Salman Rushdie (*Shame*, 1983), Toni Morrison (*Beloved*, 1987), Shani Mootoo (*Cereus Blooms at Night*, 1996) and Arundhati Roy (*The God of Small Things*, 1997), all of whom have turned the Western-dominated gothic genre to their own purposes in engaging with the legacies of colonial violence and slavery.

Oyeyemi wrote her first novel, *The Icarus Girl*, whilst she was still at school in London. It was published in 2005 whilst she was reading political and social sciences at Cambridge University. The novel is set predominantly in contemporary London, but it also includes sections set in Ibadan, Nigeria and the 'Bush', or wilderness of the mind. These settings allow Oyeyemi to explore what would become key paradigms of her subsequent oeuvre: the dislocation and alienation wrought by colonial ties and ruptures experienced by those from migrant communities, and fantastic or gothic spaces that overlap and imbue otherwise all-too-real spaces with richly symbolic meaning. In what becomes her trademark postcolonial gothic style, Oyeyemi's first novel draws on the language of haunting and monstrosity familiar to aficionados of an Anglo-American gothic tradition, interspersed with Yoruba mythologies that both recall Britain's former colonial ties and rework the gothic genre.

The Icarus Girl follows the story of eight-year-old Jessamy Harrison, a mixed-race girl with an English father and Nigerian mother, as she attempts to negotiate her identity and a sense of belonging in a place where both Britishness and beauty are associated with whiteness. A reclusive child, Jess frequently takes comfort in small spaces where she is isolated from human contact, until her parents decide to take her to Nigeria. Jess considers 'Nye. Jeer. Reeee. Ah.' to be 'ugly' (Oyeyemi 2006: 9), the defamiliarising rendering of the word reflecting a fear that she feels of the place that she perceives as liable to claim her for its own and 'pull her down against its beating heart' (Oyeyemi 2006: 9). Once there, Jess is addressed by her Grandfather as Wuraola, her Nigerian name that she has never previously heard. This is a moment of rupture, as she associates the name with 'another person [. . .] someone who belonged here' (Oyeyemi 2006: 20). The passage functions as an early signal that Jess is unable to reconcile facets of her identity and heritage that she perceives to be in conflict.

It is in Nigeria that Jess meets Titiola, whose name she fears mispronouncing and therefore renders TillyTilly. TillyTilly follows Jess back to England, claiming that her and her parents have just moved into the neighbourhood, but it becomes increasingly apparent that no one else can see her. Interpretations proliferate around this character, who is variously constructed as an imaginary friend, as a stand in for Jess's dead and previously forgotten twin, Fern, and as an abiku, or evil spirit, that is possessing Jess in order to bring about her demise. TillyTilly starts out as Jess's friend and confidante, but her actions become increasingly malignant as she 'gets' people and punishes them on Jess's behalf, often without Jess's consent. Though Jess is initially enthralled by TillyTilly's magical abilities to fly, become invisible, and switch places with her, she ultimately finds herself struggling for control of her own body. Jess's relationships with her peers and family become increasingly fraught as she is possessed by the jealous TillyTilly, who smashes possessions, makes Jess's Dad sick, and alienates Jess from her closest friend, Shivs. The novel ends with Jess and TillyTilly struggling for Jess's body following a car crash in Lagos that leaves Jess in a coma.

Published in 2005, *Juniper's Whitening* and *Victimese* are Oyeyemi's only dramatic works to date. Though they represent a departure in form from *The Icarus Girl,* these plays work to develop themes and concerns inaugurated in Oyeyemi's debut novel. Oyeyemi wrote both plays whilst studying at Cambridge University, initially penning them for performance by friends and colleagues at Corpus Christi College. *Juniper's Whitening* was performed over the period of a week in April 2004 at the Corpus Playroom, by the Fletcher Players Society. For Oyeyemi, the plays were an 'experiment' in producing an immediate result from her writing; they allowed her to see an audience's reaction to her words and characters (Lyons 2006: n.p.). Character is central to *Juniper's Whitening* and *Victimese,* as both explore the psychological consequences of trauma suffered by a young adult woman. As in *The Icarus Girl,* psychological breakdown intertwines with supernatural horror so that the audience cannot tell where one ends and the other begins. These plays locate their small cast of characters in claustrophobic one-room settings that evoke a particularly female gothic sense of entrapment.

Victimese is set in the college residence of troubled student Eve, and centres on her attempts to fend off various visitors. Seeking to preserve her isolation, Eve does not wish to interact with others; she refuses food and drink and is determined not to leave her room. However, the room is as much a prison as it is a safe haven, a space in which Eve is compelled to inflict harm on her body and begins to lose the threads of her identity. *Victimese* is not simply a study in psychological breakdown, though. Eve is represented as a figure of sacrificial female subjectivity, unable to bear the burden of guilt and sin placed upon her. An explicitly gothic literary tradition is also signalled in Eve's fear that leaving her room will bring her face to face with her nemesis and double, 'that person who's carrying my death for me' (Oyeyemi 2005: 43).

More surreal than *Victimese, Juniper's Whitening* is ostensibly a domestic drama about a troubled relationship between lovers Aleph and Beth, both of whom are haunted by past transgressions. The titular Juniper functions as an unstable third position in the drama, variously functioning as the child of the household, as Beth's rival, and then her double. The domestic setting of the play is in fact the gothic house, both because it is home to a gothic family haunted by secrets, and because its topography is determined by a critical tradition that reads the gothic house as a symbol of the psychological interior. As in *Victimese,* the action occurs in one room, but characters are warned not to ascend to the attic. The recesses of this gothic house are haunted by past trauma, as Beth realises when she cries, 'someone's coming from the attic, someone's treading on the air; making it sink' (Oyeyemi 2005: 26). As well as this ghostly presence, Beth is haunted by Juniper, her double and avatar of the gothic child. In the gothic tradition the child often figures as an ambivalent symbol for the sins of the past and the hopes for the future of the gothic family. Juniper is the receptacle for Beth's repressed trauma – namely her child abuse at the hand of a parent and the subsequent murder of her own child – and also its manifest inescapable presence. *Juniper's Whitening* thus shifts register from domestic drama to gothic horror.

Taken as a pair, *Victimese* and *Juniper's Whitening* stage concerns central to Oyeyemi's later novels, here formulated as two distinct problems: the impossibility of a meaningful connection between self and Other and the difficulty of writing, voicing or otherwise performing an identity marked as Other by the politics of gender and race. The aggressive dialogue that characterises both plays dramatises the impossibility of forging meaningful connections with another through language. As characters struggle to make themselves understood, they become cynical: 'I'm supposed to honour you with the pretence that you can reach me,' scoffs Eve at her former lover (2005: 38). Taking up E. M. Forster's exhortation to 'only connect', Oyeyemi dramatises over and over the failure of interpersonal relationships forged through language (Forster, *Howard's End,* 1910). This is later explored in dialogue with the promises of romance fiction in Oyeyemi's *Mr Fox,* though this latter text is markedly more hopeful than Oyeyemi's plays. Failure thus seems to characterise both *Juniper's Whitening* and *Victimese* since neither suggest that a fragmented self can be made whole, either through articulating and assimilating past trauma or by forging connection with others.

The title of Oyeyemi's second novel, *The Opposite House*, is taken from an Emily Dickinson poem that is referenced through the epigraph: 'There's been a Death, in the Opposite House.' The novel is concerned with the death of certain cultural practices and the process of forgetting that accompanies doubly displaced peoples and traditions. The house that Oyeyemi uses to evidence this symbolic death, or passing away, is the 'somewherehouse', which is inhabited by Orisha: gods of the syncretic Santería religion that evolved in the Spanish Caribbean as a means of allowing enslaved Africans to continue worshipping Yoruba gods in the guise of Catholic saints. The somewherehouse has doors in London and Lagos, the latter of which becomes impossible to open as the narrative unfolds. To borrow Arundhati Roy's terminology, this is the first of Oyeyemi's 'history houses', in which the physical space of the building is used to reflect a particular history – in this case one of displacement and cultural amnesia (Roy, *The God of Small Things,* 1997). A second iteration of the 'history house' motif is to be found in Oyeyemi's subsequent novel, in which a Dover guesthouse embodies a xenophobic national(ist) history.

The fantastic and richly symbolic Santería plot is one of two narrative strands, which reflect each other but do not meet. The second plot is focussed on Maja, a black Cuban who has been living in London with her family since they emigrated when she was five years old. Now in her early twenties, Maja is pregnant with her first child and living with her partner, white Ghanaian Aaron. Plagued by morning sickness and struggling to find a memory from her past to pass onto her child, Maja is haunted by what she terms 'my Cuba' (Oyeyemi 2008: 45). Maja's solitary memory from Cuba is from their farewell party, during which she sits under a table with another child, listening to a woman sing. The memory is one of guilt and trauma, as Maja witnesses the other child having a fit and shies away without thinking to report the incident to an adult. However, when Maja meets Magalys – the girl from the memory – many years later in the UK, she is shocked to find that it was in fact herself who had had the fit. This drives Maja's desire to return to Cuba, as she finds herself with no memories to pass on. Yet despite buying a plane ticket, Maja never returns. Read in conjunction with the Orisha strand of the tale, in which return to Nigeria through the Lagos door becomes impossible, the implication is that whilst the past may haunt, historical wounds incurred by rending people from places cannot be healed through return.

The Opposite House explores the intersection of different forms of oppression based on ethnicity, class and gender. Not only does Maja witness the atomisation of black identities through a multicultural discourse that insists on distinguishing her from 'roots' Africans in a way that denies commonalities of oppression, but she also experiences oppression along gendered lines, as her pregnancy renders her an object in the service of her foetal subject in the eyes of Aaron. In her chapter on 'Intersectionality and Monstrosity', Anita Harris Satkunananthan focuses on the interconnectedness of different manners of oppression, arguing that it is important to bring culture, class and gender into conversation together.

The plight of the formerly colonised subject residing in the former colonial centre remains a significant concern in Oyeyemi's *White Is for Witching,* though the focus of this novel is more ambiguous than either *The Icarus Girl* or *The Opposite House*, with multiple narrative voices producing a deliberately discordant polyphony of themes and ideas. Set in the seaside town of Dover, *White Is for Witching* foregrounds its concern with racism in two ways: first, it describes the suffering of non-white subjects tortured by a racist and inhospitable guest house, 29 Barton Road; second, it explores the plight of asylum seekers being held at a detention centre on the outskirts of the town. However, the novel is also ostensibly a Bildungsroman, focusing on the coming-of-age of twins, Miranda and Eliot Silver, following the death of their mother. Miranda is particularly affected by grief, which leads to a worsening of her eating disorder, pica. The disorder manifests both in the refusal of food and in a craving for non-nourishing substances, which in Miranda's case is chalk, as befits the Dover setting and the novel's concern with whiteness and Englishness. As Miranda's condition worsens and she grows ever thinner, she is increasingly unable to account for her whereabouts and fears she is subject to possession by the evil spirit animating the guest house, known as 'the goodlady.' Miranda is then implicated in a series of vicious attacks on Dover's asylum seekers as well as complicit in the guest house's increasingly violent attempts to expel its unwanted non-white guests. Animated by the goodlady, or Miranda's great grandmother, Anna Good, 29 Barton Road is also reluctant to let Miranda go, even as she prepares to leave for university at Cambridge. The novel diverges along multiple narrative threads, at turns narrated by Eliot, by 29 Barton Road and by Ore, Miranda's black British girlfriend. These multiple threads and conflicting voices function to lose track of Miranda, who fragments and eludes the house, her family and readers.

White Is for Witching is also an explicitly psychological story, drawing on psychoanalytical ideas to explore not only the plight of the non-white subject living in England, but also the trauma produced at the heart of white identity predicated on an ambivalent and unstable racist discourse. Though the fates of Ore and other non-white characters in *White Is for Witching* are not incidental to the plot, these characters are placed at the novel's periphery since its main focus is the psychological unravelling of white British Miranda. Miranda's dissolution is due in part to a racist discourse that haunts English identity, here embodied by the spirit of Anna Good and symbolised by the chalk that Miranda compulsively consumes. Anna Good's hatred of those she terms 'blackies, Germans, killers, dirty' (Oyeyemi 2009: 118) reveals what Homi Bhabha has termed the fetish at the centre of colonial and racist ideology. This fetish of 'the Other' is necessary to white identity, but it reveals that this identity is predicated on anxiety and defence even as it seeks to assert its mastery (1983: 27). Racist discourse constructs 'the Other' in a stereotypical way in order to assert its mastery and coherence in opposition, but this coherence is simultaneously threatened by the division signalled by the racist fetish and by the possibility of 'the Other' returning the look, or gaze, cast upon it. Miranda's desire for Ore represents this fetishistic desire to consume the skin and body of 'the Other' desired and feared simultaneously for the difference it signals and its permeability. Natalya Din-Kariuki offers a reading of *White Is for Witching* in the context of race and psychology alongside others of Oyeyemi's works, complementing a psychoanalytical reading of the double with West African narratives of duality and returning spirits. For Din-Kariuki, the idea of the double is crucial to understanding Oyeyemi's negotiation of the problem of mimetic representation for raced bodies, the blurring of lines between 'real' and fictive bodies, and the problems of writing more generally. Din-Kariuki's reading of the novel adds to a body of scholarship that reads Oyeyemi's work alongside other African diasporic literature.

Oyeyemi's fourth novel, *Mr Fox* (2011) represents a shift away from the concerns and styles demonstrated in her earlier work. Foremost, *Mr Fox* is a collection of short stories linked by a connecting narrative that acts as a portmanteau for a series of fairy tale retellings. The overarching narrative is significant in itself, but each short story can also be read in isolation. There is a shift from an explicitly gothic register into a playful metafictional mode that sees Oyeyemi experimenting with fairy tale, the romance genre and 'screwball' comedy. Oyeyemi locates the novel in the United States, in a loosely rendered 1930s New York, conjured out of 1930s and 1940s Hollywood depictions in 'screwball comedies' such as Hitchcock's *Mr and Mrs Smith* (1941) – whose bickering high society couple recall St. John and Daphne Fox – as much as out of historical record. *Mr Fox* retains threads from Oyeyemi's earlier fiction. Primarily, the novel expresses a deep concern with interpersonal relationships and the troubled connections between self and other, rendered here as 'fraught and painful' (Bender 2011: 16). Furthermore, Oyeyemi draws the literary playfulness that characterises *Mr Fox* from her long-running interest in intertextuality. The intertextuality of *Mr Fox* is signalled overtly as the novel sets about rewriting the tropes of traditional fairy tales. Oyeyemi's short stories concern themselves with a cycle of tales depicting a tyrannical and murderous spouse and his trembling, virginal bride. The most famous of these is the French folktale 'Bluebeard', first published in Charles Perrault's *Histoires ou contes du temps passé* in 1697. Oyeyemi takes her title from a rewriting of the Grimms' tale, which features in Joseph Jacobs' *English Fairy Tales* as 'Mister Fox' in 1890. *Mr Fox* transposes these tales of misogyny, male privilege and male violence and places them in dialogue with both the promises of romance fiction and the threat of slasher horror. In this way, male-female relationships, and concomitant concerns of power, privilege and voice, are unravelled and reconfigured.

The plot of the novel centres on the turbulent but creative relationship between New York novelist St. John Fox and his made-up muse, Mary Foxe. Both characters contribute to a storytelling competition, initiated by Mary, who has become tired with St. John's penchant for killing his heroines in a variety of gruesome ways. The stories within the novel and the overarching narrative also explore the marriage between St. John and Daphne as a rivalry that brews between Mrs Fox and Mary Foxe. As the novel progresses, this rivalry blossoms into a tentative friendship, which comes to be as important as the twisted romance between Mary and St. John. Mary Foxe increasingly draws on Daphne's strength in her attempts to assert her independence from the male novelist who brought her into being. More hopeful than Oyeyemi's preceding works, *Mr Fox* reveals the misogyny at the heart of literary and social convention, and struggles to establish successful channels of communication between its central characters, but its ambivalent ending also promises the possibility of emancipation for the initially incarcerated Mary Foxe and gestures towards a more equal and satisfying relationship between Daphne and St. John in the future.

Mr Fox has not yet garnered much academic critical attention, and has received a mixed reception in the broadsheet and literary press, where its deliberately fragmented narrative structure is met with some dissatisfaction. Reviewers praise *Mr Fox* as a more mature novel than its predecessors, describing it as ambitious and complex (Sethi 2012: n.p.; Nazaryan 2014: 1). In contrast, critics also suggest that the novel feels incoherent. One critic calls it a 'paradoxical read'; each short story satisfies in itself, but the 'general muddle' of the whole does not (Williams 2011: n.p.). Aimee Bender, writing in the *New York Times* wonders if 'some readers may crave more overt connections between the stories' (2011: 16). The fragmented shape of *Mr Fox*, however, and the fragmented experience of reading it, are crucial to the novel's revisionist agenda. Oyeyemi reveals and disrupts what she posits as a fundamental human need to order fragmentary experience into a structuring narrative, warning how such narratives limit and ensnare those who weave them. In the short story 'Fitcher's Bird', the protagonist Miss Foxe loves fairy tales because they offer a narrative of experience in which all is 'overcome by order in the end' (Oyeyemi 2012: 65). Unfortunately, Miss Foxe's love of fairy tale, and its generic cousin, the romance, leads her to a cruel end. Submitting herself to the violence of Fitcher, she expects to be transformed into a princess – 'dazzlingly beautiful, free' – but, as the closing lines of the tale relate 'this is not what happened' (Oyeyemi 2012: 69). Miss Foxe's beheading at the hands of Fitcher seems at first a straightforward feminist cautionary tale, warning of the dangers of attempting to mould oneself in the image of femininity demanded by patriarchy. However, placed in context with the rest of the stories, this tale becomes more than a feminist reinvention of the cautionary tale: this is not the end for Miss Foxe. Though the protagonist does not become the princess she imagines in this particular tale, she is revived in subsequent tales, which allow her to undergo reinvention and transformation. As suggested above, Mary Foxe is constantly in motion, a nomadic and adaptable subject. David Punter's chapter in this collection examines the motif of the fox, suggesting that the terror in Oyeyemi's work is located through the trauma of finding inside the self a foreign body that troubles fantasies of wholeness.

Whilst some of the promises of romance are preserved in this collection, *Mr Fox* is nevertheless ethically concerned with the relationship between women and men in patriarchal society and literature. Many of the stories reframe violence against women, but they do not efface it. Thus, the novel should also be read in a tradition of feminist rewritings of fairy tales, one of the most famous examples of which is Angela Carter's *The Bloody Chamber* (1979), which is most concerned with wolves but opens with a rewriting of Bluebeard. Assessing the novel as part of this feminist tradition, Natalya Din-Kariuki claims that Oyeyemi's rewriting of the Bluebeard tale 'remoulds and eventually smashes traditional gender relations' (2013: n.p.). Certainly, in terms of its structure, *Mr Fox* upsets the hierarchy of writer and muse. All three characters – St. John, Mary and Daphne – contribute to the collection, but the author of each tale is never made clear.

Oyeyemi's fifth novel, *Boy, Snow, Bird*, retains a thematic engagement with some of the topics that have become integral to her oeuvre, including madness, the harmful relationships between women, and alienation that occurs on the level of family drama but is reflective of greater political forces. She also engages once again with the alienation experienced by minority communities. However, like *Mr Fox*, this is transposed to a specifically North American context, engaging with racial passing amongst African-Americans rather than the British multiculturalism of her earlier works. Set in 1950s New England, *Boy, Snow, Bird* is a reworking of the fairy tale 'Little Snow White' (Brothers Grimm, 1812) that interrogates the tale's concern with a 'snow white' version of beauty. The specific setting in McCarthy's US ensures that the fairy tale rewriting moves beyond the psychological symbolism of characters that are reduced to stock types (the crone, the wicked stepmother, the virginal innocent) and sees individual character and action as deeply imbued with the specifics of socio-political circumstance.

Boy Novak, the novel's protagonist, is born in the Lower East Side of Manhattan in the 1930s and grows up without a mother, whose absence is never discussed by her physically and psychologically abusive father. The protagonist's childhood is rendered in the second person, which has the effect both of interpolating the reader and suggesting the trauma incurred by the young woman who tries to distance herself from the events: 'He'll punch you in the kidneys, from behind, or he'll thump you on the head and walk away sniggering while you crawl around on the floor, stunned' (Oyeyemi 2014: 6). After a particularly horrific punishment that sees her tied up in a rat's cage in the cellar with a hungry rat taking bites from her face, Boy takes a small sum of money and catches a bus out of New York, riding it to the last stop at Flax Hill, an artisan town where 'People make beautiful things' (Oyeyemi 2014: 22). Despite some initial resistance to Boy on account of her name, her origins and her lack of skill, she soon settles into the area, takes up a job in a second-hand bookshop, and meets the man who will be her husband: Arturo Whitman.

It is made clear from the outset that Boy's marriage is not one borne out of love, an emotion that she reserves for her childhood sweetheart, Charlie Vacic. Rather, Boy is pragmatic about her relationship with Arturo, and 'halfway to smitten' with Arturo's daughter, Snow, whose beauty and charm ingratiates her to all those around her (Oyeyemi 2014: 78). However, the relationship between Boy and her step-daughter turns sour when Boy gives birth to her own daughter, Bird. As a nurse proclaims when she is born, 'That little girl is a Negro', leading Boy to see what she had not noticed before: that Arturo's family are black and have, for generations, been attempting to pass as white, even sending away Arturo's sister Clara to live in Mississippi with an Aunt on account of her dark skin (Oyeyemi 2014: 131). Yet Boy surprises her relatives by sending not Bird but Snow away to live with her Aunt Clara, in an attempt to prevent Bird from living in the shadow of her sister.

The trope of motherhood is particularly emphasised through a sub-plot involving Boy's journalist friend, Mia, who goes on the trail of Boy's mother in order to discover 'what someone goes through when they refuse to be a mother', having herself recently undergone an abortion (Oyeyemi 2014: 289). What Mia discovers, is that Boy's mother, Frances, is now Frank, the man that Boy believed to be her rat-catcher father. Frank is described as an alter-ego, adopted following a rape that led to his daughter's birth. Frances, an outgoing and intelligent lesbian embarked on doctoral study, becomes Frank, an abusive and violent man who assaults his subsequent girlfriends and his daughter. A further intertext for *Boy, Snow, Bird* is thus Iain Banks's *The Wasp Factory* (1984) in which the young protagonist, Frank, finds out that his birth sex was female and that he is not in fact a mutilated man as his father has led him to believe. In this Frank-enstinian construction of identity, transgender is associated with monstrosity and the result of trauma. This has led to a number of criticisms pertaining to the apparent transphobia of Oyeyemi's novel, in which 'trans-ness is the result of trauma, and the trans parent is evil and abusive' (Anon 2014: n. p.). The revelation of Frank's trans identity does seem rather abrupt, a convenient device that leads to an ending that implies resolution and the healing of the relationship between Boy, her daughter and her recently-returned stepdaughter, as they travel to New York in order to 'wake up' Frances (Oyeyemi 2014: 305). This unusually redemptive ending is at odds with an oeuvre that elsewhere resists closure and the sense of unified, complete or 'true' selves that exist without reference to social context or the influence of others. We might instead read the ending as indicative of the social damage done when certain modes of identification (as homosexual, as black, as a mother who does not want children) are socially proscribed, a position that is explored in far more detail and due complexity in the narrative of racial passing that runs throughout.

Snow's beauty is prized, particularly by her elderly relatives, because it enables her to pass as white, with the pale skin, dark hair and red cheeks of her fairy tale counterpart. It is this reification of Snow's skin that causes Boy to send her away, redrawing an us/them, white/black binary by aligning herself with her biological daughter. As she suggests, 'it is not whiteness itself that sets Them against Us, but the worship of whiteness' (Oyeyemi 2014: 275). In this manoeuvre, Oyeyemi foregrounds the internalised racism of the Whitman family that causes them to prize whiteness and thereby alienate members of their own family. A focus on beauty not as a static characteristic but as a process of becoming is foregrounded at the outset through a description of the artisan town of Flax Hill in which people 'make beautiful things' but are 'interested in the process, not the end product' (Oyeyemi 2014: 22–3). Beauty is also thematised throughout the novel through a focus on characters' ambiguous relationships with mirrors that often fail to behave in an appropriate manner, as is the case with the wicked stepmother of the source fairy tale. Cousins's chapter on 'gender, race and beauty', places Oyeyemi's works in dialogue with other 'revisionist mythmakers', considering the ways in which a desire for beauty plays out alongside constructions of race.

Works Cited

Anon. 2014. For Angel H: Boy, Snow, Bird by Helen Oyeyemi. Feministe. http://www.feministe.us/blog/archives/2014/10/23/for-angel-h-boy-snow-bird-by-helen-oyeyemi/ Barthes, R. 1974 / 1990: *S/Z*. Oxford: Blackwell.

Barthes, R. 1977: *Image Music Text.* Translated by Stephen Heath. London: Fontana Press.

Bender, A 2011: A Writer of Slasher Books Finds More than a Muse. *New York Times*. http://www.nytimes.com/2011/10/30/books/review/mr-fox-by-helen-oyeyemi-book-review.html?_r=0.

Bhabha, H. 1983: The Other Question: Stereotype, Discrimination and the Discourse of Colonialism. *Screen* 24 (6), 18–36.

Bhabha, H. 1994: *The Location of Culture*. Oxon: Routledge.
Braidotti, R. 2011: *Nomadic Theory: The Portable Rosi Braidotti*. New York: Columbia University Press.
Brett, M.G. 2016: *Political Trauma and Healing: Biblical Ethics for a Postcolonial World*. Grand Rapids: Eerdmans.
CCRT (Community Cohesion Review Team). 2001: Community Cohesion: A Report of the Independent Review Team, chaired by Ted Cantle. *Cohesion Institute*. http://resources.cohesioninstitute.org.uk/Publications/ Documents/ Document/DownloadDocumentsFile.aspx?recordId=96%26file= PDFversion.
Cousins, H. 2012: Helen Oyeyemi and the Yoruba Gothic: *White Is for Witching*. *The Journal of Commonwealth Literature* 47(1), 47–58.
Craps, S. 2012: *Postcolonial Witnessing: Trauma Out of Bounds*. Basingstoke: Palgrave Macmillan.
Deleuze, G. and Guattari, F. 1983: What is a Minor Literature? *Mississippi Review* 11(3), 13–33.
Deleuze, G. and Guattari, F. 1987: *A Thousand Plateaus*. Translated by Brian Massumi. Minneapolis: University of Minnesota Press.
Din-Kariuki, N. 2013: Natalya Din-Kariuki on Helen Oyeyemi. *Asymptote*. http://www.asymptotejournal.com/special-feature/natalya-dinkariuki-on-helen-oyeyemi/.
Ferguson Ellis, K. 1989: *The Contested Castle: Gothic Novels and The Subversion of Domestic Ideology*. Urbana; Chicago: University of Illinois Press.
Foucault, M. 1984: Of Other Spaces: Utopias and Heterotopias. Translated by Jay Miskowiec. *Architecture /Mouvement/ Continuité* 5 (1), 46–49.
Ifowodo, O. 2013: *History, Trauma and Healing in Postcolonial Narratives: Reconstructing Identities*. Basingstoke: Palgrave Macmillan.
Ilott, S. 2015: *New Postcolonial British Genres: Shifting the Boundaries*. Basingstoke: Palgrave Macmillan.
Kiely, R. 1972: *The Romantic Novel in England*. Boston: Harvard University Press.
Lyons, G. 2006: Interview: Helen Oyeyemi. *Aesthetica*. http://www.aesthetica-magazine.com/helen-oyeyemi/.
Martin, M. 2007: Oyeyemi's Opposite House. *NPR*. http://www.npr.org/templates/story/story.php?storyId=11384738.
McLeod, J. 2004: *Postcolonial London: Rewriting the metropolis*. London: Routledge.
Moers, E. 1985: *Literary Women: The Great Writers*. Oxford: Oxford University Press.
Najita, S.Y. 2006: *Decolonizing Cultures in the Pacific: Reading History and Trauma in Contemporary Fiction*. Abingdon: Routledge.
Nazaryan, A. 2014: Here Comes Helen. *Newsweek Global* 162 (12): 1–4.
Nazaryan, A. 2014a: Helen Oyeyemi, a postmodern literary wizard. *Independent*. http://www.independent.co.uk/arts-entertainment/books/features/helen-oyeyemi-a-postmodern-literary-wizard-9213132.html.
Oyeyemi, H. 2005/2006: *The Icarus Girl*. London: Bloomsbury.
Oyeyemi, H. 2005: *Juniper's Whitening and Victimese*. London: Methuen.

Oyeyemi, H. 2007/2008: *The Opposite House*. London: Bloomsbury.
Oyeyemi, H. 2009: *White Is for Witching*. London: Picador.
Oyeyemi, H. 2011/2012: *Mr Fox*. London: Picador.
Oyeyemi, H. 2014: *Boy, Snow, Bird*. London: Picador.
Sethi, A. 2005: I didn't know I was writing a novel. *The Guardian*. http://www.theguardian.com/books/2005/jan/10/fiction.features11
Roy, A. 1997: *The God of Small Things*. London: Fourth Estate.
Sethi, A. 2012: Review: *Mr Fox* by Helen Oyeyemi. *The Guardian*. http://www.theguardian.com/books/2012/may/13/mr-fox-helen-oyeyemi-review.
Todorov, T. 1973: *The Fantastic: A Structural Approach to a Literary Genre*. Translated by Richard Howard. Cleveland: Case Western Reserve University Press.
Ward, A (ed.). 2015: *Postcolonial Traumas: Memory, Narrative, Resistance*. Basingstoke: Palgrave Macmillan.
Ware, V. 2010: The White Fear Factor. *Terror and the Postcolonial*. Edited by Elleke Boehmer and Stephen Morton. Chichester: Wiley-Blackwell, 99–112.
Williams, C. 2011: Helen Oyeyemi: *Mr Fox*. *The AV Club Book Review*. http://www.avclub.com/review/helen-oyeyemi-emmr-foxem-62444.

CHAPTER

1

Witches, Fox-Fairies, Foreign Bodies: Inflections of Subjectivity in *White Is for Witching* and *Mr Fox*

DAVID PUNTER

When approaching a novelist, it would be good to feel that one had a clear grasp on her work; no doubt this offers a kind of stability, a sense of knowing where one is coming from and where one is going to. But even while restricting myself to two of Helen Oyeyemi's novels, *White Is for Witching* (2009) and *Mr Fox* (2011), I have found this quite impossible, and this essay constitutes an attempt to wonder why. In fact, most of it is a meditation on why it is so difficult to feel 'anchored' in Oyeyemi's work, and how this sense of disorientation contributes to the appeal, the success and the challenge of her novels.

I would like to begin with what is perhaps a rather obvious formulation, which is that the subject, subjectivity itself, is displaced in these novels. The subject – in the sense of the individual, certainly, but perhaps also in the alternative sense of the topic – is not centre-stage; instead it is 'subjected' to all manner of interference. From the beginning, the novels seem to say, there is something outside the self, beyond the subject, which haunts you; which may even in some strange sense want you, but for what purpose is never fully imaginable. The boundaries of the self are unstable, permeable, they do not protect, and here it may be that, according to the ongoing logic of the uncanny, it is twins and doubles which represent the most dangerous uncertainties of all. As we know from Freud, doubles may promise survival, in the sense that they provide an assurance that one may, in some sense, 'outlive oneself.' Else, they may presage death, in that the presence of the double demonstrates that the self is putatively fully replaceable, and occupies but a temporary role in a continuing narrative of which one is not the centre (Freud 1919). In Oyeyemi, this twin, or double, takes many forms; it can be a brother, it can be the author, it can be a surrogate – *mon semblable*, one might say, *mon frère* (Baudelaire 1993: 6).

In fact, it sometimes seems in Oyeyemi that the central problem – if there can be such a thing – is about trying to invent, from scratch what a fully human relationship might be. And this occurs in terms of relationships to the other, but also in terms of the relationship to the self. It is not, in Oyeyemi, as though we are born with an innate understanding of what it means to be human; for many of her characters, there are no suitable models from which inferences might be drawn. Instead, each event occasions a new response, and the process of becoming human is everywhere confronted with difficulties and obstacles. An example occurs in *White Is for Witching*:

> She tensed, and I cracked her open like a bad nut with a glutinous shell. She split, and cleanly, from head to toe. There was another girl inside her, the girl from the photograph, all long straight hair and pretty pearlescence. This other girl wailed, 'No, no, why did you do this? Put me back in.' She gathered the halves of her shed skin and tried to fit them back together across herself. (Oyeyemi 2009: 230)

This raises a crucial question about Oyeyemi, which is whether this alienation, this sense that the unprotected self is too weak, too vulnerable to confront and engage with the outer world, is an unconscious product of traumatic circumstance, or a willed defence against the unacceptable. This is a reminder, whether conscious or not, of some recent developments in psychological theory and practice. Where the psychoses had formerly been thought of as a controlling set of behaviours with their own internal, albeit devastating, logic, it is now more customary to think of psychotic symptoms, however dire and however far they might go in preventing the subject from engaging with what we consider to be a 'normal' life, as themselves protections or defences (see, for example, Pillmann and Marneros 2004). They can be seen as defences against a fate even worse than having to live with florid symptoms, with all the difficulties that entails, namely the complete dissolution of the self. Such disintegration is an ever-present threat for Oyeyemi's characters.

One might be reminded of the array of horrifying symptoms of dissociation displayed by Annabel in Angela Carter's startling novel *Love* (1971), who has continually to reinvent herself because nothing around her seems fully recognisable; or of Beryl Bainbridge's even more terrifying *An Awfully Big Adventure* (1989), in which the protagonist is, in the search for an identity and reassurance as to her own presence in the world, continually making phone calls apparently to her mother and receiving helpful replies. In fact, it turns out at the end that she is phoning the speaking clock. Meanwhile, she is trying out a sexual relationship but only, as she says, as a 'preparation' for what it might be like to have such a relationship in the 'real' world, whatever that might be. The issue here is of the difference between experiencing a world into which one might naturally fit, and a world from which one might feel constantly alienated.

Just so here in *White Is for Witching* there is a doubling of the self, the inside and the outside: the inside needs protection and cannot stand exposure, it has to gather around itself a camouflage, although the problem then becomes that this camouflage might be all too readily taken for 'the real thing', and thus the inner self moves farther and farther away from genuine engagement. Or, perhaps, what Oyeyemi is questioning is whether there is indeed such a thing as genuine engagement. In some kind of post-Baudrillardian world, are all our encounters mirages, are they all simulacra, and if so of what (Baudrillard 1995)? Is there a level of the real to which we might all ascend, or is that too a delusion, a cover-story for a multitude of radical isolations?

To return to the title: the implications of 'white is for witching' are, of course, manifold. First we might think of the white witch, the apparently benign figure who will preserve us from the darknesses that might otherwise threaten to engulf us. But we need to think also of skin colour, of cross-cultural witches, and what might be concealed inside. Here we could turn, although it is not my major concern in this essay, to Oyeyemi's *Boy, Snow, Bird* (2014), the entire plot of which hinges on an uncanny series of inter-generational passings – a passing on of secrets, naturally, but also passing in the racial sense – we are frequently unsure of racial issues, as we turn out to have been, by the end, even of the gender of one of the significant characters.

In *White Is for Witching* there are also the white cliffs of Dover – an ironic guarantee of national identity and hence cultural order, and also, in the novel, an ever-present, hovering possibility of death, of suicide (Oyeyemi 2009: 88). This scenario would be the culmination of estrangement, of alienation. Yet some of Oyeyemi's characters are stranger than this, 'strangers', to take Julia Kristeva's words in a different direction, 'to themselves' (1991). What hovers around this constellation of the estranged, around this feeling of never being 'at home', is not only the perpetual isolation of being a foreigner in a foreign land, but also the sense of inhabiting a foreign body. The terrors of Asperger's syndrome and autism are never far away, whether in the sense of the unquiet self or in the symptoms of the fetish, the obsession which run through the novels. And it would be too simple to say that that 'foreign body' is *outside* the self; instead, it is *inside* the self, inescapably at home where it should not be, sitting by the fire-side, an interloper in the very spaces which one had thought most truly one's own:

> A light goes on in the house. It goes on on this floor. And each time I dream this, I try to work out what room the light goes on in, as if that matters. But I just can't work it out. It's not mine, it's not yours, it's not the light in the psychomantium. It's not the bathroom light. It's like there's an extra window, or an extra room I haven't seen before. Three figures come to the window. One is in the middle and has her arms around the other two. I can't see them, just their silhouettes through the blind. (Oyeyemi 2009: 133)

These strange presences which are also not presences pervade the text. Miranda is haunted by problematic absences, things which are simultaneously there and not there. Such present absences are also important in *Mr Fox*, where they may remind us of the fox-fairy, and to its numerous examples and avatars in Chinese fiction, where the fox-fairy is silky, seductive, full of purpose (Kang 2006). To be directed by (or to) the fox-fairy is the alternative to drifting, to not knowing how to make a self. The fox comes to supplant an internal lack of direction with a sense of purpose, whether that be social or sexual, but it turns out that this direction is inevitably towards death, the death of the self, its replacement by a different image. In many of the tales, the fox appears as a beautiful girl to a hapless young man, and immediately fills him with all the feelings he has thus far failed to experience; but then reveals herself in fox form, thus becoming simultaneously a figure for the supernatural (for the fox in Chinese mythology has celestial properties) and also as the elusive harbinger of death, as the victim is led down paths and byways in an endless pursuit which can end only in catastrophe. Some of these fox-fairies have a provenance in a process of gendered revenge: they are a response to violence towards women, whether this has been perpetrated by the victim himself or whether he has been chosen as a sacrifice for ancestral patriarchal practices. And this leads us to motifs of return, and to how Mary Foxe, in *Mr Fox*, might counter or circumvent her endless deaths at the hands of the writer. It is, of course, no accident that the writer is male.

To stay for the moment, however, with *White Is for Witching*: we might say that much of Oyeyemi's concern here is with the problematic ingestion of the Other – what it is that we can say about ourselves if our 'selves' are formed from bits and pieces, shards and remnants, of other people, other cultures, other practices, which we have incorporated or introjected, depending on the psychological success or failure of the ingestion process. This is symbolised in *White Is for Witching* by 'pica', which is the term for the ingestion of foreign bodies, foreign substances – chalk, coal, pebbles – from which no nutrition can be derived. It is described at some length as a 'medical term for a kind of disordered eating' (Oyeyemi 2009: 22). It is worth noting that it is not, as might be initially supposed, solely a term from a modern or contemporary lexicon of psychic ailments: its first recorded usage is in 1563, and is commonly attributed etymologically to the magpie, in its legendary role as the 'miscellaneous feeder' *par excellence.* Medically the only creatures who have actually been known apart from humans to have practised pica are dogs, but, presumably, only after their domestication. A connection here might be made with Jon McGregor's extraordinary novel *even the dogs* (2010), which is also crucially about addiction and the ingestion of foreign bodies. But then, it is true too that in *Mr Fox* the writer-in-the-text Mr Fox does not offer nutrition, he offers death; but more, he offers fragmentation of the self, and thus we might make a link to what 'writing as a fox' might produce in terms of the complex fragmentation in *Mr Fox*, the novel within a novel. The most obvious connection here would be to the tropes advanced by Deleuze and Guattari about 'writing as a wolf' and what that might entail in terms of questioning our habitual thinking about writing, indeed about language itself, as a peculiarly human achievement, and about writing as the outstanding guarantee of human supremacy, a supremacy which, in Oyeyemi, is always under siege (1980: 36).

So these two novels are about problematic ingestion and about the inescapability of a foreign body, of something which should be strange to the self and thus makes the self – itself – feel, to use Bob Dylan's formulation, 'violent and strange' (Dylan 1978). What they are also about is the paradoxical prospect of vanishing; they are about people who have an 'insubstantial' life, people who fade away. Miranda in *White Is for Witching* is, for example, only uncertainly *here*; she comes and goes, her sense of subjectivity (formed, for example, by resistance to the house which is also a central character in the novel, having, as it were, a speaking part) is spasmodic, a thing of fits and starts. Mary Foxe is, in a complex sense, not *here* at all; where, indeed, could she be if she is only a construction, a character in a story or set of stories – but of course that is true of all figures in writing, as it is true, although on a different level, of Mr Fox itself, the author's double or avatar.

And thus we find ourselves in a receding hall of mirrors, of bodies in flight, never quite surfacing to the reality which, we suspect as readers, might consume such characters if they were ever to be fully 'in contact.'

The point of the foreign body, we might say, is that it is never fully *here* at all; it is always in exile; and there is again a connection to the issues of race and skin colour in Oyeyemi, which have also to do with exile and a sense of not being allowed to be at home in one's own skin. And yet that formulation itself may be rather crass, for there is a circumspection, a reticence, what others might call an evasiveness, on these issues in Oyeyemi's writing, which forces us as readers to question our own constructions, our own assumptions. As we have seen, white may be for witching in several senses; but white may also be for the draining of blood, for terminal pallor, for the absenting of the longed-for vivid body. Here we may be dealing not only with pica, but also with a different medical condition, the Lesch-Nyhan Syndrome. The major feature in this rare but appalling state of mind and body is the consumption of one's own body parts. Normally, of course, this is quite mild, if such a term is appropriate: the human body can only withstand so much torture and disintegration. Common occurrences concern the consumption of lips and fingers rather than arms and legs. The biting of fingernails and the eating of one's own hair are residual symptoms of Lesch-Nyhan Syndrome. We can see much of this constellation of afflictions in Anna Good's self-consumption (Oyeyemi 2009: 23–24).

But beyond, or perhaps around, this lies the wider constellation of self-harm – in Oyeyemi's case sometimes in its more florid senses – and this can take us back to the all-embracing question of witches. Can witchcraft cause self-harm – a question which has been asked, from more or less prejudicial viewpoints, down the centuries (see, for example, Hutton 1999; Levack 2013)? I have no space here to go into a general history of witchcraft, but my main point is that witches and self-harm have been associated for a very long time. What is it that, for example, has caused the village girls to undergo an epidemic of diseases? What has caused the very cattle in the fields to manifest symptoms, whether it be those of illness or those of chronic disobedience to human domination? One of the most ready explanations down the ages has been witchcraft, in the sense that the age-old connection between the witch and a knowledge or understanding of natural process is all too available to be misinterpreted as a means of domination, as the prelude to an exercise of power which is beyond the reason of the male-dominated world. A witch, we might say, speaking in the language of patriarchal fear, is she who has achieved quasi-total control over her own life, and thus shows signs of escaping from conventional orders of gender. This, however, is also true in another sense of the author, in relation both to characters and to the reader, and this is an analogy on which Oyeyemi plays. Here is Mary Foxe talking with Mr Fox, her creator:

> We came to a halt by a lake that seemed to have clouds in it even though it was a clear day. The moor swept on after the water interrupted it, and looking at the other side I felt doubled; without turning I could see what was behind me. S.J. told me stories about the lake. He was a good storyteller; matter-of-fact, convincing. Excalibur had come out of this lake, he said, and I saw no reason to disbelieve him [. . .]. I want to stay here, I thought. I want to stay. (Oyeyemi 2011: 165)

The clouds in the lake, we might say, are stories; it is these stories which 'cloud' what might otherwise, in a fantasised world untroubled by fantasy or narrative, be a clear blue sky – although also it is only the clouds which give colour, shape, pigment, striation to the otherwise bland, colourless exterior.

We might say that two worlds intersect here, or perhaps live side by side. There is the world of shaped, but also inevitably fragmented and fragmenting, story – stories told in fragments, to be sure, but also stories which fragment clarity, which force us to accept that different subjectivities are in play in the world around us. We are, as it were, interrupted everywhere. But there remains the world on the other side, the unattainable world of the uninterrupted moor, a fantasy of childhood omnipotence, of a time when we were, or thought we were, in control of what was happening, kings or queens in our own castles.

This, then, is a further example of doubling; what is implied here is that there might be a possibility, on whatever psychic plane, of knowing what lies behind as well as what lies in front, the past as well as the future, where one has come from (even if that is only from some other author's imagination) as well as where one might be headed. But of course where one might be headed might be merely towards a further imbrication with narrative, the telling of one's own story, if one can still have a self around which to organise such a story, after so many foreign bodies – fragments of myth, metaphors, legends, elements of dream – have been ingested. One might refer to this as a kind of plea of the soul, a plea for some simple account which would be uncontested, a thanatic resignation which will avoid or circumvent all the challenges posed by 'difference', of whatever kind.

And if such a conclusion were ever to be possible, then the appearances of the world would be stable, things would not mutate into other things – girl into fox, fox into girl, or fox into woman, or indeed fox into ghost, for ghosts and haunting are always very close to the surface in Oyeyemi's fiction. Miranda, for example, is constantly haunted by her 'familiar' haunts – or, thinking again of witching, by her haunting 'familiar', one of the most common of all the tropes in stories of witchcraft. In *White Is for Witching*, nothing is less familiar – in Freudian terms of the uncanny – than the utterly familiar, than house and home. But the fox, to take the trope a little further, to go deeper into the den, can perhaps actually turn into the wolf. When we are greedy, perhaps with that unassuageable greed which is both the provocation to and the consequence of pica, with a greed for foods which give us no nutrition and leave us hungrier than when we started to eat, then we conventionally say that we 'wolf it down.' This phrase suggests an attempt to incorporate all that we suspect may be otherwise denied to us as we chase the fleeing animal of our desires through unimaginable thickets, always hungry, always running on an absolute hope, which would also be a figure for 'running on empty.' In the final story of *Mr Fox,* simply titled 'some foxes', a nameless girl chases a fox that never looks back before sinking into the snow and succumbing to the cold (2011: 266–69). Who or what is the hunter here, who or what the hunted?

And so, perhaps, the vulpine and the lupine interconnect and may even be mistaken for each other. The imagery of the wolf is everywhere in fairy story, and it is precisely this imagery of the wolf that is taken up by Carter in the stories in *The Bloody Chamber* (1979); and the question behind this, as it is behind Oyeyemi's potent uses and abuses of legendry, is about what can be tamed, what can be brought in from the wild? Is it, for example, even possible to tame one's own digestive system, to command it to one's bidding, or is that physical system itself a foreigner in the midst, obeying a different set of dictates of which the assumed self knows little or nothing?

In fact the point may be put more broadly as one which concerns who actually has command or control. Is it, for example, the fictional writer Mr Fox? Is it, in *White Is for Witching*, Miranda's father? Even knowing one's father to be in some sense innocent may be no guarantee of stopping the flow of unconscious symbolism which accumulates around fathers and daughters, made perhaps most manifest in recent times in Sylvia Plath's 'Daddy' (1962), where the father turns, or is turned, into a vampire, but one which only serves to conjure a further panoply of female vampires – just, of course, as Count Dracula does, to the joy and terror of Jonathan Harker.

But the consumption of blood is not pica, blood is nourishing, nutritional – perhaps; depending on the question of whence the blood flows. And blood, in a different sense, also guarantees continuity with the past, and this is what lies behind the insistence on female generations, the female bloodline, in *White Is for Witching*. What Oyeyemi describes – in fits and starts, as a matter of secrets and occlusions, half-glimpses in darkened and curtained rooms – is an alternative genealogy, one which is not dependent – or less dependent – on the patriarchy, one where habits and inclinations get passed down through the female line. What, however, is significant here is that this attempt at an escape from patriarchal domination does not result in any recognisable form of freedom: repetition remains, indeed it may be the only thing that does remain; we live, or so Oyeyemi seems to claim, amid the remains of repetition.

Accompanying this (and again this is a theme repeated, although with many differences, in *Boy, Snow, Bird*) is the issue of adoption (or, the adoption of 'issue', in the sense of offspring). The senses and meanings of adoption proliferate. There is indeed parental adoption; but there is also a concern about the adoption of a 'native' place or space, the possibility of finding oneself 'at home', in a world to which one has been born, even though no such world might seem immediately available. And there is, further than this, the adoption of tongue, of a language: for Miranda it sometimes seems as though she has no 'native' grasp on language at all, as though all is artificial, as though even with this most primal of gifts she is making it up as she goes along, constantly surprised when any kind of communication is effected. At one point, for example, she shakes her head, and then nods, 'unsure which movement was appropriate' (Oyeyemi 2009: 31).

But the flow of metaphor goes farther than this: for if the tongue in this sense is language, then the tongue is also the tongue that tastes, as that which might be trusted to distinguish, however faultily, between what is nutritious and what is non-nutritious. Some witches are those who up to a point feed on what is non-nutritious – we need only think of the contents of the witches' cauldron in *Macbeth* (Shakespeare 1611). Yet at the same time, and this strikes to the heart of white and dark witchcraft, they are the only possessors of the true secrets of nutrition: they bear the knowledge of what will heal, what will mend a broken heart, what will enable survival against the vast odds of being born a woman, with all a woman's vicissitudes, in a world where the stories get written by men. Witches are herbalists, and they are also poisoners: the hopes and fears of patriarchy are both abjected into the figure of the witch, as Miranda – the name, of course, signifying 'she who is to be wondered at' – becomes the receptacle of the desires and anxieties of others. It may be going a little far, but it is the case that the only things which are nutritious for some young creatures are those which have been already digested by their parents; it is only through such pre-preparation that we can be sure that our food will not, as the old saying goes, 'stick in the craw', will not choke us in the very act of consumption. But in Miranda's case, there is a further dilemma: if she does not eat 'normal' food, then the threat is that she will be fed by the Goodlady, who embodies tradition and a poisonous nationalism.

We could also consider Mary Foxe as an example of what it might be like to be brought up on the non-nutritious, in this case on mere fantasy, in a world where time and time again there is death in the air, and where the urge to substantiate is constantly thwarted: Mary cannot 'become real', she can no more 'incarnate' than any (other) words on the page can become the objects, emotions, thoughts they appear to represent. There is, to put the point in a different rhetoric, a permanent separation between sign and referent (see Saussure 1983). And this can return us to pica; for perhaps pica is not only about ingesting, but also about wanting to be *turned into* the non-human, the non-suffering, the non-passional. It may be about the wish, the need, to construct a stony self – made of marble, perhaps, but more probably of chalk, like the white cliffs of Dover, that strangely paradoxical symbol of permanence and the well-defended which can yet be so easily eroded that it becomes its own opposite. The kind of chalk being spoken of here appears to be capable of resisting all onslaught, when in fact we know that, at least in terms of Miranda's fragile sense of self, it will nevertheless be capable of shattering at the least touch. The self here may appear strong but it is fatally striated, marked with fault lines inherited from an unstable past, a cover-story for a weakness which no petrification, no formation of a 'heart of stone', can ever fully erase.

To turn again to the house, which is all-important in *White Is for Witching*, as emblem of security and yet at the same time as the holder and perpetuator of secrets which we may never fully grasp. We can connect this with vampirism, with the reduction of the bloodline to pallor, as we see all too vividly in *Dracula* (Bram Stoker 1897), where one of the major tropes is of the endless extension of the house as family, as *oikos*, as bloodline. Yet it may be said that it is precisely that 'house' – the physical housing, the constructions of the body – which has to be shed, with all its contents and paraphernalia, in order to ensure continuation of the race, the family, if such continuation is possible. Here is the house of death in *Mr Fox*:

> The morticians had done well with my father. He didn't even look that stiff. There was a waxiness to him, but it was more like that of a new doll's [. . .] I hadn't expected to be able to see that he had suffered. Now he looked cordial; it felt impossible that he could have done anything terrible, could ever have felt or thought or planned . . . if you didn't know, you could believe that this man had never done anything at all but lie there, patiently waiting for whatever happened next. (Oyeyemi 2011: 154)

It is true that we have already learned, a few pages earlier, that this stillness in death represents the withdrawal of all protection, the end of all communication, with the past; but we might also feel that it represents the possibility of a new beginning, a wiping clean of the slate.

With the father gone, perhaps life can begin afresh, but of course matters are not so simple: 'I have my father's nose. I have his ears. I touched my nose and ears. Soon they would be ashes' (Oyeyemi 2011: 154). It is this premonition of death, this awareness of the temporary and the fleeting, which is the hallmark of so much of Oyeyemi's fiction. Yet there is no terror here, instead a matter-of-fact acceptance that in the end we cannot be free from the past, that the bloodline continues to run, that unless the utmost care is exercised, then all there is is the repetition, the filling out of a predetermined set of prophecies from which there is no escape.

Mr Fox ends with a fable, and it is a variation on the fox-fairy legends I have already mentioned; it is simply called 'some foxes.' 'What can it mean', the question goes,

> for a fox to approach a girl? Foxes are solitary. A fox that seeks out human company is planning evil. Or it has something the matter with it. Rabies, or something worse. The fox watched the girl at play, and he didn't understand what she was doing – it certainly wasn't fox business. Still it interested him, and he gazed and gazed at her. (Oyeyemi 2011: 263–64)

But this fox certainly is not evil, and the 'something' that is the matter with it is, in a sense, the same 'something' as that which is 'the matter' with Oyeyemi's human characters: namely, that they are on the outside looking in, they do not have an innate sense of what it is to be human. Everything is to be interpreted from scratch: the fox has a 'sensation of a deep scratch in his side' (Oyeyemi 2011: 264). And no interpretation can ever be complete or satisfying: the fox has a 'certainty that the girl would put out the lamps before he had looked his fill' (Oyeyemi 2011: 264).

And this fox becomes human, in a sense: by the end he 'stood a head higher than she did' (Oyeyemi 2011: 77). They have lived together for a long time: she 'put down her bucket and tried to count years on her fingers. He watched her until she gave up' (Oyeyemi 2011: 277). Fox into human; 'lady into fox', to quote the title of David Garnett's strange novella (Garnett 1922). If none of Oyeyemi's girls, estranged as they are, can find solace from mortality in human relationships, perhaps there is a least the vestige of a possibility that other relationships altogether might be possible. If one can teach – as the fable here goes – the dumb to speak, then what one hears may be voices that speak something truer than the deceits and evasions of merely human interaction. But in order to enter this different realm – a realm, perhaps, of magic – then certain risks have to be run, and death has to be encountered without protection, without the defences that allow the vulnerable self to hide itself away and sleep through the years of change.

It is, then, arguable, that Oyeyemi confronts us in these two novels, *White Is for Witching* and *Mr Fox*, with a series of conundrums. The major one, to be exact, is about whether it is better to be subjected to the repressive but sometimes, in fact, quite benevolent rule of the father (as Miranda says at one point, although her father may be 'brief', it is 'all in the most likeable manner possible' [Oyeyemi 2009: 15]); or whether it is better to be subjected to the compelling violent generational rule of the female line – if indeed these two courses are entirely exclusive. Escape from repetition is not possible, although some modification of it is. Some gestures will interrupt the endless procession of noses, ears, habits, looks that otherwise maintain a rigidity which will, in the end, lead us down to the underworld without ever having looked around us, taken the opportunity to observe with the senses of the fox, of the wolf, of the other that is incorporated within us and can grant us a limited freedom at the same time as frightening us to death.

What, again, is a witch? It is a word often purely associated with women. There were men too, albeit very few, who were burned at the stake in the sixteenth century as witches – the apparently cognate terms 'wizard' and 'warlock' were not used; a witch, apparently, is a witch. But witchcraft is about power as well as about weakness; it is an entangled sign of authority and despair. Jeanette Winterson argues the case brilliantly in her novel *The Daylight Gate* (2012), where a group of disenfranchised, deprived, desperate women falsely accused of witchcraft decide to accept the label, without any idea of what it might fully mean, in the last hope that some supernatural being, impressed by their conversion and late allegiance, might ride to their rescue. This, of course, does not occur.

But the true complexity of Oyeyemi's fiction is wider than this, and concerns the possibility of a 'rule' that lies beyond the human altogether, and this is where these two books take us: towards the ingestion of the Other, towards the inescapable need to accommodate ourselves to the difficult fact that, beyond one's death, one's story, such as it is, will be told by an other. Yet if Oyeyemi's stories tell us that we can never tell our own story, that we are always subjected to somebody else's narrative, and that there is no clear path of escape from that rule, then they also simultaneously subvert that assumption, or at least challenge us to ask the question: can we tell a story which will move beyond the subjection of our own subjectivity? And beyond this, running like a thread through Oyeyemi's work, is the question of who this 'we' might be anyway, striated as such a subject position always is by the considerations of gender and ethnicity.

To tell that story, that *other* story, that story of how we have all our lives been subject to an external regime, whether it be by witchery or by the constant refusal of the author to remain dead, as in the question posed by *Mr Fox* but also in Roland Barthes's by now all too familiar dictum, is a challenge with which Oyeyemi engages, and this brings us back to the notion of the subject, in all its multifarious forms (1967). On this topic, the *subjected* in the subject, here is *Mr Fox*:

> All the times I've been frightened because of my father. My need for night-lights, my inability to sleep in a room unless I'm able to clearly see all corners from the bed – and dreams, bad dreams like messengers he sent. All the times he's frightened me. Die, then, I thought. *Die.* And I wondered when he would be gone. (Oyeyemi 2011: 135)

There is, of course, a terrible tension throughout this passage; but it really comes into shape in the last few words, for it is the case that for the father to die is not to imply that, then, he 'would be gone'; this would, indeed, be far too simple.

And here also is *White Is for Witching*, and in particular the characteristically ambiguous figure known as Sade:

> I stared at the tribal marks on Sade's face. She took my hand and drew it across the scar tissue, her expression matter-of-fact. 'Only the men are marked, usually. It would be the men who go to war, I suppose. But I wanted marks. So I copied my father's.' (Oyeyemi 2009: 212)

Sade has voluntarily undergone a process of ritual scarification, has acquired the cicatrice usually reserved for men. Seen from one angle, this might mean that she has freed herself from the plight of the woman, from the condition of being of 'the sex which is not one', in all the manifold senses of Luce Irigaray's caustic phrase (1977). But under another light, as it were, this too has been a process of subjection, going under the knife to imitate the father in a savage parody of castration. Sade (the name too is obviously significant, echoing as it does the Divine Marquis) has taken on part of the panoply of power; but perhaps in seeming to do so she has merely acquired the outer sign, or, indeed, been subjected to it.

And so, to conclude, there is throughout Oyeyemi, or at least through these two books, a measure of fear; or an attempt to measure fear; or an engagement with the impossibility of measuring that fear when one cannot be sure how far even the fear is one's own, or a function of the repetition: 'my father's nose [. . .] his ears' (Oyeyemi 2009: 154). It is possible to take on the outer signs which may instil fear in others; but the question would be at the cost of what violence to the self. Does the intensification of the signifiers of patriarchy serve to rob them of their power, or does it merely reproduce the signs of the established order?

What is clearly at stake here too is the issue of colour, of what colour itself might mean in opposition to 'whiteness' in all its ramifications, and this concern of Oyeyemi's runs like a half-concealed vein through her writing, which is itself 'marked' by questions of 'passing', issues to do with what the consequences are if one's inside world is always already pre-construed by the outer appearance and with what the further results might be if and as one takes steps to conceal or evade this stereotyping. Oyeyemi addresses these questions with a persistence which is, nonetheless, the mark of an absolute singularity, and it is here that the remarkable strength of her writing lies: in a refusal to succumb to obvious revolt, to overt anger, but instead an insistence on marking the haunting, the ambiguity, which attends our endeavours, however difficult and doomed, to construct a subject while avoiding the constructions of others.

Works Cited

Bainbridge, B. 1989: *An Awfully Big Adventure*. London: Duckworth.

Barthes, R. 1967: The Death of the Author. *Image-Music-Text*. New York: Hill and Wang.

Baudelaire, C. 1993: 'To the Reader'. *The Flowers of Evil*. Translated by James McGowan. Oxford: Oxford University Press.

Baudrillard, J. 1995: *The Gulf War Did Not Take Place*. Bloomington, IN: Indiana University Press.

Carter, A. 1979: *The Bloody Chamber*. London: Gollancz.

Carter, A. 1971: *Love*. London: Hart-Davis.

Deleuze, G. and Guattari, F. 1980: *A Thousand Plateaus: Capitalism and Schizophrenia*. Translated by Brian Massumi. Minneapolis: University of Minnesota Press.

Dylan, B. 1978: No Time to Think. *Street Legal*. Columbia Records.

Freud, S. 1919 / 1955: The 'uncanny'. *The Standard Edition of the Complete Psychological Works of Sigmund Freud. Vol. XVII (1917–1919)*. Edited by James Strachey *et al.* London: The Hogarth Press.

Garnett, D. 1922: *Lady into Fox*. London: Chatto and Windus.

Hutton, R. 1999: *The Triumph of the Moon: A History of Modern Pagan Witchcraft*. Oxford: Oxford University Press.

Irigaray, L. 1977: *This Sex which is not One*. New York: Cornell University Press.

Kang, X. 2006: *The Cult of the Fox: Power, Gender and Popular Religion in Late Imperial and Modern China*. New York: Columbia University Press.

Kristeva, J. 1991: *Strangers to Ourselves*. Translated by Leon Roudiez. New York: Columbia University Press.

Levack, B. P. (ed.) 2013: *The Oxford Handbook of Witchcraft in Early Modern Europe and Colonial America*. Oxford: Oxford University Press.

McGregor, J. 2010: *even the dogs*. London: Bloomsbury.

Oyeyemi, H. 2014: *Boy, Snow, Bird*. New York: Riverhead.

Oyeyemi, H. 2011: *Mr Fox*. London: Picador.

Oyeyemi, H. 2009: *White Is for Witching*. London: Picador.

Pillmann, F. and Marneros, A. 2004: *Acute and Transient Psychoses*. Cambridge: Cambridge University Press.

de Saussure, F. 1983: *Course in General Linguistics*. Translated by Charles Bally and Albert Sechehaye. La Salle, Illinois: Open Court.

Winterson, J. 2012: *The Daylight Gate*. London: Hammer.

CHAPTER
2
Gothic Children in *Boy, Snow, Bird*, *The Opposite House*, and *The Icarus Girl*

CHLOÉ BUCKLEY

The Gothic and the (Postcolonial) Bildungsroman

The child recurs as a gothic and unsettling figure throughout Oyeyemi's novels, revealing a concern with the symbolic work that the child performs in a contemporary project of writing postcolonial identities. Two narrative traditions – the gothic and the bildungsroman – form an uneasy coalescence in *Boy, Snow, Bird* (2014), *The Opposite House* (2008), and *The Icarus Girl* (2006), all of which explore their young protagonists' struggle to navigate key coming of age moments, from early adolescence, to leaving home, marriage, and pregnancy and motherhood. The young female protagonists in these novels belong to gothic families, threatened by secrets in their past and troubled by their future survival. In *Boy, Snow, Bird,* the family's decision to 'pass' as white in the racist society of early twentieth-century United States also prompts anxieties over the family's social legitimacy. At the centre of these typically gothic concerns about the family is a child, upon whom is placed the burden of the family's future. This gothic child unsettles the teleology of the traditional bildungsroman form and so counters a narrative found in postcolonial writing and criticism that figures the child as a hopeful marker of transformation or affirmation.

Oyeyemi's gothic children offer an unsettling alternative to the ways the child has recently been imagined in discussions of what I will call here the 'postcolonial bildungsroman', borrowing the term from Feroza Jussawalla (1997). Jussawalla argues that the bildungsroman is used by postcolonial writers in a variety of contexts and cultural locations to chart a growing-up process that sees the young protagonist turn towards an indigenous culture in an assertion of self-realization and self-affirmation (1997: 30). Similarly, discussing the more specific context of late twentieth-century black British writing, Mark Stein argues that the bildungsroman form is used by second and third generation black writers in Britain to carve out 'new spaces' that bring about the transformation of their young protagonists and of British society (2004: 21, 22). Oyeyemi's use of gothic speaks both to the body of late twentieth-century black British fiction that Stein explores, which includes novels such as Zadie Smith's *White Teeth* (2000) and Meera Syal's *Anita and Me* (1997), and to the wider category of the 'postcolonial bildungsroman' outlined by Jussawalla, which incorporates American coming of age writing as well as the European bildungsroman tradition.

Oyeyemi's British novels, *The Icarus Girl* and *The Opposite House*, are set in a postcolonial London. As Britain's former colonial centre, London is shaped by the lingering effects of Britain's past acts of colonisation. John McLeod offers the concept of 'postcolonial London' to describe the way writers from, or who have ancestral links with, countries with a history of colonisation, represent the former British colonial centre in their writing (2004: 15). McLeod suggests that London continues to be shaped by the legacy of British colonialism through post-war migration and settlement. He further insists that writings from and about postcolonial London do not suggest that colonialism is done with; it charts the ways colonialism continues to impact London's immigrant communities, often in negative ways (2004: 3). Oyeyemi's London-based novels bear up McLeod's analysis of postcolonial London, focusing on the experience of young protagonists who moved to Britain at a young age, from Nigeria and Cuba respectively. The continuing effects of colonisation and colonial ideology are seen most obviously in the racism encountered by Jess and Maja in London, but also in the characters' feelings of dislocation. They cannot connect with a 'homeland', a location which increasingly becomes inaccessible, but nor can they find an affirmative location within London itself. Jess's London home becomes haunted by the gothic spectre, TillyTilly, and Maja's London flat becomes oppressive as an inexplicable water leak, associated with the displaced Santeriá Goddess, Aya, reinforces Maja's aversion to the other tenant in the building, Miss Lassiter, making Maja increasingly desperate to leave.

Oyeyemi's British-based protagonists struggle to achieve a state of comfortable hybridity and optimism figured through the experiences of second generation immigrants in other contemporary postcolonial

British bildungsromane. Novels such as Zadie Smith's *White Teeth* (2000) mark a late twentieth-century moment of optimism about multicultural Britain that Oyeyemi's novels look back on with suspicion. McLeod notes that a 'sense of optimism about London as a multicultural and hybrid city [. . .] pervaded much opinion at the end of the decade – as evidenced by the reception of Zadie Smith's novel' (2004: 21). Though McLeod notes the existence of 'more sceptical and troubled visions' of postcolonial London, optimism continues to influence early twenty-first-century criticism (2004: 21). This is evident in Stein's analysis of another critically lauded bildungsroman of this period, Meera Syal's *Anita and Me* (1997). Stein notes that the novel offers a hopeful ending when its young protagonist discovers that the resident of the 'big house' in the town where she lives is actually an Indian man, like her father. Seeing a man who looks and speaks like her father occupying a position of wealth and status in a largely racist society 'suggests a host of future options for the protagonist' and possibilities suddenly become '*conceivable*' for her (Stein 2004: 38. Emphasis in original). This optimism about the possibility of carving out spaces of belonging, present in both the novel and Stein's analysis, is absent in Oyeyemi's British-based gothic bildungsromane, which leave their protagonists dislocated and fragmented. Jess remains in a coma, trapped in the 'Wilderness of the Bush', whilst Maja remains unable to reconcile herself to the impending birth of her baby. She returns to take up temporary residence in her childhood bedroom, neither able to settle in her London flat, nor to return to Cuba. The regression and disintegration of the protagonists' identities vigorously deny 'the postcolonial rewriting of London as a utopian space of cultural and social transformation' expressed by McLeod and unsettle Stein's assertion that the black British bildungsroman offers 'a widening of scope and a furthering of subject positions' (McLeod 2004: 16; Stein 2004: 38).

Oyeyemi's later novel, *Boy, Snow, Bird* constitutes a different intervention in the category of the 'postcolonial bildungsroman', relocating its young protagonists to the early twentieth-century United States. Within this location, Oyeyemi's characters negotiate the racism and social segregation resulting from the United States' role in the slave trade, itself a part of the machinery of European colonisation. The novel evokes a postcolonial context both in the sense of exploring the far-reaching consequences of European colonisation and slavery, and in the sense of engaging with the idea of America itself as a former colony. *Boy, Snow, Bird* evokes these postcolonial contexts whilst also writing back to a tradition of American 'coming of age' novels, in which the bildungsroman form is used to express an often 'utopian vision' of America as a young colony, freed from the strictures of its parent state, undergoing its formative adolescence (Millard 2007: 5). Kenneth Millard affirms that the American bildungsroman continually re-evokes, and thus reinvigorates, a coming of age mythology that shapes American culture (Millard 2007: 6). Stories of youthful protagonists asserting their independence and rebellion also invoke a sense of the nation as an innocent, an image that often denies its darker histories (Millard 2007: 7). The rebellion of Boy, asserting her independence by moving to Flax Hill, evokes the American coming of age narrative, as does her name, which suggests the particularly male rebellion represented by characters such as Huck Finn and Holden Caulfield, in *Adventures of Huckleberry Finn* by Mark Twain (1885) and *The Catcher in the Rye* by J. D. Salinger (1951) respectively. The bildungsroman form that figures America as an innocent asserting its rebellion as it forms a new identity is disrupted in *Boy, Snow, Bird* by a gothic structure in which the past erupts into the present, implicating characters in secrets and anxieties they attempt to escape. This irruption of the past manifests at the birth of Bird, whose dark skin colour reveals the secret the Whitman family have tried to hide: they are black Americans passing for white. This revelation evokes not only personal secrets, but the present social and cultural segregation of black and white Americans and its origins in the slave trade. The novel's shift of focus from Boy's youthful rebellion and incipient freedom, to the gothic children, Snow and Bird, unsettles the trajectory of the coming of age novels, as its protagonists are caught in a tension between future hopes and past trauma.

The first of Oyeyemi's gothic children appears in *The Icarus Girl*, which is focalised from the perspective of a haunted child, Jessamy Harrison, and evokes the twentieth-century horror film tradition of the 'evil' child through Jess's uncanny double, TillyTilly. TillyTilly radically functions to disturb the trajectory of the bildungsroman form and prompts disintegration in both the protagonist and the narrative itself. As Jess fights with TillyTilly for control over her body and identity, the narrative culminates in a car crash, and Jess becomes trapped in the non-physical location of the 'Wilderness of the Bush' where it is increasingly unclear whether she is possessed by or finally free of TillyTilly, or even whether she is dead or alive. *The Icarus Girl* draws on a gothic narrative described by Robert Kiely as aiming at the breakdown and disintegration of character and narrative coherence (1972: 193, 153). Oyeyemi's second novel, *The Opposite House*, moves away from explicitly evoking a horror tradition, but nonetheless continues to draw on the gothic in its figuration of the child as uncanny in relation to the adult protagonist, Maja. Maja is unsettled by the image of herself as a child, which she constructs out of nostalgia and unreliable memory. As the narrative progresses, Maja's sense of her identity, anchored on this unreliable childhood self, unravels. Maja is further troubled by the idea of her unborn child, which she paradoxically conceives of as symbolic of a hopeful future *and* as a parasite that threatens to take over her body. Oyeyemi's later novel, *Boy, Snow, Bird,* a fairy tale narrative centring on the antagonistic relationship between mother and child, evokes the unsettling logic of replacement from traditional gothic, and recasts the figure of the innocent child as potentially monstrous in the context of racial passing in the mid-twentieth-century United States. The beautiful whiteness of Snow modulates into an unsettling blankness as the burden of representation and hope for transformation placed upon the postcolonial child is called into question.

Constructing the Child

The bildungsroman, or novel of formation, is now frequently used to denote a form of storytelling that imagines the transformation of a child into an adult in a variety of contexts, but it is a form shot through with tension and contradictions. As Tobias Boes notes, in its original formulation, the bildungsroman's staging of the teleological development of the individual emphasises the change in its protagonist in relation to a specific national setting, and imagines 'the positive effect that the depiction of this change will have on the reader' (2012: 5). As well as a novel of personal and national transformation, the bildungsroman is also a novel invested in youth. Franco Moretti's analysis of the European bildungsroman argues that the form codifies 'youth as the most meaningful part of life' (1987: 3). However, this investment in youth sits in tension with the bildungsroman's teleological structure, in which the transformation of the character only makes sense in relation to the novel's ending (Moretti 1987: 7). Thus, youth is paradoxically 'subordinated to the idea of "maturity" [. . .] it has meaning only in so far as it leads to a stable and "final" identity' (Moretti 1987: 8). Boes further argues that though Bildungsroman criticism emphasises finality and closure, 'hardly any actual novel' offers such closure (2012: 7, 4). Boes argues that the bildungsroman always leaves some 'remainder' that resists closure (2012: 3). Oyeyemi draws out these tensions of the bildungsroman form in her invocation of a gothic structure of character and narrative disintegration, and her use of unsettling gothic children who refuse to be co-opted into a process of maturation, their presence an unsettling 'remainder' within a narrative left open and unfinished.

In the bildungsroman, the child symbolises variously incompletion, innocence, dependency, wildness: all that the self must cast off in order to enter the adult social realm. In Moretti's formulation, 'the bildungsroman attempts to build the Ego, and make it the indisputable centre of its own structure [. . .] connected, of course, to the theme of socialisation – this being, to a large extent, the "proper functioning" of the Ego' (1987: 11). In this psychoanalytical narrative of maturation and socialization, the child's incompletion and wildness functions to shore up its opposite: the unified, socialised adult subject. However, this psychoanalytic figuration of the child as the incomplete adult, a subjectivity not yet put in order by the Ego, is paradoxical. On one hand, this child is constructed positively as the self capable of growth and unification. On the other hand, this child represents all that must be cast off, abjected, repressed, for the adult self to emerge. Virginia Blum argues that there is a desire at the heart of psychoanalysis to destroy the child so the trauma it represents will 'never re-emerge to plague the adult' (1995: 157). This negative and contradictory psychoanalytic construction of the child gives rise to gothic representations of it in Western literature and film.

Anxiety over the contradictory status of the child certainly manifests in gothic and horror, but so, too, does the image of the child as essentially hollow, unable to represent a stable identity or guarantee a stable meaning. Sue Walsh suggests that 'there is a problem with reading gothic child characters either as "children", or as "characters", since these two concepts suggest entities that are somehow separate from the narration that produces them and of which they are constitutive' (2007: 184–85). Walsh follows the theories of Karín Lesnik-Oberstein, who argues that the 'child' is 'an identity which is created and constructed differently within various cultures, historical periods, and political ideologies' (1998: 2). Lesnik-Oberstein's central argument – that 'the child does not exist' – is central to understanding the way gothic children function in Oyeyemi's novels (1994: 9). In Oyeyemi's novels, child characters reveal themselves as empty frames, or fantasy screens. TillyTilly is an apt figuration of this since at first she seems to promise Jess an ideal image of herself, demonstrating the power and knowledge Jess lacks. However, as I have argued elsewhere, TillyTilly is revealed not to be a child at all, but a deconstructive force that fails to signify one meaning and leads instead to the absence of identity (Ilott and Buckley 2016: 413). *The Opposite House* further reveals the way that the child functions as an adult construction that (inadequately) covers over the absence of meaning and a secure identity. Maja's nostalgic recollections of her own childhood in Cuba prove to be false and she becomes increasingly anxious about what future her unborn son represents as her pregnancy progresses. Blum argues that 'the terrain of childhood [. . .] is a mythical country mapped out by an adult consciousness ceaselessly in its search of its subjective experience in another time and place' (1995: 14). In *The Opposite House* neither Maja's past in Cuba nor her future in Britain can be guaranteed by the image of the child, who is increasingly figured as 'a blind spot' for the characters and the readers alike (Blum 1995: 89).

Reworking the bildungsroman, Oyeyemi reconfigures the construction of the child and draws attention to the paradoxical desires and fears woven into it. Moreover, Oyeyemi's novels point to the fact that the child is always the product of retrospective narration on the part of an adult. As Blum argues, the story we tell about the child is always a story about adult subjectivity (1995: 4). In Oyeyemi's novels, the act of writing or telling the child manifests as problematic; the adult subject cannot be guaranteed or shored up through the act of writing the child. Oyeyemi's critique of narrating the child manifests in *The Opposite House,* in a scene where Maja recalls her mother reading a copy of Heinrich Hoffman's *Struwwelpeter* (1845). *Struwwelpeter* is an infamous nineteenth-century children's book that contains vividly illustrated didactic tales intended for the moral instruction of bourgeois children. Maja catches a glimpse of 'a giant in yellow trousers [. . .] dipping two squirming boys headfirst into a cauldron of ink' (Oyeyemi 2007: 86). This is a passing reference to Hoffman's 'Story of the Black Boys', in which a giant, Agrippa, catches three boys teasing a black child and dips them in ink to teach them a lesson. Oyeyemi's playful reference to the tale suggests that the antiracist efforts of white, colonial societies leave a lot to be desired since both Maja and her brother, Tomás, encounter racism in the contemporary setting of the novel. The encounter with Hoffman also overturns paternalistic and colonial didacticism, since its reader is a black girl and not Hoffman's intended white, European, bourgeois, male child. John Morgenstern asserts that the middle-class school-boy is both the 'consumer' of nineteenth-century children's literature and the 'object of its representation' (2002: 136). Hoffman epitomises the didactic paternalism of this middle-class literature, claiming to write the book for his sons' entertainment, but using the gruesome stories to impart moral and behavioural messages. Maja's reading subverts this didactic intent because not only does she incorrectly recall the book (Agrippa wears an orange robe, not yellow trousers), she also omits the details of the story and its concomitant 'moral' lesson so that the image presents simply a senseless scene of adult brutality. This recollection of

Hoffman also recasts the image of Agrippa as communicating something of the violence behind the narration of the child. The giant, with his oversize quill and ink pot, roughly dips the children into ink. Likewise, adult writers call up children out of their 'ink', forming them into examples that shore up social structures, morality and adult identity. In its original context, Agrippa's black ink figures as a punishment. Here, the black ink suggests that it is specifically the writing of the black postcolonial child that proves difficult for writers located within white, racist societies. Oyeyemi's black children in their differing postcolonial locations, of contemporary postcolonial London and 1930s segregated America, either experience their childhood as gothic, or manifest as uncanny or preternatural figures in the eyes of the adult protagonists.

The Gothic Past

I want to draw out further the way Oyeyemi problematises ideas such as multiculturalism, hybridity and transformation in postcolonial writing and criticism by exploring her use of a particularly non-linear gothic narrative structure in which the past always returns to disrupt the present. What disrupts the trajectory of the bildungsroman first and foremost is a classic gothic structure in which a 'fearful sense of inheritance in time' combines 'with a claustrophobic sense of enclosure in space [. . .] to produce an impression of sickening descent into disintegration' (Baldick 1992: xix). In recent critical discourse, the child bears the burden of either gesturing towards a positively transformed future multicultural society, as in Stein's account of black British novels of transformation from the late twentieth century, or of guaranteeing an affirmative link to a native culture, as in Jussawalla's analysis of the postcolonial bildungsroman. Though at first seeming to fit Stein's description of a black British novel of transformation, both *The Icarus Girl* and *The Opposite House* draw on a gothic concern with the returning past and with claustrophobic domestic spaces in which their female protagonists become trapped, a location from which the protagonists are unable to affirm a positive, hybrid identity. Both *The Icarus Girl* and *The Opposite House* also disrupt the structure of the postcolonial bildungsroman as formulated by Jussawalla because they do not allow for the 'assertion of an indigenous selfhood' (1997: 30). Instead, the knowledge of both Jess and Maja's 'indigenousness' asserts itself as a gothic irruption from the past that destabilises their present location. It is because Oyeyemi's children return to the postcolonial bildungsroman the problems and anxieties that are often repressed in a hopeful construction of the postcolonial child that they manifest as uncanny and gothic.

Stein's analysis of the black British bildungsroman is pertinent to Oyeyemi's British fiction, which speaks back to the works he identifies as transformative and hopeful. These black British bildungsromane chart the identity formation of young people who arrived in Britain at a very young age, or who were born in Britain to immigrant parents. The liminal position of these late twentieth-century British writers manifests as precarious, but Stein argues that the bildungsroman emerges as a form through which this liminality can be narrated and transformed (2004: 7). In Stein's formulation, the black British bildungsroman is a novel of 'subject formation under the influence of social, educational, familial and other forces' that entails the maturation of its protagonist 'as well as the transformation of British society and cultural institutions' (2004: 22). In Stein's analysis the child is an important symbol of an emergent, but affirmative, subjectivity that guarantees the transformation of wider society. Stein locates the child in a position of futurity to a present moment in transition, since it belongs to the 'next' generation of black British subjects and can thus chart a movement forward and away from present problems and anxieties. In Stein's analysis, the young protagonists' conflict with the previous generation, along with their unique hybrid position within British society, allows the novels to approach a happy ending, albeit with some reservations, in which protagonists begin to come to terms with their identity (2004: 25–26). For Stein, the children and adolescents of these novels are able to carve out a space for themselves, undertaking a journey of discovery and maturation that allows for a coming to terms with blackness and may even have the potential to redefine Britishness itself to incorporate blackness and other forms of difference (2004: 40, 30). Stein's utopian narrative places upon the textual child a huge burden: the responsibility to transform models of black subjectivity and the power to bring about social change beyond the pages of the novel itself. Here, the child is associated with the new, with progress: the child is 'better equipped to survive and succeed in a racist society than her parents [. . .] [she] is ready to assert her claim to a place in it' (Stein 2004: 47). Stein frames this discussion in terms of first and subsequent generations of immigrants from formerly colonised countries, and through this conflict creates binaries between adult and child, old and new, stagnation and progress.

I find Stein's elaboration of the child's role in the black British bildungsroman troubling in ways that Oyeyemi's fiction highlights. First, in Stein's analysis the child is a slippery figure, shifting in and out of the pages of the novel. Linking the bildungsroman to the experiences of the writers themselves, Stein suggests a direct representational link between characters and their authors, that the child within the book can be linked directly to a child without. He further suggests that the subject formation occurring within the text might incite or guarantee the possibility of transformation in postcolonial subjectivity outside the novel. Second, Stein does not question the structure of the bildungsroman, nor the linear psychoanalytic narrative of development it reproduces. Indeed, his assessment of Meena in *Anita and Me* concludes that the protagonist emerges at the end of the novel more mature, accepting of her space in society (Stein 2004: 40). This psychoanalytic reading of Meena implicitly repeats a universalizing narrative of maturation from psychoanalysis, which I have argued is shot through with troubling contradictions about the status of the child. Finally, Stein's assessment of the child in postcolonial writing is hopeful, despite identifying problems and dissatisfactions encountered by the novels' protagonists. A paradoxical child emerges from this analysis. On the one hand, the postcolonial child frees itself of the burdens of the past, and is thus able to carve out space and reconfigure Britain in ways the older generation cannot (Stein 2004: 29, 30). On the other hand, the postcolonial child is caught up in a generational and cultural conflict, weighted with a burden of continuity of origins, memories and family histories (Stein 2004: 41).

Current interpretations of the child in Oyeyemi's fiction draw on this hopeful construction of the postcolonial child, and develop it with reference to a linear psychoanalytic model of subject formation applied to the characters as though they were an analysand. Diana Adesola Mafe's analysis of *The Icarus Girl,* for example, applies a psychoanalytical framework to describe the novel as a rite of passage that 'tests' the protagonist's ability to articulate her identity as a multiracial and multicultural subject (2012: 31). Mafe appropriates Lacan's concept of the mirror stage to read the novel as a series of stages in the process of subject formation that will 'facilitate [the protagonist's] realization and her function within the social' (2012: 29). This practice of adopting a broadly developmental or ego-relational model of psychoanalysis is common when discussing children in fiction; it constructs them as subjects in process, and posits their eventual overcoming of the infantile libido as a guarantor of stable adult identity. Mafe concludes that Jess emerges triumphant at the close of the novel, articulating a viable position of hybridity and a new female voice, an 'awakening' for the postcolonial subject. Sarah Ilott and I have previously argued that Mafe's utopian reading of this novel easily unravels when other factors from the text are brought to bear – not least the figure of TillyTilly, whose possession of the protagonist results in a dissolution rather than affirmation of self (2016: 407).

This refiguring of childhood is staged explicitly in *The Opposite House*. Maja longs to return to Cuba, a place she nostalgically constructs as her homeland through a particular childhood memory. This memory, of a lantern-lit evening garden party, at which a childhood friend suffers an epileptic fit and Maja hears the hypnotic song of a woman at the garden gate, is the source of some stability for Maja, providing her with what she calls 'my Cuba' (Oyeyemi 2007: 44). At first, this link to the past through the image of the child is comforting, and draws on a literary tradition of childhood secret gardens. Susan Honeyman argues that writers often spatialise childhood, constructing the 'secret gardens' familiar to us from a Western canon of children's literature, places of magic structurally removed from the adult world (2005: 52). However, such spaces also simultaneously reveal that childhood is inaccessible to the adult; they 'surrogate our inaccessible past through nostalgia' (Honeyman 2005: 51). Revealing its inaccessibility, Maja's garden is snatched away when a chance meeting with her childhood friend reveals that there was no singer at the gate, and that it was Maja who suffered the fit. This revelation casts Maja adrift: 'I think I will pretend that I am not from Cuba and neither is my son' (Oyeyemi 2007: 168–69). Maja's anchor to her imaginatively constituted childhood self dissolves, leaving no place in which Maja can locate her identity. The memory also reveals that childhood is fraught with the same feelings of dislocation and fragmentation Maja experiences as an adult. The child's epileptic fit is recalled vividly: 'her eyes whirled blind, she slurped and dribbled and winced as she bit her tongue over and over. One of her hands drummed at the side of her head as if desperately trying to dislodge something' (Oyeyemi 2007: 45). Maja's idyllic seeming childhood is here contaminated with the same loss of bodily control and hysteria she experiences as an adult. No longer able to distance herself from this disturbing image by projecting it onto another, Maja's nostalgic construction of childhood crumbles and, with it, her anchor to an imagined stable, adult identity that she seeks through her association with Cuba.

The non-linear gothic structure whereby the past returns to disrupt the present problematises the very idea of origin and homeland. In contrast to Jussawalla's assertion that the postcolonial bildungsroman charts a growth 'towards indigenousness in language, style, religious roots and belonging', Oyeyemi's gothic use of the past reconfigures the homeland as a haunting (1997: 25). In *The Opposite House*, Cuba is figured as a liminal location through the figure of the Opposite House itself, which straddles the space between London and Lagos, its cultural heritage bearing the marks of colonial violence and slavery. Maja's father articulates this liminality in his critique of Santeriá, which he calls a 'garbled religion', noting that 'Suffering isn't transformative [. . .] You can't erase borders and stride over Spanish into Yoruba like that. You can only pretend that you have' (Oyeyemi 2007: 76). Maja's postcolonial location is doubly displaced; she cannot locate a homeland in West Africa, noting her isolation from African girls at school. She simply calls this elusive origin 'that other country' since it is too far removed from her experience. Both Maja in *The Opposite House* and Jess in *The Icarus Girl* experience a connection to an origin that troubles and haunts them, a past that they cannot escape but that does not provide a secure anchorage for their identity. Jess disavows her Nigerian origins; the word itself feels 'ugly', unfamiliar and hard to express: 'Nye. Jeer. Reeee. Ah.' (Oyeyemi 2005: 10). For Jess, Nigerian origins do not represent a 'homeland', rather they represent the origin of her haunting by the destructive spectre, TillyTilly, whom she first encounters in Lagos. The novel states clearly in its opening pages, 'it all STARTED in Nigeria' (Oyeyemi 2005: 7). TillyTilly manifests as a classic gothic haunting, the return of the repressed, both in the sense of Jess's disavowed Nigerian origins and because she also represents the trauma of losing a twin sister in infancy. Maja and Jess experience a broken attachment to Britain and cannot find an affirmative position within this liminal location between cultures. Both novels conclude by leaving their protagonists in this unsettling liminal space. Maja remains ambivalent about the impending birth of her son, her plane ticket to Cuba remaining unspent; Jess lies unconscious in a hospital bed in Lagos, the battle with TillyTilly left frighteningly unresolved. Neither novel offers the consolation of its character entering a more mature or affirmative sense of being, since the protagonists have been unable to escape the deleterious effects of the past.

Writing the Future: Gothic Lineage

The gothic, perhaps more than any other tradition, points to the paradoxical ways the child has been constructed as both a symbol of renewal and futurity on the one hand and an agent of the inescapable, destructive past on the other. Margarita Georgieva argues that the child has been central to gothic literature from the inception of the form, exhibiting a 'bipolarity' particularly suited to gothic's inherent contradictions: 'Children, adolescents and new generations are powerful symbols of rebirth and renewal, or inversely, of vengeance, destruction and ruin, which means that child figures are an extremely pliant, exploitable material' (2013: 32). Oyeyemi's construction of the child draws on a gothic literary tradition in which the child marks a site of anxiety about proper lines of descent, inheritance and legitimacy. Thus, the child in gothic is a 'coveted possession', an object over which protagonists fight for control (Georgieva 2013: 13). In the first gothic novel, Horace Walpole's *The Castle of Otranto* (1764), the villain seeks to possess the child of his rival in order that he can continue his line and legitimate his power, a position he has usurped from another. The unexpected return of that other's child, however, functions to put right the wrong the villain has committed and restores appropriate lines of descent and inheritance. Chiefly, the gothic child's function is to ensure past wrongs receive proper retribution and correct family lineage is restored. For Georgieva, the child is the object upon which the plot revolves and is able to resolve – a guarantee of retribution and renewal (2013: 16).

Oyeyemi recontextualises a gothic anxiety about the control and possession of the child in a postcolonial context, rewriting a gothic structure that promises the restitution of proper family lineage and a guarantee of the family's futurity through the child. In *The Icarus Girl* this plays out in the body of Jessamy Harrison, a child of mixed parentage, who struggles to establish an identity following either her father or her mother's image. Jess experiences this struggle partly through an indecision over her name. Called variously Jessamy, Jess, and Jessy, she discovers a further name given to her by her Grandfather, the Yoruba name, Wuraola. To Jess this 'sounded like another person. Not her at all' and she is unable to decipher from her names what is 'expected of her' (Oyeyemi 2005: 20, 19). Naming in gothic literature denotes the function of the child in the narrative (Good or Evil; Renewal or Revenge) and to whom they belong; a name confers upon the child 'a mark of belonging and distinction' (Georgieva 2013: 33). This tradition of naming as distinction and belonging is overturned in *The Icarus Girl* since Jess does not know how to 'become Wuraola', a person belonging to another place (Oyeyemi 2005: 19). Unable to anchor herself through one name, and battling with TillyTilly for possession of her body, Jess becomes lost in the spiritual 'Wilderness of the Bush', and the novel refuses to offer any certainty that she might be able to return and take up her position within the family as guarantor of its future stability and continuity.

In *The Opposite House*, Maja's unborn child, who is never named, becomes a source of psychological anxiety and physical abjection. Maja oscillates between the desire to possess her son, and the feeling that he will consume her. Echoing the gothic tradition of naming through a paternal lineage, Maja recites to herself:

> His last name shall be his father's name. His second name shall be his grandfather's name. His first name shall be a name for his ownself, but unknown to him, all those fathers before his grandfather live in this name. (Oyeyemi 2007: 5)

Maja's mantra reveals the paradox upon which the gothic child is constructed and the burden it must consequently bear: how can the child emerge as a discrete identity, capable of transformation and renewal, when it is implicated in a chain of naming as belonging that ties it inexorably to the past? Furthermore, Maja's invocation of a paternal lineage erases herself, the mother, from the family, further emphasizing the disintegration of identity she experiences as the pregnancy progresses. As in *The Icarus Girl,* the plot of *The Opposite House* remains unresolved, and the future that the baby may promise for Maja (and her troubled family) is ambiguous, though she remains pregnant at the novel's close. Maja expresses a desire to know what future her son will guarantee by naming him and seeing his likeness: 'I keep thinking, maybe if I could just know what my son looks like, who my son is, then I will be alright' (Oyeyemi 2007: 120). However, though Maja expresses the need for this consolation, it is ultimately denied.

The title of *Boy, Snow, Bird* signals its concern with naming as the act of constructing the child through narration. Each of the eponymous protagonists is positioned within their family to guarantee a whole and stable identity that has been denied to their parents: maleness, whiteness, freedom (respectively). Oyeyemi presents these acts of naming as acts of violence. Anxiety over the physical appearance of the child is also central to *Boy, Snow, Bird*, a novel that explores the trauma of racial 'passing' in 1950s USA. Though the postcolonial context is different here to Oyeyemi's British novels, the child remains implicated in a field of desire, a focal point for adult hopes that fix upon it as a guarantee of identity – here figured as whiteness. In the literary gothic, as Georgieva explains, the naming of the child and its resemblance to its parents are determined by a notion of replacement, in which the child stands in place of the parent in relation to futurity. As with likeness, naming is 'culturally and socially determined by the notion of replacement. The child is supposed to replace the parent and parents live on through their children' (Georgieva 2013: 34). In *Boy, Snow, Bird* the gothic concern with naming and resemblance plays out through Snow, a child figured as securing the continued stability of her family, who are passing as white. Her pale skin and name that doubly insists on whiteness and purity – Snow Whitman – position her as replacement for her dead mother, and as guarantee for the Whitmans' continued respectability and status. This desire for Snow to act as guarantee, however, is destructive, and 'passing' is figured as a trauma that works to fragment the family. The trauma of passing might be explained with reference to Frantz Fanon's study, *Black Skin, White Masks,* which explores the psychological trauma resulting from a colonizing process that positions black skin as other in relation to white subjectivity (2008: 174). In these terms, passing can be read as a symptom of the pathologizing of blackness imposed upon colonial subjects. The insistent naming of Snow as whiteness denotes a failure to escape the relations of otherness imposed upon the black subject, positioning the child – meant to act as guarantee of futurity – to bear the burden of continuing the trauma. Naming, then, is an act that seeks to inscribe both continuity and futurity in the child. At first, naming seems hopeful – Frank names Boy for the male identity he seeks; Arturo and Julia name Snow for the whiteness they desire; Snow names Bird for freedom from the adult expectations with which she has herself been inscribed. However, the names ultimately denote failure: Snow cannot guarantee whiteness, only bear the burden of its trauma, Boy cannot inhabit maleness, increasingly trapped by her role as step-mother, and Bird cannot be free – either from the damaging identification with her sister's whiteness, nor from the strictures placed on female identity that constrain her elders.

The 'Evil' Child

Georgieva notes that the child in literary gothic is frequently referred to as 'it', a convention which 'objectifies the child as if in support of the idea that the child is [. . .] a figure, a device, a symbol, and a characteristic with the help of which adult characters can be manipulated' (2013: 8). The gothic child is not therefore a real child, but an unsettling narrative function that acquires a 'preternatural, otherworldly aura' (Georgieva 2013: 8). Child doubles also populate literary gothic fiction, which often mirror the good child with the bad, reflecting innocence with malevolence. These uncanny, or preternatural, children of literary gothic spawn a plethora of representations of the child as evil, precocious and uncanny in twentieth-century horror film, including *The Bad Seed* (1956), *The Village of the Damned* (1960), *The Exorcist* (1973), *The Omen* (1976), *The Children of the Corn* (1984), and, more recently, *Case 39* (2009). Stephen Bruhm explores this particular aspect of the gothic child in his analysis of twentieth-century horror film, in which children most often feature as bearers of death and corruption (2006: 98).

Oyeyemi draws overtly on this construction of the child as uncanny, corrupt, even murderous, in *The Icarus Girl.* The spectre haunting Jess, the precocious and terrifying TillyTilly, is informed by Yoruba beliefs in the *abiku* (the spirit of a dead twin), but she also fits into this tradition of 'bad' children. TillyTilly's most frightening power is that of 'getting' people, something she enacts first upon Jess's Dad, leaving him 'a thing, slurred of speech, emptied, inside-out, outside-in' (Oyeyemi 2005: 284). Mimicking the horror film trope whereby the unnatural child turns to the oblivious parent as its victim, TillyTilly enacts a violence aimed at the protagonists' speech and identity. For Stein, speech plays a crucial role in affirming the identity of the black British subject, who finds a voice that permits 'expression, negotiation and transformation' (2004: xvii). Here, however, TillyTilly functions to silence. As well as 'getting' Jess's dad, she makes it so that Jess is unable to talk about what is happening to her, speaking through Jess to her friends and family so that Jess feels ashamed and cut off from individuals who show her friendship and trust. As Tilly becomes successful in her attempts to 'swap places' with Jess, Jess cannot prevent herself from also being hollowed out and erased, her identity dissolving in the face of her gothic child double.

The preternatural child proves problematic for the narration of identity in the various ways that it rejects attempts to nurture, remaining unresponsive. The opening of *The Opposite House* begins by introducing the story of the goddess Yemaya, an Orisha from Yoruba and Santeriá traditions. Traditionally linked to motherhood, pregnancy and water, Yemaya's story mirrors Maja's, as she experiences her role as mother as '*ache*' – bone deep pain.[1] She insistently feeds her charges – the Kayodes – in the Opposite House with plates piled high with nourishing food, but the Kayodes neither eat, nor speak. Yemaya's actions reveal the child as a repository of adult desire, for a deep yearning and unsatisfied 'ache.' Yet, the child remains passive and unresponsive. This image of the child recurs in Maja's brother, Tomás, who suffers from reflux well beyond his infancy. Normally a condition associated with infants, reflux causes Tomás to vomit up his food. This disturbs his father in particular who insists 'stop that, Tomás [. . .] it's unheard of. Boys don't do that' (Oyeyemi 2007: 152). Maja, of course, *is* expected to vomit, because she is pregnant. However, the novel figures her morning sickness as insupportably abject: the 'air tastes like grease; air tilts my stomach until it spills yet more' food (Oyeyemi 2007: 5). In this novel, both children and mothers regurgitate food, expressing a double abjection that suggests this pouring of desire into the child is insupportable on either side. Tomás also suffers from unexplained hearing loss that causes him to become unresponsive in class. Whilst his reflux suggests that the child cannot continue to act as a vessel for adult yearning, fulfilling expectations required of him as the 'London Baby' and thus one of the 'next' generation, his deafness presents a disturbing image of the blank child, a repository for adult desires, who reflects nothing back.

Georgieva's survey of a number of gothic texts shows that the gothic child is not necessarily a biologically immature person, but rather a location in the text in relation to an adult; the gothic child is 'someone's child' (2013: 2). Oyeyemi's work draws upon this structure, focusing upon the relationships around which the child is constructed, particularly those between mothers and their children. Maja's unborn son also functions as a repository of anxiety, lack and desire. On the one hand, Maja winces when she sees the positive pregnancy test, feeling something like dread when she anticipates her son's arrival. On the other hand, she imagines 'my boy, warm, alive, walking beside me [. . .] full of laughter and he wanted me to be happy and so I was' (Oyeyemi 2007: 6). This dream child, who allows the adult to feel the satisfaction she lacks, is quickly undercut by another image. Maja recalls how she used to watch the baby Tomás sleeping: 'Sometimes I wonder what he saw. I wonder if it seemed I had come to kill him. Babies are not trusting' (Oyeyemi 2007: 6). Oyeyemi figures mother and child antagonistically. Later, Maja feels as though her son will consume her, and her abject experience of pregnancy accompanies her psychological breakdown. Thus, *The Opposite House* both explores the burden placed upon the child and figures the child itself as burden. Though Maja achieves something like reconciliation with her unborn son near the end of the novel, she remains ambivalent about what the separation between herself and the baby will bring.

The preternatural child returns in *Boy, Snow, Bird,* figured through the character of Snow, whose whiteness and blankness become uncanny in the eyes of the novel's protagonist, Boy. Boy is disturbed by the way the Whitman family debase themselves in the face of Snow's sacred whiteness. Arturo teases that he is nobody, 'just Snow's dad', and Snow's grandmothers gaze in awe upon the girl. In Snow, they see their desires reflected, but are simultaneously othered by those desires, since she exhibits a whiteness that disavows the family's origins. Boy explains that Arturo never felt Snow was really his, that her beauty was strange, 'so blank, like a brand-new slate' (Oyeyemi 2014: 133).

Whilst Tomás and Jess in the earlier novels suffer from eating disorders, including regurgitation, in the face of adult desire, Snow remains impassive, blank like her name. In this sense, Oyeyemi borrows from the gothic that preternatural aspect of the child that threatens to become terrifying. Accordingly, Boy expresses fear on her first meeting with Snow: '"Scared" doesn't even really describe it. I almost crossed myself. It felt like the evil eye had fallen on us both' (Oyeyemi 2014: 25). Snow's picture-perfect, white beauty and the clichéd markers of childhood innocence with which she is surrounded, including cookies, flowers, and plaited hair, repel rather than attract, acting here as a warning of impending disaster. Boy's reaction reveals that the desires anchored upon the child's projected innocence are a cover for adult anxiety about what innocence hides. Bruhm identifies this anxiety in his analysis of the gothic child of Western horror film:

> The Rousseauistic innocent that is The Child in our mythology is also the Freudian child, always already corrupted, always already corruptible. To discover that child, then, is to return to that place where innocence and corruption exist, not in opposition, but in symbiosis: innocence is only knowable by those who are already corrupted; we can only know innocence by being corrupted [. . .] by knowing innocence, then, as the product of corruption. (2006: 108)

This classic horror dichotomy of the innocent/ corrupted child is reconfigured by Oyeyemi to explore how blackness is figured as the disavowed aspect in a violent black/ white binary. The beauty of Snow produces anxiety because it reveals the otherness, the black skin, the lack that the Whitmans seek to cover through her. Boy initially desires Snow in order to cover lack, too, though in her case it is the lack of a nurturing parent-child relationship in which she can ground her identity. At first she thinks she can possess Snow: 'this girl is mine [. . .] we're giving each other something we've never had' (Oyeyemi 2014: 109). Later, however, Boy recognises that Snow's innocence is a performance of childhood resulting from adult projections and desires, and she begins to read Snow very differently:

> She gave me a look of radiant, innocent virtue that made my skin crawl [. . .] spontaneous and calculated at the same time. My hand came up to knock that look off her face [. . .]. I wouldn't have seen the rat catcher in my actions until much later. (Oyeyemi 2014: 141–42)

Snow's whiteness manifests as a blankness, a fantasy screen that ultimately reveals the lack it seems to cover. Snow's performance of the innocent child proves unsatisfying for Boy's desires to become a parent, and Boy increasingly identifies with the monstrous Frank, her father, in her desire to punish Snow.

As well as invoking the step-mother relationship of *Snow White,* Oyeyemi also invokes Mary Shelley's gothic novel, *Frankenstein* (1818) in this antagonistic relationship between parents and children. The name of Boy's father, Frank, makes this self-reflexive connection, invoking the infamous gothic paternal relationship as well as its later rewriting in Iain Banks's *The Wasp Factory* (1984). As a story about a parent and child, *Frankenstein* depicts the tragic consequences of failing to act upon parental responsibility. Anne Mellor argues that the central theme of the novel is Victor Frankenstein's total failure as a parent (2003: 10). Banks's rewriting of *Frankenstein* introduces into this antagonistic relationship a transgender narrative in which the main character, also called Frank, discovers at the close of the narrative that he is a girl, not a boy, and has been fed male hormone drugs by his abusive father. Drawing on Banks's interpretation of *Frankenstein*, *Boy, Snow, Bird* returns 'Frank' to the role of parent. In Oyeyemi's version, Frank was once a woman and so is Boy's mother, not her father. This reconfiguration of Banks's transgender narrative redirects Oyeyemi's readers to the fact that *Frankenstein* is a gothic novel about motherhood; its 'birth myth' central to a 'female gothic' tradition (Moers 1985: 92). Shelley's gothic anxiety about the trauma of motherhood, including a moral concern about failing to be a good mother, as well as concerns with how the body and identity are reconfigured in becoming a mother, thus shape the way *Boy, Snow, Bird* constructs the child as frighteningly unknowable. For Mellor, Shelley wants the reader to understand the consequences of imposing meanings on that which we cannot truly know and constructs the monster as 'a sign of the unknown, the never-before-perceived' (2003: 22, 20). The characters in the novel assume that the monster's outer appearance is a valid index to his inner nature, though Shelley complicates this by narrating some of the text from the monster's perspective. Drawing on this confusion over appearances and inner depths, Oyeyemi suggests that the characters of *Boy, Snow, Bird* wish to make Snow into a clear indexical sign guaranteeing that others will read the Whitman family as they appear, that is, as white. Snow's whiteness, however, offers a blankness that guarantees nothing, only resulting in her banishment and abandonment by Boy, seeking to give her daughter freedom from the trauma of racial passing self-imposed by the Whitmans in their attempts to escape the cultural and social stigmatisation of blackness. In turn, this banishment figures Boy as a cruel mother, seemingly doomed to repeat the sins of her parent, Frank.

Oyeyemi draws upon a variety of images of the gothic child in order to counter a postcolonial narrative in which the child figures as hopeful guarantee of futurity and transformation. Gothicised in various ways – either by experiencing their identity as fragmented and haunted, or by becoming uncanny figures themselves – the children in these novels suggest that the myth of the child is liable to dissolve under the weight of the burdens it is made to carry. As Marina Warner notes in her analysis of monstrous representations of the child, 'childhood doesn't occupy some sealed Eden or Neverland set apart from the grown up world: our children can't be better than we are' (1994: 46). For Oyeyemi as a writer, the child proves an unstable construction on which to anchor and inscribe identity. Thus, the child becomes an accusatory figure, calling into question the troubling desires with which it is freighted. It resists pressure to conform to the psychological maturational journey, and instead threatens to disrupt the emergence of a whole, stable postcolonial subject. I do not read Oyeyemi's fiction as entirely negative about a creative postcolonial project, but I contend that it manifests doubts about unproblematic narratives of postcolonialism, which might imply that colonialism is over, and of positive accounts of the hybridity and transformation of postcolonial subjectivity, pointing instead to the gaps and problems still faced by the postcolonial project in fiction and criticism.

Note

1 The word *ache* is italicised in the novel, suggesting its further meaning in Yoruba as denoting a divine life force. Here its English meaning sits in uneasy tension with its Yoruba meaning as Aya's role as a diving, life bringing mother is refigured here as bringing trauma and pain.

Works Cited

Baldick, C. 1992: Introduction. *The Oxford Book of Gothic Tales*. Oxford: Oxford University Press, xi–xxiii.

Blum, V. L. 1995: *Hide and Seek: The Child Between Psychoanalysis and Fiction*. Champaign, IL: University of Illinois Press.

Boes, T. 2012: *Formative Fictions: Nationalism, Cosmopolitanism, and the "Bildungsroman"*. Ithaca, NY: Cornell University Press.

Bruhm, S. 2006: Nightmare on Sesame Street: Or, The Self-Possessed Child. *Gothic Studies* 8 (2), 98–113.

Fanon, F. 2008: *Black Skin, White Masks*. Translated by Charles Lam Markmann. London: Pluto Press.

Georgieva, M. 2013: *The Gothic Child*. London: Palgrave Macmillan.

Honeyman, S. 2005: *Elusive Childhood: Impossible Representations in Modern Fiction*. Columbus, OH: Ohio State University Press.

Ilott, S. and Buckley, C. 2016: 'Fragmenting and Becoming Double': Supplementary Twins and Abject Bodies in Helen Oyeyemi's The Icarus Girl. *The Journal of Commonwealth Literature* 21 (3), 402–15.
Jussawalla, F. 1997: Kim, Huck and Naipaul: Using the Postcolonial Bildungsroman to (Re)define Postcoloniality. *Links and Letters* 4, 25–38.
Kiely, R. 1972: *The Romantic Novel in England.* Cambridge, MA: Harvard University Press.
Lesnik-Oberstein, K. 1994: *Children's Literature: Criticism and the Fictional Child.* Oxford: Clarendon Press.
Lesnik-Oberstein, K. 1998: Childhood and Textuality. *Children in Culture.* Edited by Karín Lesnik-Oberstein. London: Macmillan, 1–29.
Mafe, D. A. 2012. Ghostly Girls in the' Eerie Bush': Helen Oyeyemi's *The Icarus Girl* as Postcolonial Female Gothic Fiction. *Research in African Literatures* 43 (3), 21–35.
McLeod, J. 2004: *Postcolonial London: Rewriting the metropolis.* London: Routledge.
Mellor, A. K. 2003: Making a 'Monster': An Introduction to Frankenstein. *The Cambridge Companion to Mary Shelley.* Edited by Esther Schor. Cambridge: Cambridge University Press, 9–25.
Millard, K. 2007: *Coming of Age in Contemporary American Fiction.* Edinburgh: Edinburgh University Press.
Moers, E. 1985: *Literary Women: The Great Writers.* Oxford: Oxford University Press.
Moretti, F. 1987: *The Way of the World: The Bildungsroman in European Culture.* London: Verso.
Morgenstern, J. 2002: The Fall into Literacy and the Rise of the Bourgeois Child. *Children's Literature Association Quarterly* 27 (3), 136–45.
Oyeyemi, H. 2005: *The Icarus Girl.* London: Bloomsbury.
Oyeyemi, H. 2007: *The Opposite House.* London: Bloomsbury.
Oyeyemi, H. 2014: *Boy, Snow, Bird.* London: Picador.
Stein, M. 2004: *Black British Literature: Novels of Transformation.* Columbus, OH: Ohio State University Press.
Walsh, S. 2007: Gothic Children. *The Routledge Companion to Gothic.* Edited by Catherine Spooner and Emma McEvoy. London: Routledge, 183–91.
Warner, M. 1994: *Managing Monsters.* London: Vintage.

CHAPTER
3

'Nobody ever warned me about mirrors': Doubling, Mimesis, and Narrative Form in Helen Oyeyemi's Fiction

NATALYA DIN-KARIUKI[1]

'Nobody ever warned me about mirrors, so for many years I was fond of them, and believed them to be trustworthy' (Oyeyemi 2014: 3). This confession opens Helen Oyeyemi's fifth novel, *Boy, Snow, Bird*. When the protagonist, Boy Novak (later, Whitman), looks into the mirror, she sees 'a girl with a white-blonde pigtail hanging down over one shoulder.' She sets up mirrors to face each other so that she is 'infinitely reflected' in all directions, a proliferating effect that allows her to transcend the lonely pronominal singularity of 'I' and become 'her', 'we', 'us', and even 'Many, many me's', the sight carrying with it a 'dizzying', sometimes even erotic, charge (Oyeyemi 2014: 3).

In this scene Boy repeats, or *reflects*, an image used in Oyeyemi's first novel, *The Icarus Girl* (2005). Here the protagonist, Jessamy ('Jess' or 'Jessy') Harrison, takes to cutting out 'twin-pictures' from books. She lingers over the image, taken from the pages of a 'glossy encyclopedia', of a girl with 'short blonde hair gazing into the mirror at herself. Two girls, two smiles, snub nose pressed to snub nose. It was like twins.' Inspired by this image, Jess, a British-Nigerian girl, attempts to imitate her, gazing into a mirror herself. But her reflection is occluded: the mirror is misty, and her outline 'indistinct' (Oyeyemi 2005a: 179).

Jess's failure to see herself in the mirror has its own important precedent, this time in Frantz Fanon's revision of Jacques Lacan's 'mirror stage' as recorded in a footnote of *Black Skin, White Masks*. Fanon challenges Lacan's reading of image (*imago*) and identification with specific reference to the self-alienation of the black psyche under colonialism. Lacan's model examines the child at an age when he is able to 'recognize as such his own image in a mirror'; this is an act of misrecognition, Lacan argues, but one that transforms the subject from 'fragmented body-image' to assumed 'totality' (Lacan 2004: 441–46). The white man, in Fanon's reading of Lacan, may construct his ego on the basis of an exclusion in which the 'Negro' functions as 'The Other.' However, the black man is denied similar moments of identification. Fanon claims that the mirror hallucination is occluded in the case of the Antillean, citing a case in which his patient's reflection 'had no color.' His reflection does not grant him 'structural harmony' but division; he is forced to occupy the space of the timeless Other (Fanon 1996: 161–62). Similarly, in Fanon's re-working of the Hegelian master/slave dialectic, the colonised 'slave' is denied the violent mutual recognition crucial to self-consciousness (Fanon 1996: 216–22).[2]

Frustrating, obstructing, obscuring, and lacking in colour, the mirrors in Oyeyemi's writing bear strong affinities to, or even work to literalise, these passages in Fanon. A hallmark of postcolonial writing written during the decolonising period is its development of 'a symbolic vocabulary that was recognizably indigenous' (Boehmer 2005: 179). Oyeyemi's mirrors, and the broader motif of doubling in her novels, can be seen as a further contribution of this kind, offering a challenge to the structures of colonial narrative and subjectivity that Fanon extrapolates. But to conclude that their projects are identical would be to jump the metaphorical gun, not least because mirrors and doubling in Oyeyemi's novels do not possess any single point of origin or reference. They have a number of possible influences, including West African material and mythic cultures, Caribbean myth, the black modernist 'double consciousness', the Gothic, and the Freudian uncanny.

Scholars writing on Oyeyemi have attended to all of these links and influences in varying degrees of detail. Far less has been said about an intellectual tradition that preceded all of these, one that is so familiar to contemporary literature and criticism that its presence is now taken for granted: classical poetics. Specifically, a number of the texts and treatises comprising this tradition use the mirror as an analogy to define poetry (or art), and the capacity of poetry to imitate nature through *mimesis*. The most famous, though not the earliest, example of this occurs in a passage on aesthetics in Book X of Plato's *Republic* (Plato 2013: X.596d-e).[3] A visual map of Oyeyemi's intellectual genealogy would look like an intricately tangled 'web of filiations', not a conventional family tree (Bryce 2008: 53).[4]

How, then, are we to interpret the centrality of the mirror motif in her fiction? One approach might be biographical. Because she is a Nigerian brought up in Britain, her identity has intrigued readers, an intrigue that has been fuelled by references to her biography outside of the novels. In 'Home, strange home', a piece published in the *Guardian* in 2005, she wrote, 'I find Africa in the weirdest places, with the jolt of someone waking up in the middle of the night and catching a glimpse of themselves in the mirror across the room' (Oyeyemi 2005b: n.p.). Most scholarship has attended to biographical anecdotes of this kind and classified Oyeyemi as a 'third-generation', 'new', 'immigrant', or 'diasporic' Nigerian novelist, placing her in the company of writers such as Chimamanda Ngozi Adichie, Diana Evans, and Helon Habila. It seeks to understand 'how these late-comers are rewriting the script of national-identity construction' and negotiating 'an in-between space' in 'contemporary postcolonial society' (Bryce 2008: 50; Hron 2008: 30). These studies have much to commend them. They offer valuable insight into the forms, modes, and genres used by these writers, including the *Bildungsroman* ('coming of age' novel) and magical realism. Further, their readings of indigenous symbols of duality including twins, 'the returning child' or *ogbanje* and 'the spirit child' or *abiku* provide important critical contexts for this chapter.

In their weaker moments, though, they tend toward speculative biographical readings and rhetorical gestures that do little more than mythologise and essentialise, by turns, 'Nigeria', 'Africa', the 'migrant', and 'diaspora.' The idea of the Dark Continent has resurfaced, albeit in a softer, cosmopolitan guise: the Dark Diaspora. The lives and experiences of 'third-generation' Nigerian writers are consistently characterised in terms of 'struggle', 'perplexities', trauma and loss; their relations to citizenship and heritage are 'contested', and their knowledge of Africa is 'limited', 'partial and imaginary.'[5]

The validity of these particular claims is dubious, whether they are considered from the perspective of either literary studies or political critique. Critics attempting to read 'third-generation' writing through a biographical lens have made inferences from various forms of non-fiction by the writers in question, including the *Guardian* piece mentioned earlier. But I would suggest that more evidence is needed to make genuinely persuasive claims about an individual's affective and intellectual attachments to a nation or continent. Moreover, figuring out the relation of a given biography to literary work(s) is a fraught interpretative act in and of itself. Finally, we should avoid reifying geo-political labels and categories. To do justice to the full scale of Oyeyemi's achievements as a novelist, we must see the novels as more than fragments of autobiography. To attain a better understanding of contemporary Nigerian writing, we must challenge the assumptions undergirding the very terms and concepts currently in discursive circulation.[6]

My contention is that Oyeyemi's fiction joins the Platonic analogy of the mirror-as-art to the motifs of mirroring and doubling that are so central to conceptualisations of race in anti-colonial, postcolonial, and modernist writing. The reflections, twins, dolls, portraits, and mannequins in the novels are crucial to her engagement with issues of race and nation, the problems of mimetic representation for raced bodies, the blurring of lines between fictive and 'real' bodies, and the difficulties of writing more broadly. These doubles, in turn, offer the best interpretive guide to Oyeyemi's novels, enabling us to tease at the labelling of her work and the frameworks through which it has been read (or refracted). The novels explore various categories of identity (race, nationality, gender, sexuality) only to expose them for what they are: social constructs, not essential truths. She does so in a fashion far more sophisticated and challenging than critics have ever acknowledged. This is true of all five of her published novels, but this chapter will focus on the three in which mirroring and doubling are most formally and thematically significant: *The Icarus Girl* (2005), *White Is for Witching* (2009), and *Boy, Snow, Bird* (2014). I will consider the forms of fiction that are engendered and configured by doublings in plot and narrative, and conclude by moving excursively to questions of the 'new' Nigerian novel as world (not national) literature.[7]

But first, a note: I do not intend to undertake a comprehensive study of Oyeyemi's reading, or to make any definitive claims about the historical influence of the discourses mentioned above on 'third-generation' writers as a group. Instead, I chiefly consider them to be useful, and richly generative, theoretical paradigms. As Boy says, mirrors are not trustworthy. In all of these novels, attempts at mimetic art are shown instead to be continual deferrals or displacements of representation. *Contra Hamlet*, the mirrors they hold up do not offer explanations or answers, but only 'infinitely reflected' questions.[8]

The Icarus Girl is a *Bildungsroman* or 'coming of age' novel, inflected with magical realist and Gothic elements. The 'coming of age' trajectory that structures the novel's plot is Jessamy's encounter with Titiola, also known as TillyTilly – a haunting ghost, imaginary friend, and twin all in one. In both its form and thematic interests, *The Icarus Girl* belongs to distinctly Nigerian literary contexts. Twins feature in earlier Nigerian writing in English, including Chinua Achebe's *Things Fall Apart* (1958) and Buchi Emecheta's *Kehinde* (1994). More specifically, a number of Oyeyemi's contemporaries have recently combined the *Bildung* form and the twin trope: Diana Evans's *26a* (2006) and *The Wonder* (2009), Helon Habila's *Measuring Time* (2008), and Taiye Selasi's *Ghana Must Go* (2013), are just a few examples.

One critic writing on this phenomenon has concluded that, 'the figure of the child in these *Bildungsromane* may also *reflect* that of Nigeria itself' (Hron 2008: 30). (The latter emphasis is mine; the critic's choice of verb, however accidental or incidental, seems fitting.) This analogy makes good sense: the novels in question are written in the decades following Nigeria's independence, its own coming of age. The neatness of the child-nation analogy is compelling, but fits awkwardly on *The Icarus Girl* for several reasons. Like so many twenty-first century Nigerian-authored novels, it stretches the limits of the Anglo-American *Bildungsroman* by focusing not on one child, but two, insisting upon protocols of reading which privilege duality. The novel's point of view, its 'I' and 'me', is almost entirely Jessamy's, but the impetus for her growth, education, or cultivation (all philosophical concepts that are central to the German *Bildung* framework) is TillyTilly, a figure both within and without her. Similarly, the novel is not limited to any one geographical setting, as it travels from England to Nigeria and back again. What is more, these two children and two nations do not fall into two conveniently distinct child-nation pairings. The novel's characters repeatedly disrupt any 'black or white', English or Nigerian binarisms. Jessamy's pathology, a propensity to fits and screams, is attributed to her hybrid or 'half-and-half' identity. A child mocks, 'Maybe Jessamy has all of these 'attacks' because she can't make up her mind whether she's black or white!' (Oyeyemi 2005a: 86).

More pertinently, the novel is sceptical of the capacity of art to 'reflect' anything at all. It presents mimesis as an impossible ideal, a bar too high for any to reach. Its 'halves' and doubles are repeatedly rendered unstable, as the twins, mirrors, shadows and echoes that constitute its universe function as messy fragments and multiplicities. If Oyeyemi nods to Fanon, it is only to extend, not resolve, his problematic: Jess and Tilly may 'mirror' each other, but this mirroring is always 'out of proportion' (Oyeyemi 2005a: 43). An early indication of Tilly's presence in Nigeria is the unnerving sight of 'shadows dancing [. . .] as shadows tend to do when light shifts around its source' (Oyeyemi 2005a: 33), and Jess later overhears Aunty Anike 'singing out of sync with the radio [. . .] like an echo' (Oyeyemi 2005a: 37). The dislocated echo reappears upon the family's return to England, where Jess is troubled by the 'unnerving split-second delay' (Oyeyemi 2005a: 163) in phone calls from Nigeria. This sense of dislocation, of being 'out of sync', is foregrounded in the twins' relationship. Jess's deceased twin, Fern, seeks mimetic remembrance in the form of an *ibeji* statue.[9] However, the text repeatedly presents mimesis as structurally flawed. Tilly's 'out of proportion' (Oyeyemi 2005a: 43) body finds its parallel in the 'out of proportion' arms in the 'sketch of a black woman' (Oyeyemi 2005a: 74) Jess finds in her Nigerian grandfather's home. The sketch itself is later revealed as an imitation of an *ibeji* statue, and Tilly's body too resembles an *ibeji*'s disproportionate dimensions.

Tilly's first appearance in *Icarus* is textual, as Jess encounters her scrawl in the dust:

> On the surface of the tabletop, someone had disturbed the dust. Scrawled in the centre in lopsided writing were the words
>
> HEllO JEssY
>
> She'd always been Jess or Jessamy, never a halfway thing like Jessy. (Oyeyemi 2005a: 41)

Tilly's erratic, uneven writing renders Jess 'a halfway thing'. With the 'am' deleted from her name – a form of the verb 'to be' – Jess becomes something smaller and lesser, a 'half.' Similarly, Tilly and Jess display the willingness to re-write canonical texts, of 'amending books', with Jess heavily annotating her mother's copy of *Little Women* (Oyeyemi 2005a: 59). However, in Oyeyemi's text *all* books, both 'African' and 'Western', are vulnerable to ruin and alteration: 'Bose, with her hands coated with spicy *adun*, had nearly destroyed the wine-coloured leather bindings of his specially commissioned copies of *Things Fall Apart* and *A Dance of the Forests*' (Oyeyemi 2005a: 49).

Chinua Achebe's novel *Things Fall Apart* was published two years before Nigeria gained independence, and Wole Soyinka's play *A Dance of the Forests* was first performed during the independence celebrations in 1960. We might see Achebe's text in particular, with its iconic 'thick forest' in which twins are 'thrown away', as a crucial precursor of subsequent uses of the twin motif in the Anglophone Nigerian novel (Achebe 1976: 43). Oyeyemi adopts the twin motif, but also foregrounds the vulnerability of artistic creations, including text and painting. Any book, no matter how canonical, can be stained by food, scribbled on, or otherwise destroyed. The twins in *Icarus* are thus not subservient to their literary precursors, but assertively, even antagonistically, engaged with them. Tilly tears up Jess's *ibeji* drawings, and subsequently breaks Jess's mirror, a perfect enactment of the collapse of mimesis.

The poem that Jess and Tilly write together is semantically

ambiguous: *'I asked if I could go to her / To find my thoughts, to think one day'* (Oyeyemi 2005a: 157). Its metre recalls the iambs of spoken English, as well as the specific use of iambic tetrameter in English and Scottish ballads. The eight-line poem's rhymes (head/dead, her/prefer, day/stay) suggest a mirror-like symmetry, the possibility of being neatly cut in half. But the poem's content belies this symmetry. Like the ever-shifting boundaries between Jess and Tilly, the semantic relation of 'I' to 'her' is unclear. The speaker's mind and body are split, separated from 'my thoughts', which are with 'her.' These aesthetic tensions are what give the novel much of its life force: it dialogues with the canonical and conventional up to a certain point, until both are found to be wanting.

White Is for Witching, a Gothic novel set between Dover and Cambridge, similarly resists narrative unity and linearity. It is structured by a set of interwoven narratives, drawn together through variations in typography, including switches in font and style to signal shifts in narrative position. Oyeyemi's experimental use of lineation additionally functions as a visual code of narrative disruption. The twins' spatially appositional but disparate narratives are periodically joined by an overlapping word:

> Miranda went to see if Deme and Suryaz were all right.
> 'Who is it?' the girls said together, when she knocked on the attic door.
> 'It's me,' she said.
> They wouldn't answer after
> that
> evening, Emma and I broke up. (Oyeyemi 2010: 41)

In this instance, 'that' acts as a bridge between each twin's perspective; as a deictic word, its meaning is dependent upon context. However, it rests *between* narratives, relevant to both Miranda's stilted day-time conversation and Eliot's evening break-up. As textual points in which the two narratives converge, the bridge words – which include 'the lift', 'there', 'before', 'white' and 'the mannequin' (Oyeyemi 2010: 35, 62, 85, 115, 137), all suggestive of the text's motifs of transition, time and racial difference – visually reinforce the twins' paradoxical 'twoness and oneness' (Evans 2006: 69). The text's bridge words, like its twins, generate moments of temporal and spatial indeterminacy in which events on either side of the textual 'bridge' are forced to collide. Oyeyemi's unorthodox deployment of modern print techniques generates twin narratives coded through both visual and rhetorical modes.

The whiteness of Oyeyemi's Anglo-French twins is consistently foregrounded. Miranda and Eliot are not obviously 'postcolonial' or 'diasporic' figures, but members of a 'rosy little English family' (Oyeyemi 2010: 74). The white chalk cliffs of Dover are geopolitically and psychically crucial to the text's narrative. Miranda's eating disorder, pica, compels her to eat chalk, a literal consumption of whiteness which seems to correlate with her own 'white white face' (Oyeyemi 2010: 104). However, Miranda is simultaneously associated with liminality and foreignness. Her attraction to chalk finds intertextual resonance in Chimamanda Ngozi Adichie's *Half of a Yellow Sun*. In Adichie's novel, Olanna, also a twin, recalls the use of chalk in the Igbo kola nut ritual, in which women 'smeared it on their faces and, sometimes, even nibbled it [. . .] Olanna had chewed on the piece of chalk too' (2007: 192). The 'vast bank of chalk' on which Dover Castle stands and which Miranda consumes, then, invokes both whiteness and specifically Nigerian cultural practices (Oyeyemi 2010: 80).[10] Dover, 'the key to England' is presented as a site of national and racial anxiety (Oyeyemi 2010: 107). Miranda reads of 'the stabbing of the fourth Kosovan refugee in three weeks' and accompanies the family's Nigerian housekeeper, Sade, on trips to the Immigration Removal Centre (Oyeyemi 2010: 29).

Miranda additionally wears her deceased mother's watch, 'ticking away Haitian time, five hours behind ours' (Oyeyemi 2010: 56). Like Tilly, Miranda is out of time. These anachronistic twins, like the 'post' in 'postcolonial' suggest belatedness, a ruined originary moment which valorises fragmentation and dissonance. *Witching* rebounds with foreign doubles, each mediated through Miranda. Their mother brings back 'a pair of shrivelled corn-husk dolls' from Mexico, an image transformed later in the text when Miranda makes 'a cloth doll' for an Azeri child (Oyeyemi 2010: 19). In a search for her own double, Miranda purchases a 'very white' mannequin from an Indian trader at the Petticoat Lane Market (Oyeyemi 2010: 123).

Miranda's relationship with Ore, a black girl, figures as the text's ultimate instance of inter-racial twinning, reinforcing her proximity to 'other' cultures: 'Is it alright to say how much I like this [. . .] The way our skin looks together' (Oyeyemi 2010: 167). Ore is at the nexus of the text's racial tensions, her skin presented as a somatic site of contest. The Dover house subsequently makes explicit Ore's positioning within its racial and national schema, condemning Miranda's love for 'The skin. The skin' (Oyeyemi 2010: 194). When Ore dries herself off with one of the 'huge white towels', it becomes 'striped with black liquid', leading the house to exclaim, 'The black's coming off' and whistle the tune to 'Rule, Britannia' (Oyeyemi 2010: 214). Prior to her departure from the house, Ore's guest room is filled with a stack of British National Party leaflets. These explicit evocations of British imperialism and exclusionary nationalism are focalised in Eliot. He has access to 1940s newspaper cuttings depicting 'plucky Brits defeating the enemy by maintaining the home front', ventriloquises the racist caricatures of his grandfather's RAF slang, referring to Gauloises as 'golliwogs', and treats Dover's refugee crises with cynicism (Oyeyemi 2010: 69, 221).

Here, the doubling motif does not function in direct opposition to formal colonialism, but as an engagement with the legacies of colonialism, including the exploitation of migrated racial others. Eliot and Miranda loosely embody a Self/Other dialectic whose divisions place pressure on their twinship; Miranda's suicide is catalyzed by Ore's departure from the Dover house. Ore introduces into the text an element of Afro-Caribbean syncretism in her re-telling of the myth of the soucouyant, 'the wicked old woman who [. . .] consumes her food, the souls of others' (Oyeyemi 2010: 147). The soucouyant demonstrates an alternative form of disordered consumption, an alternative identity into which Miranda is transformed. Miranda's skin, like Ore's, is under attack. In Ore's hallucination, Miranda-as-soucouyant undergoes further self-splitting or halving: 'She split, and cleanly, from head to toe [. . .] gathered the halves of her shed skin' (Oyeyemi 2010: 230). In *Witching*, 'skin' is rendered fluid, resisting the binaries of Fanon's epidermal schema. Despite her emphasised whiteness, Miranda is irrevocably twinned to the text's racial others.

It is worth pointing out that though twins are especially important to the Nigerian novel, they also feature in wider postcolonial literary contexts, including (to name just a couple) in Salman Rushdie's *Haroun and the Sea of Stories* (1990) and Arundhati Roy's *The God of Small Things* (1997). Like Tilly in *Icarus* and Miranda in *Witching*, a number of these works feature an 'Other' twin, one characterised by darkness, illness, or evil, and each text's structure relies upon the death of this 'Other.' The necessitated death of a twin does not suggest a turn to an emphasis on the individual and the singular, an allegiance to a modernity predicated upon self-sufficiency and individuation. On the contrary, twins demonstrate the tensions inherent in such social and political frameworks. The dead twin does not disappear, but becomes a phantom other of the living, a specular substitution, which extends and develops the Lacanian mirror stage.

Now, I will consider the novel with which this essay began: *Boy, Snow, Bird*, an eclectic rewriting of the fairy tale 'Snow White' set in 1950s America. Boy Novak leaves her 'ratcatcher' father in New York and moves to the town of Flax Hill in New England, taking little but her American flag with her. In Flax Hill, she marries the jeweler and ex-academic Arturo Whitman, becomes stepmother to his daughter, Snow, and has a daughter of her own, named Bird. Bird is born 'safe and well, and dark' (Oyeyemi 2014: 131). Bird's skin and facial features reveal what the Whitmans had tried to keep hidden for years: their 'coloured' identity. Boy sends Snow away to live with Arturo's dark-skinned sister, Clara, and the sisters grow up apart, until they are brought together again at the novel's denouement.

The novel is a palimpsest of symbol, text, and historical detail, both relying upon and sharply critiquing the American national imaginary from which these symbols, texts, and details are derived. On one level, it is a story about four women across three generations, primarily written from the perspectives of Boy and Bird, alongside some letters written by Snow and, at the end, a reconstruction of the earlier stages of Frank Novak's life as a woman, Frances. On another, it is a story of a nation, in which the 'nice little system' of segregation was still alive 'down South', and where stories like the shooting of the fourteen year old Emmett Till were commonplace (Oyeyemi 2014: 49). To give an illustrative example, at one point of the novel, the sight of Boy's U.S. flag – an indicator of her continued attention to her first love, Charlie Vacic – prompts Arturo to make chains, 'Ankle chains, wrist chains, necklaces made of heavy brass links', a visceral reminder that the country, star-spangled banner and all, was built through the enslavement of black people (Oyeyemi 2014: 125).

In just one respect, this is the Oyeyemi novel that cleaves most closely to the Fanonian mirror paradigm. The white-blonde Boy sees her image in every reflective surface, from picture frames to the back of spoons, but Snow and Bird, both of whom have 'coloured' or 'dark' heritage, mostly have no reflections. In one of the rare moments that Bird is able to see herself in the mirror, it is a degrading sight: standing behind her mother, she 'looked like her maid' (Oyeyemi 2014: 185). Only a child, Bird is associated with phrases and images whose apparent innocuousness belies their immense political freight. She identifies as 'the average annoyed American' and wishes to know about the 'state of the nation' (Oyeyemi 2014: 161, 185).

The novel shows that the language and frameworks we use to describe and understand other people fail to capture the full complexity of human experience. Thus, the light-skinned members of the Whitman family successfully 'pass' as white; a violent, exclusionary nationalism set against the backdrop of the Vietnam War enables bullying schoolchildren to call Louis Chen, an American national, 'a Vietcong'; the evil 'ratcatcher' father Frank Novak was once a woman named Frances, a survivor of sexual violence. Similar tensions abound in the 'black' or 'coloured' characters' names: while the Anglo-Saxon 'Whitman' aurally suggests 'white man' and means 'white haired', the Latinate 'Clara' means 'bright' or 'clear.'

Belonging to a particular identity group is, to a significant degree, about performance and imitation. All that 'folks have to do is look the part', not *be* it (Oyeyemi 2014: 277). For instance, in one potent image, Vivian Whitman's hair begins to fall into her Thanksgiving turkey and cranberry sauce in 'sizeable clumps.' It has been damaged from the too-regular application of lye, just one part of Vivian's beauty regimen that enabled her to 'pass as white' (Oyeyemi 2014: 277). The invisible labour, pain, and potential illness that black people sacrifice to belong aesthetically to the country is brought into contact with some of its most recognisable festive symbols (the Turkey and cranberry sauce) on the most quintessential of American holidays, which itself celebrates the violent genocide of Native American people. This Thanksgiving scene is a crescendo moment in the novel because for the first time, the subject of the family's racial passing, symptomatic of a structurally embedded 'worship of whiteness', is openly discussed (Oyeyemi 2014: 275). Performative and imitative, the act of passing turns out to be another form of mimesis.

As in all of Oyeyemi's fiction, these political concerns are intimately bound up with questions of aesthetics. *Boy, Snow, Bird* is highly ambivalent about the purpose of art, history, literature, and other creative and intellectual endeavours. The terms 'beauty' and 'beautiful' are widely used elsewhere in the novel, and their meanings hotly contested. If beauty is one side of a coin, vanity is the other. In a scene that recalls Jess and Tilly's collaborative writing, Boy and her friend Mia Cabrini pass a fountain pen between them, writing a 'story' from memory about a magician who made his living by either enhancing or diminishing women's beauty. In the misogynistic moral landscape of this story, the mere possession of beauty could make a woman 'unruly' or frightening, and therefore deserving of punishment (Oyeyemi 2014: 52).

Arturo's wife, Julia, offers a damning critique of all aesthetic and intellectual enterprise, noting that it is rare for 'an idea or a piece of art' to satisfy all three criteria of 'beauty' or 'technique' or 'usefulness' (Oyeyemi 2014: 36). Arturo quits the academy for similar philosophical reasons, uncertain of the direction of historical causation: perhaps 'time just does all the deeds' and 'we pitifully try to save face by pretending we were at the controls' (Oyeyemi 2014: 30). Prior to becoming a jewelry convert, he dismissed the trade as merely making 'baubles' to 'feed vanity', an all-consuming hunger that would 'eat anything' (Oyeyemi 2014: 37). But there is some redemption to be found for a love of beauty and the beautiful: the inhabitants of sleepy

Flax Hill take pride in their craft, and in being people who 'make beautiful things.' They, including Arturo, are at great pains to show that they do not make for the sake of it: 'We're interested in the process, not the end product' (Oyeyemi 2014: 22–23).

What, then, can 'beautiful things' do? Oyeyemi makes subtle, meaningful literary allusions that align her novel with a long tradition of black American writing that is poised at the intersection of memoir and political treatise. The birdcage that Snow sends to Bird as a gift evokes Maya Angelou's poem 'Caged Bird' and her autobiography, *I Know Why the Caged Bird Sings* (1969). Importantly, the cage in Bird's hands is broken, a mere toy, its 'days as a jailhouse' well and truly over. Clara Baxter (née Whitman) purchases an 1846 edition of *The Narrative of the Life of Frederick Douglass*, a work that established the tradition of slave writing and shaped Angelou's own experiments with the autobiographical mode. *Boy, Snow, Bird* straddles several temporalities, dramatising the historical realities of slavery, imagining a freer future, and honouring the role of literary production in liberation movements by paying homage to those that came before.

Oyeyemi's fiction abnegates the timeworn notion of the empire 'writing back' to the centre from the periphery.[11] It also challenges other binary readings of recent literature that see the Nigerian diaspora 'writing back' to, or exclusively about, the 'homeland.' Just as the colonial, anti-colonial and postcolonial periods of any given nation (say, Nigeria) must be understood as shifts of power that are part of a much bigger global system, Oyeyemi's engagement with Nigeria and anti-colonial writing (the references to books by Achebe and Soyinka in *The Icarus Girl*, for instance) must be read within the broader political and intellectual contexts of her literary output. Yes, in some respects, her novels – *The Icarus Girl* in particular – present a distinctive reading of self-splitting that is largely derived from Nigerian contexts, but she writes as richly and urgently about the U.S. Civil Rights movement and migration in Europe as she does about the place of the African diaspora.

It goes without saying that the descriptors used in literary criticism are never neutral, but are themselves a form of analysis that either expand or foreclose possibility. 'Nigerian', 'third-generation', 'immigrant' and 'diasporic' are all useful and necessary terms grounded in biographical fact, but Oyeyemi's writing exceeds the boundaries of any national or diasporic paradigm. These novels are not in a birdcage, the 'jailhouse' of fixed categories and enclosure, but without it, free from it. The various motifs of mirroring explored here offer the fullest illumination of Oyeyemi's complex understanding of art and constructions of identity, challenging the current labelling of her literature and biographical readings of her work and enjoining us to consider these labels afresh. This essay has been defined by the conviction that Oyeyemi's fiction, like the 'new' Nigerian novel more broadly, is an exemplary contribution to world literature. I hope to have cleared some ground for more studies to consider her fiction in this light.

Notes

1 Without implicating them in my argument, I would like to thank Elleke Boehmer, Tamara Moellenberg, and Ankhi Mukherjee for their contributions to the ideas developed in this essay.

2 It is important to note that Fanon remains engaged in the notion of splitting even in his more explicitly political writing; in *The Wretched of the Earth* he describes communal ritual as a 'collective ecstasy.' 'Ecstasy' etymologically suggests a self-splitting, of being 'beside oneself', attesting to the paradoxical unity that comes out of being part of a disrupted group in the postcolonial state. Fanon's overlapping 'psychic' and 'political' approaches draw together the dualities of postcolonial theory itself, presenting paradigms through which questions of race and nationhood, as well as individual subjectivity, may be explored. See Fanon (2004: 83).

3 For a discussion of this idea, see Abrams 1953: 30–46.

4 Ouma makes a similar point about Oyeyemi's character, Jess: 'Jess's multiple genealogies are constituted by these varied narrative sources – literature, history, myth, and legend' (2014: 192).

5 For a representative example, see Cooper 2008: 52. For a reading of Oyeyemi's *The Opposite House* as a treatise on multiculturalism and its failure to include black people, see Cousins 2012.

6 In their reading of *The Icarus Girl* as a work of postcolonial gothic, Ilott and Buckley (2015) emphasise the significance of the novel's location in the colonial centre and make important strides in this direction.

7 In his study of *Things Fall Apart*, Abiola Irele examines the imbrication of the text's 'cultural reference' and expressive means (2001: 116). I take a similar approach in considering the relationship between the formal and figurative elements of contemporary twin texts.

8 In Act III of Shakespeare's tragedy, Hamlet turns to the classical theory of poetic and dramatic mimesis, reminding the stage players that the 'purpose of playing' is to 'hold as 'twere the mirror up to nature', hoping that their performance of the *Murder of Gonzago* will reveal Claudius's villainy (Shakespeare 1982: 3.2.21–24). Oyeyemi paraphrases a line from *Hamlet* on a similar theme – hypocrisy – in *Boy, Snow, Bird*. Hamlet notes 'That one may smile, and smile, and be a villain' (1.5.108), and Boy, using the second person to narrate her story, says 'It's perfectly clear to you that people can smile and smile and still be villains' (Oyeyemi 2014: 6).

9 Lawal notes 'If one of the pair should die, tradition requires that a memorial (ere ibeji) be procured to localize the soul of the deceased so as to

maintain the spiritual bond between the living and the dead' (2011: 85–86).

10 Oyeyemi is of Yoruba, not Igbo descent, but this intertext testifies to convergences in Nigerian cultural symbolisms.

11 The classic theoretical account of this idea is *The Empire Writes Back: Theory and Practice in Post-colonial Literatures* edited by Ashcroft, Griffiths, and Tiffin (1989).

Works Cited

Achebe, C. 1976: *Things Fall Apart*. London: Heinemann.

Adichie, C. N. 2007: *Half of a Yellow Sun*. London: Harper Perennial.

Ashcroft, B., Griffiths, G. and Tiffin, H. (eds.) 2002: *The Empire Writes Back: Theory and Practice in Post-colonial Literatures*. London: Routledge.

Boehmer, E. 2005: *Colonial and Postcolonial Literature: Migrant Metaphors*. 2nd edition. Oxford: Oxford University Press.

Boehmer, E. 2009: Achebe and His Influence in Contemporary African Writing. *Interventions* 11 (2), 141–153.

Bryce, J. 2008: 'Half and Half Children': Third-Generation Women Writers and the New Nigerian Novel. *Research in African Literatures* 39 (2), 49–67.

Cooper, B. 2008: Diaspora, gender and identity: Twinning in three diasporic novels. *English Academy Review: Southern African Journal of English Studies*, 25 (1), 51–65.

Cousins, H. 2012: Helen Oyeyemi and the Yoruba gothic: *White Is for Witching*. *The Journal of Commonwealth Literature* 47 (1), 47–58.

Cousins, H. Unplaced/Invaded: Multiculturalism in Helen Oyeyemi's *The Opposite House*. *Postcolonial Text* 7 (3) http://postcolonial.org/index.php/pct/article/view/1465/1383

Evans, D. 2006; *26a*. London: Vintage.

Fanon, F. 1996: *Black Skin, White Masks*. Translated by C. Lam Markmann. London: Pluto.

Fanon, F. 2004: *The Wretched of the Earth*. New York: Grove Press.

Habila, H. 2008: *Measuring Time*. London: Hamish Hamilton.

Hron, M. 2008: Ora Na-Azu Nwa': The Figure of the Child in Third-Generation Nigerian Novels. *Research in African Literatures* 39 (2), 27–48.

Ilott, S. and Buckley, C. 2016: 'Fragmenting and becoming double': Supplementary twins and abject bodies in Helen Oyeyemi's *The Icarus Girl*. *The Journal of Commonwealth Literature* 21 (3), 402–15.

Irele, A. 2001: *The African Imagination: Literature in Africa & the Black Diaspora*. Oxford: Oxford University Press.

Lacan, J. 2004: The Mirror Stage as Formative of the Function of the I as Revealed in Psychoanalytic Experience. In J. Rivkin and M. Ryan (eds.) *Literary Theory: An Anthology*. Oxford: Blackwell, 441–46.

Lawal, B. 2011: Sustaining the Oneness in Their Twoness: Poetics of Twin Figures (Ere Ibeji) Among the Yoruba. In P. M. Peek (ed.) *Twins in African and Diaspora Cultures: Double Trouble, Twice Blessed*. Bloomington: Indiana University Press, 81–98.

Ouma, C. 2014: Reading the Diasporic Abiku in Helen Oyeyemi's *The Icarus Girl*. *Research in African Literatures* 45 (3), 188–205.

Oyeyemi, H. 2005a: *The Icarus Girl*. London: Bloomsbury.

Oyeyemi, H. 2005b: Home, strange home. *Guardian.* https://www.theguardian.com/world/2005/feb/02/hearafrica05.development2.
Oyeyemi, H. 2007: *The Opposite House.* London: Bloomsbury.
Oyeyemi, H. 2010: *White Is for Witching.* London: Picador.
Oyeyemi, H. 2014: *Boy, Snow, Bird.* New York: Riverhead.
Plato. 2013: *Republic: Books 6–10.* Edited and translated by C. Emlyn-Jones and W. Preddy. Cambridge: Harvard University Press.
Shakespeare, W. 1982: *Hamlet.* Ed. Harold Jenkins. London: Routledge.

CHAPTER

4

'Why do people go to these places, these places that are not for them?': (De)constructing Borders in *White Is for Witching* and *The Opposite House*

Katie Burton

In Helen Oyeyemi's *White Is for Witching* and *The Opposite House*, language is frequently exposed as a vehicle for xenophobic nationalist ideologies that control and displace the Other, also limiting the dialogue available to those who are marginalised. By representing language as a barrier that often upholds ideological borders, Oyeyemi illustrates how such borders also contribute to the making up of a national identity. This chapter will show how Oyeyemi's fiction depicts Britain as a nation that strives to define itself through fixed geographical borders. These borders are then replicated through the ways in which characters are presented as national allegories, their own self-definition becoming a microcosm of the negotiation of British national identity. I argue that such an emphasis on national identity as a principal form of self-definition points towards and resists a xenophobic nationalism that isolates self and Other by highlighting the traumatic consequences such an attitude has on Britain as a whole. The portrayal of fixed geographical borders is mirrored within the novels through literal and imaginative borders that control each character uniquely. Such borders convey the limitations and the trauma of existing as one of those constructed as a cultural or racial Other within

Britain. However, the theme of haunting subsequently allows in-between spaces to enable the transgression of these boundaries. In this way, Oyeyemi creates a narrative that gives voice to those forced to occupy an 'in-between' space. Overall, this chapter demonstrates the way physical and conceptual borders are constructed within Britain to control both self and Other in order to establish a sense of national identity. Thus, I argue that Oyeyemi's use of the past to explore these borders also transgresses them, as the characters central to my readings, who can be defined as Other, are given access to the past in a way that enables control over their own identities.

In *White Is for Witching* Oyeyemi uses national allegory, borders and spaces to explore the negotiation of a national identity through questions of belonging. The characters of Miranda and Ore convey the anxieties of a postcolonial England striving to identify its 'Englishness' against the backdrop of the idea that England is a multicultural society. Here, I follow Sarah Ilott's discussion of multiculturalism as not only 'the simple fact of cultural diversity', but a problematic term that denotes an ideal image of society often taken as a political reality in a discursive move that further excludes people already excluded by racism, disenfranchisement and alienation (2015: 142). The anxieties over what constitutes a British, or more specifically English identity, is therefore just one troubling aspect of a discourse of multiculturalism that does not 'face up to social realities' (Ilott 2015: 142). This chapter shows how Oyeyemi's novels interrogate the racist idea that 'whiteness' constitutes Englishness that has continued to persist alongside, and in dialogue with, notions of multiculturalism.

That national identity continues to be constructed with recourse to racist notions of whiteness and reverse colonisation is explored by Vron Ware. She notes that

> political discourse in the UK repeatedly directs public attention to the potential disruption that 'immigrants' represent to some imagined harmonious British way of life. Led from above, these successive official scoldings, warnings, and threats, combined with ever stricter immigration controls in the name of 'fairness,' only serve to reinforce the borders held in place by intransigent racism and the 'white fear' it feeds off. (Ware 2010: 110)

Demonstrating the ways in which language and culture uphold such borders, this chapter shows how Oyeyemi's fiction highlights the hypocrisy of the 'imagined harmonious British way of life' to which Ware refers. Moreover, building upon Patrick Colm Hogan's exploration of the 'in-group' and 'out-group' divisions that form national identity, this chapter illustrates how Oyeyemi's work reveals a sense of 'Britishness' dependent upon past imperial ideologies that isolate the 'out-group.' More specifically, I examine 'The dilemma [that] comes from the fact that the national community cannot be familiar' (Hogan 2009: 95). As such, an attachment to imperial ghosts exemplifies the notion of 'Affectivity [as] the infusion of emotion into our ideas about identity' (Hogan 2009: 93). Accordingly, I argue that nostalgia and familiarity uphold the geographical and imaginative borders that denote this version of British national identity.

In reference to *White Is for Witching,* I assert that Miranda Silver offers an ambivalent response to these discourses of whiteness as Englishness. Contrary to Amy K. King's claim that 'the reader sees Miranda as a symbol (albeit unwilling) of white Britishness that can only consume the Other', I argue that Miranda actively seeks to dispel her internalised racism (2013: 69). Reading the various acts of consumption within the novel, I demonstrate that Miranda's eating habits signify more than simply consumption of the Other; instead, they exemplify the in-between space that Miranda occupies, between an imperial and postcolonial Britain. Oyeyemi uses the voice of the guesthouse (29 Barton Road) to illustrate the power of the matriarchal line as it transports its racist beliefs through time, replicating the racism and borders that exclude cultural and racial Others. Thus, the first half of this chapter engages with the construction of borders in the process of negotiating a British national identity, demonstrating ways in which Oyeyemi uses her characters as vehicles that both manifest a British 'self' and transgress constructed boundaries through their own explorations of identity.

Oyeyemi's use of language in *The Opposite House* illustrates ways in which xenophobic nationalism isolates cultural and racial Others. Ian Baucom writes: 'In describing the territories of British imperialism as spaces of bewilderment and loss which continue to trouble and confound England's subjects, Rushdie indicates that such imperial estrangements of English identity survive the formal end of imperialism' (1999: 3–4). Building upon this, I focus on ways in which national affiliations are prioritised over others and used as a means of Othering those with a national heritage originating beyond British borders. In Oyeyemi's fiction, Britain, as a former colonial power, is occupied by ghosts of an imperial past that control the Other as they internalize past ideologies that subsequently haunt British society. As such, Britain's colonial legacy restricts self-identification and identity expression for those constructed as Other. Furthermore, British imperial ideologies haunt the present day as Maja internalises a sense of disentitlement. This demonstrates the hypocrisy of a national identity that strives to uphold order in a country that uses language to create barriers around culture. As cultural Others are excluded from British history and therefore from a sense of Britishness located in the past, disorder is generated through the trauma that this triggers. My reading of Oyeyemi's work shows how reconciling more than one cultural identity is rendered problematic, as living 'in-between' creates a conflict within Maja that leads to the abjection of the self. Having established a definition of 'Britishness' that is dependent on imperial ideologies in the first half of the chapter, the second section then goes on to show how Oyeyemi transcends these borders by enabling a narrative voice that does not silence cultural or racial hybridity.

White Is for Witching

Oyeyemi uses national allegory in *White Is for Witching* to demonstrate the development of Britain as a postcolonial nation. The novel notes that the protagonist, Miranda, is born in 1982, the same year as the Falklands War. The war is described by King as 'Britain's last-ditch effort to hang onto its empire' and its association with Miranda suggests she is allegorical of Britain (2013: 63). King notes that 'Miranda and post-imperial Britain age together' (2013: 63). Whether or not Britain can be deemed 'post-imperial' is questionable, of course, and this chapter will take the uncertainty of the phrase into consideration. Indeed, Oyeyemi draws attention to the lingering effects of British imperialist ideology, particularly through the first person narration of the guest house, 29 Barton Road, which has been possessed by Miranda's great-grandmother Anna Good (the 'goodlady'). The house narrates its account of Anna Good's husband dying in the Second World War:

> 'I hate them,' she said. 'Blackies, Germans, killers, dirty . . . dirty killers. He should have stayed here with me. Shouldn't have let him leave. Bring him back, bring him back, bring him back to me.' She spoke from that part of her that was older than her. The part of her that will always tie me to her, to her daughter Jennifer, to Jennifer's stubborn daughter Lily, to Lily's even more stubborn daughter Miranda [. . .] It's Luc that keeps letting people in [. . .] They shouldn't be allowed in though, those others, so eventually I make them leave. (Oyeyemi 2009: 118)

Adopting the desires of Anna Good, 29 Barton Road embodies an imperial nostalgia that is explored by Simon Gikandi in his monograph, *Maps of Englishness: Writing Identity in the Culture of Colonialism*. Gikandi states that 'official Englishness has (at least since the 1970s) dressed itself up in imperial nostalgia, as a way of restaging its lost identity' (1996: 21). So the guesthouse acts as a neo-imperial space within the novel by demonstrating how people's racist tendencies in a 1940s Britain affected by the Second World War have been passed on through subsequent generations. This racism, along with the goodlady's ideologies of white supremacy, asserts itself in the designation of the black guests of 29 Barton road as 'those others.' Oyeyemi thus reveals how imperial nostalgia constructs and relies upon an Other, an 'out-group' that is subject to 'fear, anger and distrust' (Hogan 2009: 115). The Other is thereby demonised and placed on the margins of society. The guest house represents the borders that contain, control and ostracize the Other.

Oyeyemi portrays the fragility of ideological borders when a geographical border is jeopardized. Chaos and destruction ensue when borders are breached, revealing the hypocrisy and impracticality of an ideal national identity. Oyeyemi reveals the power of the goodlady and her fear of the racial Other after the death of Lily Silver, shot in Port-au-Prince. When the voice of the guesthouse asserts that the bullets that killed Lily were 'for' her, it suggests that Lily deserves to die. Lily is deemed unclean by the guesthouse and the implication is that her trip to Haiti is what has wronged the goodlady. Thus, Lily's death reveals the lengths to which the goodlady will go in order to uphold her imperial borders. In relation to Haiti, Gikandi suggests that it represents 'the spectral metaphor of blackness – an imminent threat to the idea of Englishness; against the metropole's idea of order and civilization, the black republic stands as the embodiment of chaos and disorder' (1996: 113). Thus, when Lily travels to Haiti, she jeopardizes the order and borders upheld within the guesthouse. Lily disobeys the goodlady and threatens the nostalgic Englishness that she represents. Noting that Haiti is a 'black well' that only yields 'black water', the guest house asserts the racist fear that Lily's venture into this space will bring contamination (Oyeyemi 2009: 9). Thus, Lily is 'pushed [. . .] outside, out of life' by an 'opponent [who] had great wings' (Oyeyemi 2009: 8). Since 29 Barton Road asserts that the bullets are intended for Lily, I read Lily's opponent as the goodlady. Thus Lily's death illustrates the goodlady's desire to control who belongs where, and the great distance her power can span. What Lily's death also reveals is the hypocrisy of imperial British ideologies, which destroy not only those constructed as Other but also elements of the self. Though the goodlady acts ostensibly to uphold the prevailing order, disorder is generated. In this way, the power structure that positions an imperial Englishness as superior is threatened. Lily's literal crossing of the national border exemplifies the size of this threat to the goodlady as a metaphor for the nation.

The connection made by the goodlady between the Silver women demonstrates the power of the matriarchal line. It is evident that Miranda has partially internalized elements of these xenophobic beliefs:

> She said, 'someone is going around stabbing these people?' She didn't want to say 'refugees'. She didn't want to say Kosovans. She didn't know why. Or maybe it seemed feeble somehow, like making a list of things that were a shame. (Oyeyemi 2009: 30)

The uncertainty Miranda feels about her 'shame' appears to imply her disgrace at the notion of identifying citizens of Dover as Other (Kosovans or refugees). What her ambivalence also suggests is that she is not fully aware of the racism she has internalised. In this way, Miranda represents a component of English identity that is also unresolved. Where the guesthouse is linked to the discrimination and imperial principles apparent in the Second World War, such as the 'Blackies, Germans, killers' already mentioned, Miranda's connection to the Falklands war illustrates a process of decolonization. As Britain was faced with negotiating a new identity in the wake of the loss of its previously vast empire, a search for a national identity became a search for familiarity. Hogan suggests that the national community 'is necessarily composed almost entirely of strangers' (2009: 95). So the development of the postcolonial Britain that Miranda embodies exemplifies a progressing nation that must fight for equality in the face of injustice based on distrust and unfamiliarity. As Hogan suggests, 'If I share language, dress, food, and various habits with my fellow citizens, unknown individuals will appear less unfamiliar to me' (2009: 95). Thus, the necessity of permeable boundaries to create a successful multicultural Britain in which racist and xenophobic attitudes no longer exist is made possible through the sharing of culture, rather than the control of the Other (Hogan 2009: 95).

The inner conflict in Miranda can be compared to Sandra M. Gilbert and Susan Gubar's study of the Grimms' tale, 'Little Snow White' (1812). By comparing Miranda's appearance – red lips, black hair, ghostly white skin – to Snow White, I read the goodlady as taking on the role of the wicked step-mother and Queen. Just as the Queen 'has internalized the King's rules', Miranda has internalised the goodlady's ideology to the extent that she somewhat lacks self control (Gilbert and Gubar 1979: 38). Miranda's self control is questioned by her twin brother Eliot after they hear the news of their mother's death:

> Later – when dad told us what the voice on the phone had told him – prim, slender Miri folded her hands on the lap of her dress. She looked down and, for a moment, appeared to be smiling. She wasn't smiling. She wasn't in control of her face. (Oyeyemi 2009: 8)

Here, features of the goodlady are at work in Miranda as she smiles at her own mother's death, a death which could only have pleased the goodlady. Although this potentially depicts Miranda, with her pale skin, as a manifestation of the white British ideology, as is argued by King, there are points in the novel when it is possible to read Miranda in alternative ways. Each character describes her possible fate differently. Ore believes that Miranda's 'throat is blocked with the slice of an apple', suggesting a link to Gilbert and Gubar's analysis of the fairy tale (Oyeyemi 2009: 1). Like Snow White, Miranda 'had to find her own devious way of resisting the onslaught of the Maddened queen, both inside and outside herself' (Gilbert and Gubar 1979: 40). By not fully ingesting the apple, Miranda refuses to allow the goodlady to control her, as she does with the other guests. At this point, Miranda occupies an in-between space. On the one hand, she exists within 29 Barton Road and is partially bound by the matriarchal lineage that exists outside herself physically, in the form of the guest house as a carrier of the voice of the goodlady and its imperial legacy. On the other hand, Miranda simultaneously strives to reject the ideologies she has inherited inside herself.

Acts of consumption within *White Is for Witching* also hold great significance in regards to a negotiation of identity, both on an individual and national scale. Miranda, and each of her female ancestors, have suffered with the eating disorder, pica. Pica is the eating of and appetite for non-nutritional substances. Miranda's habits of consumption and specific cravings signify something more than simply an eating disorder; they demonstrate a national allegory that displays her navigation through an in-between space, allowing the transgression of British geographical borders. One of the substances she chooses to eat is chalk: 'What Miri did was, she crammed chalk into her mouth under her covers. She hid the packaging at the bottom of her bag and threw it away when we got to school' (Oyeyemi 2009: 22). Ilott reads this consumption of the substance on which Miranda's hometown of Dover is built as a sign of 'the absurdity of denying the intrusion of the Other', as 'the national borders [are] resurrected within her own body' (2015: 64). Miranda's desire to eat chalk equally resembles a desire to deconstruct the physical border of the white cliffs that exist outside of her, conveying an active attempt to reject the internalised racist ideologies she has inherited from the goodlady. As a character representing her nation through acts of consumption, Miranda can be read as an ambivalent figure who transcends the boundaries that are constructed by her ancestors.

Oyeyemi further destabilises the geographical borders that define British identity through Miranda's acts of consumption. Oyeyemi explores the idea of entitlement to food in relation to Miranda, describing the guilt she feels because of her internal connection to the goodlady. Oyeyemi further evokes the eating disorder anorexia through Miranda's consumption of substances with no nutritional value. In Maud Ellmann's *The Hunger Artists*, entitlement and starvation are brought together, as the act of starving oneself is explored from the perspective of having, or feeling like one does not have, a right to food: 'People starve because they have no food, not because there is no food, and the problem, therefore, is "entitlement" to food, rather than its notional availability' (1993: 5). Miranda's act of starving herself of nutrition therefore demonstrates a need to suppress her culpability in relation to the goodlady's influence, as she strives to control the conflict within herself; in feeding herself, she recognises that she is also feeding the goodlady. Further to this, Miranda expresses a desire to expel the goodlady from within herself through her consumption of particular substances. Onyx is one of these substances, the 'properties of onyx' being that 'it helps you hold your emotions steady; side effects of onyx: it is the sooty hand that strangles all the feeling out of you' (Oyeyemi 2009: 51). As a gemstone, onyx supposedly 'removes spirit possessions,' and 'supports going on alone' (Stein 2008: 146). The goodlady is constructed as both self and Other in relation to Miranda, connected by blood yet ideologically distinct. Thus, with Miranda's own character being so bound to that of the goodlady, she potentially jeopardises her own identity in order to diminish that which is Other to and exists within her. Ellmann states: 'starvation seems to represent the only means of saving subjectivity from the invasion of the other in the form of food' (1993: 31). If food can be considered as Other in this case, then Miranda can be read as consuming only what is familiar to her: the chalk representing the whiteness of her skin and the onyx representing the blackness of her hair. As a result of her life-threatening eating disorders, Miranda illustrates how refusing the Other can cause such internal devastation.

The introduction of Ore into the novel demonstrates how borders built upon imperialist ideologies can limit and control identity. As Ore and Miranda enter into a romantic relationship, the way such borders manifest themselves within each character exemplifies the racism that is ingrained within imperialist and/or xenophobic constructions of Britishness. As Ore is a black British citizen who has been adopted by a white British family, the construction of her identity and self-definition differs from that of Miranda. Whilst Ore's parentage is unknown, Miranda's character is defined in part by the power the matriarchal line holds over her. The way each character identifies themselves again echoes Gilbert and Gubar's reading of 'Little Snow White': 'To be caught and trapped in a mirror rather than a window however, is to be driven inward, obsessively studying self-images as if seeking a viable self' (1979: 37). Miranda's room in the guesthouse highlights her need to examine her inner self:

> In a psychomantium, glass topples darkness. Things appear as they really are. Visions are called from a point inside the mirror, from a point inside the mind. Miranda looked in. She looked with the most particular care and she saw Lily Silver standing there in her room, smiling sadly. (Oyeyemi 2009: 33–34)

The vision of Lily in the mirror coming from a point inside Miranda's mind depicts the strength of the matriarchal line, which in turn implies that Miranda's own self-definition comes from fragments of others: from her ancestors, her twin brother, her lover. Her connection to the past is presented as a burden; through Miranda's struggle, the destructive potential of nostalgia for a national identity built on the premise that borders should define, control, and exclude is made apparent.

Ore's identity is constructed in relation to borders that separate 'us' and 'them.' She feels this distinction keenly whilst at university at Cambridge:

> I was taking steps to blindfold myself so that when I came out of the door of my college room this morning I didn't see the glass windows glaring at me out of the fourteenth century walls. Walls and windows forbade me. They pulled at me and said, You don't belong here. (Oyeyemi 2009: 24)

Whilst Miranda looks inward to find her identity, Ore's identity is defined by her position in relation to the outside world and, in this case, a traditional British institution. Hogan defines 'reflexive identity' as a:

> hierarchized set of properties and relations which one takes to define oneself. This set prominently includes sex, race, ethnicity, family posi-

> tion, and so forth. This set of properties and relations is first of all a matter of social attribution, not introspection. (2000: 322)

Thus, in relation to Ore, whose race is central to her reflexive identity as a black British citizen, identity becomes primarily reflexive within a former colonizing nation. Against her will, Ore is placed on the margins of ideological 'Englishness', and the window at which she stands – placed in the wall of a building exemplary of the British establishment – prevents her from taking her place within British history.

In contrast, it is possible to read Miranda's whiteness (often perceived as a lack of ethnicity, or the norm from which other ethnicities deviate) as a lack of reflexive identity, a lack which leads to her feeding off Ore:

> Then Miranda shifted and opened my mouth with her own. As we kissed I became aware of something leaving me. It left me in a solid stream, heavy as rope. It left from a hurt in my side, and it went into Miranda, it went into the same place in her. (Oyeyemi 2009: 26)

In relation to Ore, Ilott notes that 'Acts of consumption that blur the lines between bodily and national borders render Ore's body the stage on which a nationalist politics that is hostile to immigrants and their descendants plays out' (2015: 65–66). Consuming Ore as a representation of the racial Other, Miranda negotiates a hybrid identity within herself that is a microcosm of a multicultural Britain being negotiated around her, one that can be seen to consume the racial Other even as it seemingly celebrates racial diversity. This relationship of consumption between Miranda and Ore also demonstrates the absurdity of the fears described by Ware in relation to Britain being 'full up', as the only person who feels the debilitating effects of this consumption is Ore, the racial Other (2010: 102). When the role of the Other is denied in history through a language that seeks to control, the borders that are formed contain and control elements of the self too.

The Opposite House

Nationalism and national identity also play a key role in demonstrating the isolation of the Other in *The Opposite House*. Hogan defines nationalism as 'any form of in-group identification for a group defined in part by reference to a geographical area along with some form of sovereign government over that area' (2009: 4). In *The Opposite House* it is made evident that drawing on national identity as a primary point of affiliation is considered integral to existing within the boundaries of British society. Oyeyemi's narrative draws attention to the ways in which British society reacts to cultural hybridity by emphasising the importance of the 'in-group' identification to which Hogan refers. The protagonist, Maja, is a black Cuban living in London; she has Cuban and West African roots, a complex heritage that positions her as Other due to her lack of a single national identity. Maja's own struggles in defining herself are made evident when she reacts to the prejudices she faces from her African classmates as they evaluate her 'roots' in comparison with another girl:

> 'You know, a lot of the others have been saying that out of you and Dominique, we like you better. You're all right. You're roots.'
>
> I must have seemed stupid to her. I said 'Huh?' I thought a black girl was a black girl. Why did it come down to a choice between me and Dominique, and not any of the other girls? We were both black without coming from the right place. We were the slave girls from Trinidad and Cuba; not supposed to speak Spanish, not supposed to speak English either. (Oyeyemi 2007: 97)

This exchange demonstrates that Maja is polarised by her heritage and displaced within the wider community as she is deemed not 'right' because her blackness is not the same as her peers'; she does not conform to their in-group identification. The situation reflects more widely upon the alleged importance of a 'sense of [national] identification' that allows the superior identity in question – be it Maja's classmates or the British government – to control their boundaries and the subjects within them (Hogan 2009: 4). That which may be deemed integration within a multicultural nation is therefore merely a mechanism to create a hierarchised structure that removes the agency of the Other.

Location and cultural heritage work simultaneously to place this novel within the Gothic genre. Through an exploration of the past through haunting, this brings to light histories that have been repressed by Britain as a formerly colonizing nation. In the introduction to *The Routledge Companion to Gothic*, Catherine Spooner and Emma McEvoy state that the Gothic can be 'defined according to its emphasis on the returning past' (2007: 1). The protagonist's younger brother, Tomás, exemplifies this return to past. At the beginning of the novel Tomás is referred to as 'the London baby' by his parents (Oyeyemi 2007: 7). Immediately, he is assigned an identity that is dependent upon the nation in which he was born. The pressure to perform this identity is suggested by the '[T]ubes of face paint [that] form a deliberate circle on Tomás' dresser. His paintbrushes are gelled stiff and white' (Oyeyemi 2007: 78). When Maja witnesses him using his paints, the burden of existing as a black person subjected to British imperial ideologies is made evident: 'The eye set in the white is cold and black and bright to excess, as if it contains him' (Oyeyemi 2007: 54). The image of containment and the rigidity of the brushes on his desk demonstrate the way Tomás is controlled and confined by the identity given to him; he is unable to escape the legacy of white superiority as a boy with black Cuban heritage, just as he is unable to escape his parents' definition of him as the London baby. Thus Britain's colonial past is still a factor that holds significance, demonstrated by Tomás's need to assimilate, and the location of London is used as a vehicle to show the constraints of being given an identity that is tied to the nation.

In *The Opposite House,* Oyeyemi uses the concept of displacement to highlight the way Britain and its multicultural population are haunted by a colonial past, as imperial ideologies are *also* ingrained in the minds of those constructed Other. In relation to colonialism, Ngũgĩ states that: 'the most important area of domination was the mental universe of the colonised, the control, through culture, of how people perceived themselves and their relationship to the world' (1986: 16). With slavery forming part of her cultural heritage, it is this power dichotomy of white ownership and black subordination that dictates Maja's perception of herself and her relationship to the world. Maja's inability to feel at ease or welcome in her white Ghanaian partner's apartment replicates the way the racial Other is not able to feel welcome in a predominantly white society:

> I'm still not used to Aaron's flat, even though I moved in four months ago, even though he calls it 'ours' [. . .] I approach it with caution. I feel like an interview candidate arriving to be considered for tenancy by the house itself. I lost myself so far as to raise a hand to knock at the door though the keys are already dangling on their ring from the index finger of my other hand. (Oyeyemi 2007: 18)

The idea that Aaron, the owner of the flat, believes that Maja and himself can successfully share the space, places him in a similar position of power that was held by the British as colonisers. Maja's existence within the flat relies on his permission, so her hesitance arises from a lack of a sense of entitlement. Through this portrayal of internalised racism experienced by Maja, Oyeyemi demonstrates an imperial past that still haunts the British population.

Language and culture are closely enmeshed and *The Opposite*

House portrays how this bond can work to exclude: 'books are conversations that are not addressed to me and I want to sneak up and listen but I also want to be invited in. If I was invited in the conversation would not be what it was' (Oyeyemi 2007: 14). Books are a way into the history of a culture, often containing plots that mirror their contemporary culture's social issues and concerns. As Ngũgĩ states:

> Language, any language, has a dual character: it is both a means of communication and a carrier of culture [. . .]. For the British, and particularly the English, it is additionally, and inseparably from its use as a tool of communication, a carrier of their culture and history. (1986: 13)

Books use language to communicate and translate ideas within a culture: Maja's inability to access British language and history highlights the way racism becomes internalised, so the ghosts that haunt Britain are still very much alive. Furthermore, through Maja's difficulties Oyeyemi demonstrates the hypocrisy of multiculturalism in Britain. According to Ngũgĩ, the aim of language is to carry culture through communication. *The Opposite House* reveals language's ties to history that work to exclude anyone who poses a threat to the perception of British history. Whilst offering a critique of this exclusion, *The Opposite House* also establishes a framework for these silences to be discussed so that an inclusive discourse can occur.

The occupation of an 'in-between' space positions Maja as the Other in the society in which she lives. Maja's hybrid identity stems from her experiences as a black Cuban migrant living in London with parents of West African and Cuban heritage. *The Opposite House* both posits childhood as an ideal state and critiques the preference for an overriding national identity as essential to one's self-definition. Maja presents the reader with an account that portrays the effects of being relocated as a young child:

> I was seven years old when we came here. I've come to think that there's an age beyond which it is impossible to lift a child from the pervading marinade of an original country, in another country, another language like hot oil scalding the first language away. I arrived here just before that age. (Oyeyemi 2007: 12)

This vividly illustrates the way identity in childhood is not fixed, but a malleable state. There is a point in time in which Maja's identity is able to shift, but the image of the 'hot oil scalding the first language away' indicates that there is also a juncture at which the opportunity to choose a national identity is removed. The language used indicates the traumatic nature of having an identity constructed by factors beyond one's control.

Reconciling two or more cultural or national identities is presented as problematic in *The Opposite House*. Maja feels excluded from British history and sees the language she learnt as a child being 'scalded away.' It is evident that she fears being silenced as a result of her hybrid identity by being allowed to choose only one language. Oyeyemi challenges this notion using an in-between space that gives Maja the ability to voice her hybridity:

> I start to hum, and to speak tunefully to myself, the way I do when I'm climbing into song. I am nervous because it's been a few days and the most terrifying thing for someone whose vocal chords are strung for both song and speech would be to reach into the dark between one and the other for melody and find nothing. I find it. (Oyeyemi 2007: 44)

The space in between song and speech for Maja, in between Cuba and Britain, is dark. This darkness represents the lack of certainty that is felt as a result of Maja's conflicting identity. Instead of constructing the space between song and speech, where she is afraid she will 'find nothing' as oppressive to Maja, Oyeyemi uses it as an opportunity to establish a dialogue that does not position Maja as the Other to herself. Janet Wilson and Daria Tunca argue that the '"middle ground" of the postcolonial, [is] where identities can metamorphose or be transformed and power relations negotiated' (2015: 1). Oyeyemi uses Maja as a vehicle to explore the 'middle ground' between song and speech as Maja is able to 'reach into the dark between' song and speech, and find melody. So her fear of finding nothing is overcome, and this in-between space enables Maja's voice, thus becoming a space in which hybrid identity can be voiced.

To emphasise a championing of unfixed identity, Oyeyemi presents childhood as a state of being with permeable boundaries that can transgress national borders. Helen Cousins states that Maja seeks a 'simply "black" identity', however the references to Maja's childhood in Cuba depict a desire for an identity that defies any specific label (2012: 1). Referring to the function of the child within narrative, Sujala Singh states that: 'the very search for the past in each of us changes the past as we go along, so that the lost thing is not the same now, as it was before' (2004: 15). I read the past, therefore, as an unpredictable space that can be explored by the characters as a way of gaining control of their self-definition in the present. Maja repeatedly refers back to a childhood memory in which she inhabits a moment and place entitled 'my Cuba.' Chloé Buckley notes that this memory of an evening garden party 'is an experience from which Maja draws strength and identity' (2015: n.p.). The protagonist's desire to return to 'my Cuba' and not simply 'Cuba' represents a desire to return to a period where having a malleable identity is accepted as the norm: childhood. If the 'lost thing' is Maja's identity, she demonstrates how an attempt to search for a national identity on a larger scale is of no use, as the past cannot be used as a stable point of origin from which an identity can be formed. So although Maja believes 'her' Cuba to exist in the physical sense, I perceive it as a representation of the part of her identity that desires the freedom to defy a static identity. This is portrayed with the way Maja describes 'her' Cuba: 'My Cuba is a hut with a tabletop for a roof, wall-less and unmoored by strange music and feet and fruit juice' (Oyeyemi 2007: 45). The image of a wall-less space that could be seen as a sanctuary – both emotionally and physically – underscores the idea that the state of being to which Maja desires to return is an identity with permeable boundaries.

The abject plays a significant role in depicting the traumatic consequences of possessing two conflicting identities. In *Powers of Horror*, Julia Kristeva describes the abject as 'a repulsion [that] places the one haunted by it literally beside himself' (1982: 1). Maja's ambivalence regarding her own national identity results in the death of the ego as a result of an inability to identify with something outside the self as 'nothing is familiar' (Kristeva 1982: 5). At the beginning of the novel she describes her repulsion of food: 'Food: everything I eat, my mouth lets it go, my stomach heaves painful, sour streams' (Oyeyemi 2007: 17). Kristeva describes the act of expelling food as abjecting oneself. Maja abjects food because she does not feel entitled to it. If 'food is not an "other" for "me"' then the abjection of food is Maja's abjection of herself (Kristeva 1982: 3). Referring back to Ellmann's argument that people starve because 'the problem [. . .] is "entitlement" to food, rather than its notional availability', Maja's abjection of food also implies that she does not feel entitled to herself as she is rejecting the 'notional availability' of food (1993: 5). The conflicting identities that are thrust upon Maja as a black Cuban woman living in London remove her agency, shown through her abjection of food and the lack of entitlement it represents. The abjection of food thus displays the self-deprecating nature of possessing a hybrid identity when it results in disintegration of the physical self.

Oyeyemi subverts dichotomies of self and Other in relation to national identity, as the novel depicts the internal trauma that manifests in those constructed as Other. Key to Maja's identity are her

Cuban roots. Maja is a jazz singer, and the act of singing for her is intertwined with memories of Cuba: 'It's the five-year-old Maja that brings jazz into me, blocking my chest so I have to sing it out' (Oyeyemi 2007: 44). It is evident how part of Maja's Cuban identity is effectively silenced by the 'courteous, clipped white noise' that is presented as the antithesis of the voice she sings with 'tunefully' (Oyeyemi 2007: 22, 44). As her singing voice and her speaking voice are represented to be inassimilable, one being tied to the Cuban part of her identity and the other to the British part, it is her singing voice that becomes Other. In this way, Maja's identity represents the way hybrid identities appear unstable, as there exists within her two cultures that are driven apart by the imperial ideologies of white superiority that haunt contemporary Britain and Maja herself. The way in which Maja is silenced due to her otherness is made evident through the violent depiction of the way her words feel 'battered' down (Oyeyemi 2007: 22). Oyeyemi illustrates the governing British powers as barbarous and anachronistic as Maja is presented as having an affinity with her Cuban roots, yet she is unable to explore them fully. Through her memories and through song, Maja is able to access the part of her history and her identity that is silenced. This allows a space in which the trauma of existing between two cultures can be expressed, highlighting ways in which Maja can use the past to reclaim a measure of control over an integral part of her identity that is denied by the country she lives in.

The novel emphasizes the way Maja is silenced by the need to alter the way she speaks. Readers are presented with residual imperial ideologies inherent in a language constructed as superior. Oyeyemi's novel tackles this by employing characters who assert control over their own identity. Ngũgĩ states that:

> It is an ever-continuing struggle to seize back their [African] creative initiative in history through a real control of all the means of communal self-definition in time and space. The choice of language and the use to which language is put is central to a people's definition of themselves in relation to their natural and social environment, indeed in relation to the entire universe. (1986: 4)

Although Ngũgĩ refers here specifically to African Literatures, there are resonances with Maja's identity both in terms of her West African heritage and the treatment of her Cuban heritage. Maja describes her parents speaking: 'their voices smoothed to calm, placeless melody through academia' (Oyeyemi 2007: 22). Identifying their voices as placeless illustrates the way Maja's parents use voice to traverse the borders and language barriers that exist within Britain. Thus, their identity is not defined by their relationship with the colonizing nation, yet they are still understood. Subsequently, Oyeyemi's use of voice within the novel allows an ownership of identity that does not rely on a single national identity; in this way, language is presented as an opportunity for reasserting control over the past rather than isolating the Othered subject.

In showing how language reinforces British imperial ideologies that control and isolate the Other, Oyeyemi demonstrates how imperial nostalgia haunts contemporary notions of multiculturalism. This chapter has established how Britain's colonial legacy still haunts the nation, as the characters within Oyeyemi's novels internalise the racial and cultural hierarchies that remove their agency. In *White Is for Witching*, by using 29 Barton Road to carry the voice of the goodlady through four generations of women, Oyeyemi presents a nation that is still tainted by ideologies of its colonial history. As an image of imperial Britain, the guesthouse portrays the anxieties of a past generation whose fear of the Other is destructive, both for the self and the Other. As another allegorical representation of the nation, however, Miranda Silver represents a generation that is trying to progress to form a multicultural Britain devoid of the hypocrisies of imperialism. Oyeyemi uses acts of consumption in the form of eating disorders throughout the novel, which display how Miranda herself attempts to fracture the borders that exist in both the literal and abstract sense. So as opposed to being a symbol of white Britishness, Miranda is a manifestation of diversity within Britain whilst also showing the self-destructive results of imperial ideology. The borders that Miranda works to deconstruct are overwhelmingly present for the character of Ore, exposing the effect the conflicted national identity has on the Other. By interpreting Haiti as '"the savage slot" that enhances the utopian possibilities of the domestic epos' and refugees, immigrants and asylum seekers as people who 'bring disease, violence, rape and anti-social behaviour', I show how the Other is constructed by imperialism as intrusive and unwelcome into 29 Barton Road (Gikandi 1996: 113; Ware 2010: 103). However, Oyeyemi's novel works to dispel these prejudices.

In *The Opposite House*, the hypocrisy of Britain's 'political discourse' is made evident as language is frequently constructed as a bar to communication, emphasising the retrogression that arises from drawing on national identity as a primary point of association (Ware 2010: 110). The traumatic inner conflict that develops as a result of possessing a hybrid identity is depicted through Maja's fear of the silence and uncertainty that exists in between the apparently inassimilable British and Cuban cultures. However, Oyeyemi creates an in-between space as a platform to give voice to these issues surrounding hybridity. *The Opposite House* does present some instances in which its characters are offered an opportunity for such in-between spaces to enable freedom and control over one's own identity. However, Oyeyemi's narrative principally acts to voice the trauma that arises from being forced to assimilate with a specific British national identity. Overall, Oyeyemi's fiction demonstrates how imaginative and physical borders are cultivated within perceptions of 'Britishness.' Her characters function as microcosms of the nation and make evident the struggle to negotiate a multicultural British identity that does not exclude the Other. Oyeyemi's novels demonstrate how in-between spaces enable a narrative that gives voice to the Other by emphasising characters' desires for an identity with permeable boundaries. As they occupy these in-between spaces, the characters in Oyeyemi's fiction allow a transgression of the borders that control, exclude and marginalise the Other.

Works Cited

Baucom, I. 1999: *Out of Place: Englishness, Empire and the Locations of Identity.* Princeton: Princeton University Press.

Buckley, C. 2015: Helen Oyeyemi: *The Opposite House. The Literary Encyclopaedia.* http://www.litencyc.com/php/sworks.php?rec=true&UID =35616.

Cousins, H. 2012: Unplaced/Invaded: Multiculturalism in Helen Oyeyemi's *The Opposite House. Postcolonial Text* 7 (3), 1–15.

Ellmann, M. 1993: *The Hunger Artists: Starving, Writing & Imprisonment.* London: Virago Press.

Gikandi, S. 1996: *Maps of Englishness: Writing Identity in the Culture of Colonialism.* Chichester: Colombia University Press.

Gilbert, S. M. and Gubar, S. 1979: *The Madwoman in the Attic: The Woman Writer and the Nineteenth-Century Literary Imagination.* New Haven: Yale University Press.

Hogan, P. C. 2000: *Colonialism and Cultural Identity: Crises of Tradition in the Anglophone Literatures of India, Africa and the Caribbean.* New York: SUNY Press.

Hogan, P. C. 2009: *Understanding Nationalism: On Narrative, Cognitive Science and Identity.* Columbus: Ohio State University Press.

Ilott, S. 2015: *New Postcolonial British Genres: Shifting the Boundaries.* London: Palgrave Macmillan.

King, A. K. 2013: The Spectral Queerness of White Supremacy. In L. Kröger and M. R. Anderson (eds.), *The Ghostly and the Ghosted in Literature and Film: Spectral Identities.* Lanham: University of Delaware Press, 59–74.

Kristeva, J. 1982: *Powers of Horror: An Essay on Abjection.* New York: Columbia University Press.

Mighall, R. 2007: Gothic Cities. In C. Spooner and E. McEvoy (eds.) *The Routledge Companion to Gothic.* New York: Routledge, 54–62.

Ngũgĩ Wa Thiong'o. 1986: *Decolonising the Mind: The Politics of Language in African Literature*. Portsmouth: Heinemann.
Oyeyemi, H. 2007: *The Opposite House*. London: Bloomsbury.
Oyeyemi, H. 2009: *White is for Witching*. London: Picador.
Singh, S. 2004: Postcolonial Children: Representing the Nation in Arundhati Roy, Bapsi Sidhwa and Shyam Selvadurai. *Wasafiri* 41, 13–18.
Spooner, C. and McEvoy, E. 2007: Introduction. In C. Spooner and E. McEvoy (eds.) *The Routledge Companion to Gothic*. New York: Routledge, 1–4.
Stein, D. 2008: *Gemstones A to Z: A Handy Reference to Healing Crystals*. Berkeley: Crossing Press.
Ware, V. 2010: The White Fear Factor. In E. Boehmer and S. Morton (eds.) *Terror and the Postcolonial*. Chichester: Blackwell, 99–112.
Wilson, J. and Tunca, D. 2015: Introduction: Postcolonial Thresholds: Gateways and Borders. *Journal of Postcolonial Writing* 51 (1), 1–6.

CHAPTER

5

Sensory Signification in *Juniper's Whitening* and *Victimese*

Nicola Abram

'Our world is trembling in the void of strangers'
– Wole Soyinka, *Death and the King's Horseman*

After penning *The Icarus Girl*, Helen Oyeyemi briefly turned her attention to playwriting. Two dramas followed that debut novel: *Juniper's Whitening* and *Victimese*. The first was given a production by student acting company The Fletcher Players Society at the Corpus Playroom in Cambridge, opening on 27 April 2004. This was during Oyeyemi's own studies at the University of Cambridge, in Social and Political Sciences. No performance history is recorded for *Victimese*, but both playscripts were published by Methuen in a combined volume in 2005.

Though Oyeyemi has not published or had any plays produced since, much of her work actively blurs the generic boundary between prose and drama. Such genre-crossing is exemplified in the opening of her novel *White is for Witching*. The typography of its first pages resembles that of a playscript: text is attributed to characters by name, and their sequential speech is given no expository frame:

ore:
Miranda Silver is in Dover, in the ground beneath her mother's house.
[. . .]
eliot:
Miri is gone.
[. . .]

> **29 barton road:**
> Miranda is at *home*
> (Oyeyemi 2009: 1, 3)

In this instance, the effect is of a series of soliloquys; the individual characters share a space on the page but are effectively spotlit as occupying distinct and distant positions. This dramatic quality of Oyeyemi's prose was recognised with Holly Race's stage adaptation of *The Icarus Girl* for the Arcola Theatre, Hackney, which ran from 17 to 28 April 2007. Unfortunately, Kieron Quirke's review for the *Evening Standard* found the production 'underdeveloped', 'dully staged', and 'stolidly literalist' (2007: 449). While commending 'The power of story' – attributing this success to Oyeyemi herself, as the original author – Quirke lamented that her innovative novel was reduced to dialogue rather than receiving the non-linear, non-naturalistic dramaturgy it demands. It seems that the mask work and physical theatre promised in the pre-production marketing materials were not realised.

Despite this apparently imperfect adaptation, Oyeyemi's autographic playscripts are worthy of attention. Not for nothing have West and East African and Caribbean authors and activists invested in theatre as a tool for raising anticolonial consciousness; it is an appropriate response to the 'drama [that] is enacted every day in colonized countries' (Fanon 1986: 145). Oyeyemi's plays align with the resistant and revolutionary work of Frantz Fanon, Ngũgĩ wa Thiong'o and Wole Soyinka through the use of form, in particular; and it is the same form that sets such plays apart from the 'conventions of European realist drama' (Innes 2007: 25). Indeed, as with much theatre originating from Africa and its diasporas, the clean application of European interpretive categories – realism, naturalism and supernaturalism – is confounded by the unremarked slippages between psychological interiority and supernatural events (Jeyifo 1985: 58). This chapter examines the particular qualities that the dramatic form offers to Oyeyemi's own anticolonial project. By locating *Juniper's Whitening* and *Victimese* within Yoruba epistemology, I read Oyeyemi as answering to the classical mimetic tradition: she offers her Anglophone audiences an alternative mode of spectatorship, grounded in a conceptual context where 'knowledge' is not an object to be acquired but an event to be experienced. Rather than participating in the circulation of fact, or even the representation of reasonable fictions, both plays signify instead through affect.

'A forestful of seeking eyes': *Juniper's Whitening*

Juniper's Whitening exemplifies a wilful refusal of 'narrative articulation and character development', features identified by C.L. Innes as characteristic of postcolonial performance (2007: 25). This renders any attempt to précis the plot extremely reductive. The following gestures are therefore consciously incomplete. In fact, as I will go on to argue, this blunting of Eurocentric critical tools is a vital part of Oyeyemi's political project.

Juniper's Whitening sees Aleph, Beth and the titular Juniper animate a curious triangle of fear, care and coercion. The play begins with a non-naturalistic prologue, where the alternating voices of Beth and Aleph speak a self-consciously imagistic sequence: 'A tree of tongues. A sea of pens – / A forestful of seeking eyes' (Oyeyemi 2005: 3). Stage directions specify that the actors remain out of sight during this scene, and that darkness follows it; this withholding of orientating information continues throughout the play. But when Juniper then appears onstage, dishevelled and disorientated, the strangeness of the story is announced explicitly: she plainly accuses Aleph of killing Beth, *again*. Juniper fears Aleph, flinching at his approach, and he manipulates her. But Beth, it seems, will not stay dead; over several scenes we hear of Aleph bringing her back by repeating her name.

This first play in the collection is sparse in its staging, with the script specifying only a few simple props to signify a domestic scene: a table, a single chair, and a bed. Though the scenery suggests the experience of occupying a shared space, the characters fail to interact effectively: the play echoes its sparse staging with similarly economical dialogue. Efforts to communicate only emphasise the gulf between characters, as statements go unheard, and questions – especially Juniper's – often remain unanswered: 'Who did that?', 'Is that what you did?' (Oyeyemi 2005: 4, 9). Juniper seeks an explanation for Aleph's violent treatment of Beth; Aleph questions why Juniper wants to run away, and why she stays; Beth demands to know who else is there; and Juniper doesn't want to know what's outside. Indeed, for much of the play the characters seem to know little more than the audience, leaving the action unanchored and oddly disorientating: Who are they? Where are they? What happens – and why?

This deliberate withholding of knowledge appears as theme as well as form. Juniper complains that Aleph and Beth 'both know the truth' (Oyeyemi 2005: 14), but Aleph insists that they understand no more than she does: 'You're inside as far as you can go. You're here just as much as we are' (Oyeyemi 2005: 15). The climactic revelation of an earlier trauma – the incestuous rape of a daughter by her father –

suggests an explanation for this silence; perhaps 'there is no story' because there are no words suitable to form and to fit it (Oyeyemi 2005: 15).

Instead of a verbal sign system, the trauma is made manifest through sounds: examples include the choking noises produced by Beth in the darkness of the prologue, or the eerie peal of laughter in the closing moments of the play (Oyeyemi 2005: 3, 34). Anita Harris Satkunananthan reads these nonverbal utterances as the somatising of psychopathology: 'the fear of articulation rendered complex and physiological' (2011: 44). For Harris Satkunananthan, such moments of elision are indicative of the abject. They signal material that is 'passed over in the dramatic text precisely because [it is] too terrible for the human mind to contemplate directly' (Harris Satkunananthan 2015: 24). I would answer that such content is not exactly unknowable, but unspeakable; it can *only* be known, first-hand and in full sensory perception, never simply spoken. Trauma refuses to be ordered and organised into the systematic relationship of signifier and signified. But it can be communicated in other ways: reading Oyeyemi's plays in conversation with Sarah Kane's, Harris Satkunananthan admits that Kane's *Blasted* does make the central trauma visible onstage through the silent performance of a violent act. Conversely, Oyeyemi enacts the world-unmaking effects of such trauma directly on her audience; the dramatic form allows her to bypass the distancing mediation of a narrative guide, instead placing each spectator at the centre of the senseless traumatic experience.

In *Juniper's Whitening*, characters sometimes refuse to speak as a means of securing their autonomy. It is a purposeful resistance to the demands of others, a determined assertion that the prospective speaker and their subject are not available for another's consumption. Twice, characters in *Juniper's Whitening* express their reticence to talk as a means of keeping the subject for themselves:

> **Beth** It doesn't matter – just tell us anything. Tell us about . . . your mother.
> **Juniper** No. She's mine.
> **Beth** She'll still be yours when you've told us about her.
> **Juniper** No.
> (Oyeyemi 2005: 16)

> **Juniper** What did you see out of the window? Tell me.
> **Beth** I saw outside. It's daytime, and someone is there.
> **Juniper** Tell me.
> **Beth** No, it's mine.
> (Oyeyemi 2005: 24)

As Harris Satkunananthan writes, the 'struggle for articulation' demonstrated by the characters in Oyeyemi's fiction is 'a defiance of the commodification of truth and experience' (2011: 41). As well as displaying a communicative gap between characters, this stubborn silence also measures the distance between character and audience. Those observing the action – whether watching or reading – are made aware that access to the characters' interior lives is not to be expected through the spoken word.

Further complicating the audience's ability to comprehend – and thereby straightforwardly consume – the play, it refuses to authenticate itself against a knowable reality and recorded history. There is no sense of geographical location or chronological occasion; objects enter into the characters' existence, such as the strawberries and tomatoes that Beth demands are brought to her, but the stage is never made to be a space in which these journeys visibly occur. The outside world appears only as projection and phobia of the characters, not as a fully realised scene. This recalls South African playwright Athol Fugard's dramaturgy as described by Biodun Jeyifo: 'this "outside" world [is] indirectly insinuated into the dramatic action largely as the introjected fears and pathological maladjustments of the characters' (1985: 99). While they write from and of different (post)colonial contexts, it is significant that both Oyeyemi and Fugard centre the individual onstage. This makes global history subordinate to the intimate details of human stories; it insists on emotional welfare as an important site in the struggle for independence, and a legitimate object of dramatic study. The audience is asked to suspend their prior knowledge of relevant geopolitical events, and attend instead to the present depiction of intra- and interpersonal realities.

The absence of adult figures completes the lack of a determining context for the play's events. Instead, we are presented with three young people, whose navigation of the borderlands between childhood and maturity offers a productive site for problematising what is known and knowable in the world. As Madelaine Hron observes, youth protagonists serve a special purpose in postcolonial writings, which cannot be explained away by the generic categorisation of juvenile literature or a reductive assertion of the newly independent nation's youth: 'Childhood [. . .] represents a particularly resistant space of complex, on-going negotiation and articulation of difference that is perhaps not as readily accessible in the stable, socially structured world of adults' (2008: 30). The youth of the characters populating *Juniper's Whitening* and *Victimese* – and, indeed, regularly appearing as protagonists in Oyeyemi's fiction – enables an exploration of liminality, hybridity, possibility, and resistance.

In terms of setting, *Juniper's Whitening* is recognisable only as contained within a house. This choice recurs in Oyeyemi's fiction: 29 Barton Road features as a malevolent and sentient presence in *White Is for Witching*, manifesting 'the goodlady' as an agent of its racist revenge; in *The Opposite House*, the 'somewherehouse' both straddles Lagos and London and blends the real with the magical; the House of Locks in '"sorry" doesn't sweeten her tea' is rendered deliciously surreal through the spontaneous opening of interior doors. Much has been made of Oyeyemi's inheritance of a Gothic literary tradition, and her innovation in its contemporary configurations (cf. Cousins 2012, Mafe 2012). In the conventions of nineteenth-century Gothic literature, the haunted house makes visible the psychic complexity of the human. *Juniper's Whitening* would seem to continue this investment of domestic architecture with symbolic resonance. Harris Satkunananthan rightly reads the setting of the house as physically figuring the themes of the play: 'a claustrophobic enclosure which mimics the culturally unsettling liminal space between life and death' (2015: 18).

Beyond the immediate, interpersonal significance of the house as a particular and precisely inhabited space, the lack of locational specificity also gives the setting a metaphoric significance. Of Soyinka's play *The Road*, Biodun Jeyifo writes: 'We perceive in the stifling space of this claustrophobic milieu, and in this one day, a day like any other day, the cracks in a social order which masks by myriad devious means its explosive contradictions and antagonisms' (1985: 21). The same could well be written of *Juniper's Whitening*: in this single story set in a specific house we might also read the fault-lines that carve up a destructive patriarchal culture in which women are complicit in the continuation of epistemic, ecological, and bodily violence. The 'stifling space' of the house is breached only by a rumoured window in the attic. It makes possible a means for looking beyond the claustrophobic interior; as a metaphor, it promises perspective by revealing context. Aleph instructs Juniper: 'You mustn't look outside. The safest way is to close your eyes, because then nothing you see inside yourself can hurt you. I promise' (Oyeyemi 2005: 19). In this inverted onstage world, the (attic) window is the eye to one's own soul. Invoking another literary tradition built on domestic architecture, the unknown interior of the attic is suggestive of the fictional madwomen confined there – first figured by Charlotte Brontë's Bertha Mason, in *Jane Eyre*. Oyeyemi offers no 'angel of the house', a figure named by Coventry Patmore's 1854 poem, and later dethroned by Virginia Woolf in her 1931 essay 'Professions for Women.' Instead, in *Juniper's Whitening*, madness indwells the house, and to breach its boundaries is taboo.

On stage, another literary lineage also moves into view; staging the domestic setting makes reference to the so-called 'kitchen sink drama' of 1950s social realism, echoing its interest in the casual brutality and normalised violence enacted in the domestic interior. Indeed, the house that features in *Juniper's Whitening* is made meaningful when Beth tells Juniper the 'story' of 'a girl who lived in a small house with her parents' (Oyeyemi 2005: 30). The ostensible safety of the domestic scene – a local school, friendly neighbours – becomes the sinister site of incestuous violence, as the girl's father is revealed to sexually abuse her at home over an extended period. The architectural 'close places' provide the proximity required for the abuse, and conceal the daughter's suffering when her father crosses bodily boundaries: 'he would tell the little girl to come closer. He wanted to touch her' (Oyeyemi 2005: 31). This shared domestic space also facilitates the mother's complicity: she knows of the horrors that occur inside the house, and within her family, but neglects to act. The home is therefore made *unheimlich* – or translated from the German, 'unhomely.' *Juniper's Whitening* cleverly plays with the two meanings of *heimlich* that Sigmund Freud identifies: first, 'belonging to the house', 'familiar', and 'intimate'; second, that which is 'Concealed, kept from sight' (1919: 222–23). The final revelation of the dark, domestic secret is not just for the information of the audience, then, but is also an uncanny return of what has been repressed by the play's central character, Juniper.

Confirming the recurrence of this hidden past in the present, Beth's tale continues: from the rape a child is conceived and born. The daughter subjects her baby first to neglect and then to deliberate harm. Thus, not only does the sexual and psychological abuse directed at the daughter produce a son, but the abuse is then *re*produced as her physical abuse of that son. The daughter harms Gimel to somatise the emotional harm that she herself experiences, and to externalise her internal anguish.[1] The newborn victim symbolises her own helplessness against both the sexual violence committed by her father and the symbolic violence of the Law of the Father. Borrowing from Carl Jung, Harris Satkunananthan reads the abused infant as metaphoric of traumatic circumstances for which the conscious mind can neither compensate nor correct (2015: 22). The child, as trauma made flesh, is tasked to bear the burden of the mother's suffering. The messianic resonance is not incidental, but his punishment brings her no peace and his wounds bring her no healing.[2] Further, in a disturbing distortion of Christ's resurrection, it seems that Gimel will not stay dead. He haunts the text and the attic of the house, out of sight but sonically present as a series of unexplained crashing sounds (Oyeyemi 2005: 16). Complicating the Christian mythology, Gimel also invokes the figure of the *abiku*, the Yoruba concept of a spirit child who is destined to die and repeatedly to be reborn.

The strange exchanges between the three characters include several moments that articulate with tingling horror the human capacity to harm. Beth speaks:

> I've realised what it is about children that tempts you to murder. They have this littleness to their skulls, and their placid expectancy, like they know it's a rule that they have to be loved – when things are that small and well-formed, you have such a terror of someone or something coming along and bursting them that you suddenly have a crushing strength in your fingers. (Oyeyemi 2005: 12–13)

In a play where murder has become a mundane nightly ritual, there is no 'good.' Here, children are not avatars of innocence but a means of revealing the evil that inheres in all humanity. Aleph insists that even kindness is quickly perverted: 'It becomes like a debt you owe the other one. You cast yourself as decent, and you can't stop' (Oyeyemi 2005: 14).

This lexicon of performance – 'you *cast* yourself as decent' (emphasis mine) – speaks forward to the final scenes, where it is implied that these three characters are, in fact, one: psychically split by the trauma of the incestuous rape. This manipulation of the relationship between cast and character – here, three actors animate aspects of a single character – has a long history in black British women's theatre. In *Pyeyucca* (1985) by Theatre of Black Women, the character Laura (played by Patricia Hilaire) is split by the internalisation of racist ideals of beauty to produce her alter ego, Pyeyucca (Bernardine Evaristo); their eventual healing reunion is signalled by careful choreography. In *The Story of M* (1994), SuAndi performs as both her mother, Margaret, and as herself. The recurrence of this technique points to the shared circumstances of simultaneous racism and sexism, which inevitably and indelibly impact on mental wellbeing and psychological integrity as well as having socio-economic and cultural consequences. In Oyeyemi's play, the fluidity between the characters is signalled in the shifting possession of the mysterious 'Whitening.' In the title it is attributed to Juniper, while in the first spoken lines Beth claims it as her own, before Aleph corrects her with the use of the first person plural:

> **Beth** So, here it is? My whitening?
> **Aleph** *Our* whitening!
> (Oyeyemi 2005: 3)

But this unmasking of the characters as constitutive parts of a human whole offers an uneasy denouement.

If the characters somatise the fragments of a fractured psyche, then the murders become legible as episodes of self-harm.[3] Aleph murders Beth because she remembers the violence that Juniper tries to forget: it is 'self-defence [. . .]. As in, defence against yourself' (Oyeyemi 2005: 21–22). Overwriting the usual meaning of the term, here the 'self' is not that which is to be defended, but that which must be defended against. Later, Beth admits that Aleph 'came because I needed him. And then he wouldn't go away. Because it's possible to invite madness [. . .] it's possible to open your arms wide and hug death' (Oyeyemi 2005: 32). And Aleph affirms: 'I'm here because you need me – I'll always be here, for as long as you need me' (Oyeyemi 2005: 34). There is an early attempt at healing: at the start of the third scene, Juniper is seen 'sprawled on the floor, looking at herself from different angles in a hand-mirror' (Oyeyemi 2005: 11). This mirror is more psychomantium than incidental instrument of vanity; Juniper is attempting to perceive herself as a coherent whole, not fractured or in fragments. But Beth is directed to seat herself in the chair behind Juniper, a move which implies the insertion of her reflection into the mirror's face. Juniper's need to recognise herself as a singular being is answered by the assertion that her shadow is ever present; her self-regarding gaze is forced to accommodate the proliferation of those selves. In another gesture towards resolution, and reunification of the daughter's psyche, the final scene sees Juniper become Beth, with Juniper reportedly dead. Yet the shadow self still speaks, as Juniper recites words Beth has voiced previously (Oyeyemi 2005: 19, 22, 33).

The metaphoric resonance of this climactic moment is that the past persists into the present. It must be acknowledged if it is to be endured – though even this does not guarantee the future. As playwright Tsegaye Gabre-Medhin has written of an Ethiopian cultural context, 'today's inquisitive generation [. . .] must be encouraged to come to terms with its historic past; even that historic past often torn and denied against [them]' (1977: n.p.). The nature and content of this repressed past is noteworthy in *Juniper's Whitening*: the play dramatises the effects of a personal, individual, familial violence, rather than a national colonial conquering – though echoes of this historical trauma remain. This personal past is part of the political past; the political past and present are peopled by persons with histories. The central event of the play is a perversion of parenthood made possible by both a specific and systemic patriarchal violence, for which the young, female body figures as primary location.

Connections – both formal and thematic – can be made with plays by Oyeyemi's contemporaries. The strange simplicity of *Juniper's Whitening* finds particular parallels in the work of British playwright debbie tucker green. Like tucker green, Oyeyemi is careful to designate overlapping, interrupted and simultaneous speech. This insists on the audience's responsibility to select the object of their look and listening. The two playwrights also share an interest in active silences. Oyeyemi gives exquisite detail to her stage directions for these: 'Aleph looks at [Juniper] as if about to explain something, then looks away, hands in pockets, brow creased in frustration, as if he thinks that his theory is too weighty for her' (Oyeyemi 2005: 4). tucker green's plays are similarly punctuated with ellipses and unspoken exchanges between characters, so that silence comes to scaffold meaning rather than subdue it. For both playwrights, the focus is on the social and emotional consequences of an unrepresented action. tucker green is notable for her characteristic refusal to stage the central 'event' of her plays' plot; *Juniper's Whitening* withholds the vital details until the end, and even then they are spoken rather than shown. Thematically, too, the playwrights overlap: tucker green's *born bad* (2003) exposes the effects of incestuous rape on a 'Dawta' and her siblings, complicating the situation with the mother's complicity. This examination of the ethics of witnessing recurs in tucker green's work, given a context of domestic violence in *dirty butterfly* (2003), complex injustices in *stoning mary* (2005), and racialised knife crime in *random* (2008).[4] Likewise, Juniper knows of the violence Aleph inflicts on Beth but does nothing. Both Oyeyemi and tucker green were based in Britain at the time of writing their plays, though the situations they depict range in setting: tucker green crosses nations, traversing Europe, Africa, and the Americas, while Oyeyemi ventures into indeterminate spaces that symbolise the universal psyche. But both playwrights are engaged in a shared political project: not only do they examine the effects of trauma on its victims and survivors, but they also insist on the responsibilities of others other than the perpetrator to intervene.

There are also allusions to a more established English literary canon layered beneath Oyeyemi's silences and strange domestic scenes. The play's prologue cites the soliloquy that Shakespeare gives to Hamlet:

> To die, to sleep –
> To sleep – perchance to dream: ay, there's the rub,
> For in that sleep of death what dreams may come
> When we have shuffled off this mortal coil,
> Must give us pause.
> (Shakespeare 1982 [1601]: 278–79)

In harmony, Beth and Aleph echo Hamlet's line 'what dreams may come', adding 'Why do we say we fear to die?' (Oyeyemi 2005: 3). This frames the content to follow as an exploration of the nightmarish illogic that may attend death. Pursuing the same theme of mortality while updating the literary referent, Beth's repeated death and resurrection mirrors the suicidal cycle in Sylvia Plath's poem 'Lady Lazarus': 'like the cat I have nine times to die. / This is Number Three' (1981 [1962]: 244–45). Beth is reported to die at least twice in *Juniper's Whitening*, and Aleph once, numerically confirming the allusion. In addition, Beth's plea 'Tell me, tell me all of it' (Oyeyemi 2005: 23) invokes T.S. Eliot's poem 'The Love Song of J. Alfred Prufrock', ghosted by that same biblical figure who bears knowledge from beyond the grave:

> Would it have been worth while,
> [. . .]
> To say: 'I am Lazarus, come from the dead,
> Come back to tell you all, I shall tell you all'
> (1980 [1917]: 6)

By invoking this canonical collection of texts, Oyeyemi situates her play – and interpellates her audience – within a particular circle of knowledge: literary, Anglophone, elite. Yet if this recognition of a shared cultural context entices the audience to presume the reassuring solidarity of common referents, that sense of an epistemic community is soon confounded.

After the apparent revelation of the daughter's trauma and the characters' interconnectedness, the ending of the play resolutely refuses the audience's knowing. The climactic events take place offstage, and consist of sounds – laughter and breaking glass – rather than comprehensible speech. There is no comic resolution, cathartic purgation, or even the clarity of a tragic denouement; instead, this ending produces an unsettling, *unheimlich* experience that is to be carried away from the theatre or the final pages of the playtext and into the world. Oyeyemi offers chaos not order, suspense rather than stability.

Coupled, the two key objects that feature in the play – the mirror and the window – have a history as metaphors of mimetic representation: they depict works of art as, respectively, a reflection of the world and an opening onto it. Thus, these objects together invoke the idea of art as a way of knowing the world, and of that world as real, knowable, and existing prior to its representation. This model prioritises the visual, as if seeing in itself guarantees comprehension. But the metaphor does not hold for *Juniper's Whitening*. This play positions its audience to see but not to understand. Other ways of knowing are needed.

'Glass in the act of splintering': *Victimese*

The second play in Oyeyemi's publication, *Victimese*, also stages the experiences and interactions of young people. Here, four characters congregate in Eve's college bedroom. Similarly subversive in content, the play begins with Eve's apparent acts of self-harm – stage directions specify her bloody, bandaged wrists – and her social withdrawal. It proceeds to lay bare the disordered dynamics of the relationships between Eve and her sister Megan, with her college friend Ben, and with her prospective or perhaps previous lover, Toper. Eve is clearly experiencing some mental distress: she explains that she is afraid to leave her room for fear of meeting her 'nemesis' – a figure described as 'incidentally beautiful, and purposefully cruel' – and thereby accelerating her death (Oyeyemi 2005: 73). The other characters come and go, and after various cyclical conversations, events culminate in a strange deathday celebration, where the four eat and drink to mark the day that Eve expects to die.

This is a play with a relatively naturalistic setting: stage directions specify a 'cluttered, harshly lit college room [. . .] full of posters and soft toys' (Oyeyemi 2005: 37). Again, the implication is of a liminal space between childhood and adulthood; this is also a space contingent on and adjacent to a place of formal education, and it proves to be the classroom in which the characters are inducted into a more sophisticated interpersonal awareness. Revisiting the Gothic house that contained the events of *Juniper's Whitening*, the figurative significance of the closed domestic setting – as a symbol for psychic interiority – is explicitly debated by characters in *Victimese*:

> **Eve** Oh . . . like reality's a kind of house that we all concede to share, but everyone has their own private room that they slip into under pressure.
>
> [. . .]
>
> **Toper** No. If we're talking rooms, then we're all in our own private rooms already. (Oyeyemi 2005: 42)

It is unclear – perhaps even to Eve – whether she welcomes the visitors to her 'private room.' Toper and Megan knock at the door and are bidden to enter, if reluctantly, but directions specify that Ben 'bursts in without knocking' (Oyeyemi 2005: 50). Collectively occupying this confined physical space does little to guarantee the success of their interactions, though. Returning to the above excerpt, Toper's negative response and Eve's initial scepticism combine to confirm the failure of communication between characters; the relational breach between them is always already in effect. This can be read as a radical statement on the status of the real: if reality is not collectively occupied, as Toper asserts, then relationality is clearly threatened.

Toper describes the friends' failure to meet meaningfully through speech, saying 'The words are falling right through me' (Oyeyemi 2005: 41). Yet this statement suggests that it is actually himself, not (only) the language, that lacks a concrete quality; though he invokes himself in the first person, he does so only to describe being passed through – his personhood penetrated – by the others' utterances. Megan, too, makes reference to the incongruity between body and discourse, saying that Eve's words are less comprehensible than her bodily presence. She complains that Eve's labours to reassure her are uncharacteristic and empty: 'I can't understand you when you're fitting your lips around the words you think you should say' (Oyeyemi 2005: 46). The recurrence of the second-person address here insists on Eve's material reality; the five instances of 'you' in this sentence declare that Eve is, thinks, speaks, and takes shape, whereas Megan's single evocation of 'I' only serves to state her negative actions: she cannot understand.

Eve's relationship with Toper is figured differently. His words are made material through inscription on paper: a pile of old letters represent his previous efforts to communicate. Eve rejects both their form and content, cutting the paper in a refusal to indulge the victim/saviour relationship that the letters describe (Oyeyemi 2005: 38). Disfiguring the 'flesh' that Toper's words take, she reshapes the fragments into an ironic collage for her bedroom wall (Oyeyemi 2005: 41). Continuing this distant posture throughout the play, Eve regularly polices the other characters' language. She addresses them urgently if she suspects that they are slipping into the self-pitying pleas she terms 'victimese', and subjects her own speech to similar scrutiny:

> there's a formula – you know what I'm talking about. I'd need to start speaking victimese to you; tell you about how much I'm hurting and how it all seems so hopeless – I'm supposed to honour you with the pretence that you can reach me, that you can actually make a difference to what's happening in my head, and then, when you have these ego-coins in your hand, you'll lavish your help on me. Only it wouldn't really be help at all. Besides, I can't remember the victimese for 'thank you.' (Oyeyemi 2005: 38)

Paradoxically Eve's refusal to mean the words she says is the most overt explication of the play's themes that is offered. Her hurt and hopelessness signal a state of mental ill health. Certain words become a means of payment, exchanged according to a social contract that benefits only the benefactor of the 'help.' Toper reinterprets Eve's cynicism, suggesting that she 'tries to undo other people, just because she doesn't know how to be whole. They offer her love, and she despises them for it' (Oyeyemi 2005: 55). In Toper's estimation, Eve's motivating problem is an issue of knowledge – or, rather, its lack – of 'how to *be*' (Oyeyemi 2005: 55, emphasis mine). Being and being whole are not given as natural states but as learned postures predicated on particular information being understood and correctly acted upon. But while she lacks this knowledge of 'how to be whole', Eve exemplifies another kind of knowledge: the experience of being-as-fragments. Clearly, this revisits the psychic fragmentation structuring *Juniper's Whitening*; I shall return to its importance in due course.

Most of the dialogue in *Victimese* is minimal: it is limited to sleepy nonsensical statements, mundane exchanges about domestic arrangements, or silencing eruptions of emotion or judgement. But there are moments of expansive monologue as characters take turns to share secrets. Ben speaks of a childhood realisation that his family's care for him is partial and contingent; Eve explains that she injures herself to relieve the emotions her parents prohibited expression of; Megan reveals her disordered relationship to her sister, by turns demanding her concern and punishing her for not reciprocating the dependence. These revelations make Eve's strange 'deathday' party into a kind of confessional space. But despite this exchange of intimate knowledge, communication does not result in empathic connection. Eve complains 'it's gotten so everything you say to me is pre-muted; like you don't expect to be heard' (Oyeyemi 2005: 72). Evidently, the act of telling does not guarantee understanding. Secondary knowledge about something offers no substitute for first-hand experience of that thing; neither does such knowing necessarily entail empathy for its orator. Here, the testimony of another does little to secure a climate of care or compassion among its audience.

Compounding the failure of the characters' staged communication, allusions to literary texts fail to confirm a common canon. Such statements simply echo between the characters, adding to the sense that everything spoken between them has been said before. For example, Ben addresses Megan as Megaera, one of the furies from classical Greek mythology. His instruction to Eve to 'Shuffle over here and let me place my fingers in your wounds' puts Eve in the place of the resurrected Christ, offering empirical assurance of his living identity to salve the doubts of his disciple, Thomas (Oyeyemi 2005: 52). Yet none of these allusions are decoded in the characters' conversations. Unacknowledged – and, indeed, hardly heard by her interlocutor – Megan cites several lines from a poem by Emily Dickinson to describe her insomnia. The rhythmic recital becomes a kind of incantation, punctuated by Ben's mundane responses:

> **Megan** Some polar expiation . . .
> **Ben** Well, I don't get that.
> **Megan** An omen in the bone –
> **Ben** It's just that terrible, taut buzz for me –
> **Megan** – of death's tremendous nearness.
> (Oyeyemi 2005: 57)

The destination of these fragments is, finally, the reader. If we recognise their source – or even simply sense that they originate beyond the present text – we are addressed as a community of knowledge. Oyeyemi's appropriation of these citations rewrites known texts with new meaning. Here, then, we are asked to renew our knowledge: literally to know *differently*.

Despite the failure of verbal communication to secure any connections between characters, their interpersonal intimacy is announced in other intriguing ways. Megan somatises Eve's distress during her dreams; she describes experiencing a strange sensation in her forearms that seems to signal a sibling connection to her sister's self-harm (Oyeyemi 2005: 46). This technique of embodying another's pain makes available a further connection with debbie tucker green's work: her 2008 play *random* directs the character of Sister to incarnate her murdered brother's wounds through the performer's gestures to her own body. I read this stage technique as a way of insisting on the co-constitution of the self, so that subjectivity is determined not by a solo body but in interaction with others. If the boundaries of the body can be transgressed, so that one person's pain is transferred to another, then the psychic borders between self and other are also called into question. In both cases, the corporeal connection is made between siblings. The body of one is made to stand in for the other, as if experienced first-hand.

Victimese is an appropriately desolate depiction of depression: though crowded by characters coming and going, Eve remains decidedly alone. It seems Eve's description of her expected 'nemesis' is a construct to incarnate and then engage with her own suicidal feelings. In the closing moments of the play, Eve makes her first and final exit. After several long and freighted moments of indecision, no one follows. The scene fades to black. The implication – perhaps, more strongly, the instruction – is that she alone, and without an audience, will and must enact the confrontation. This final event of the play is clearly signalled as a liminal situation, but the outcome for Eve is not predetermined. Thus, the emotional effects of the scene pile upon the audience as well as arresting the characters' action. More than simply mirroring a complex world, *Victimese* has its audience and readers enter and experience it.

'Oh, do not ask, "What is it?" / Let us go and make our visit': Knowledge and/as experience

Both plays offer themselves as allegories for psychoses relating to a prior (childhood and/or colonial) trauma. But this interpretative possibility is sufficiently submerged that the staged experiences – rather than their explanations – retain primacy. Oyeyemi's drama modifies naturalistic theatre tradition; she defamiliarises recognisable spaces, creates strange characters who evade critical scrutiny, and withholds a climactic resolution. In both plays, a single setting preserves Aristotle's unity of place: *Juniper's Whitening* is set in a dark house, while *Victimese* shrinks the scene to a college bedroom.[5] Time, too, is limited according to the rules of ancient tragedy, with both plays seeming to span a single day. Yet action is lacking and the narrative arc is deflated; form and feeling come to the fore. I therefore argue that Oyeyemi's plays are primarily sensory – rather than sense-making – events. As Aleph himself says, 'there is no story' (Oyeyemi 2005: 15). Juniper agrees that there are no words to tell it with. And, as Beth cautions, 'Stop going on about the words – it's not them but the feeling I get from them' (Oyeyemi 2005: 24).

Aleks Sierz's category of 'in-yer-face' theatre goes some way towards describing the visceral content of Oyeyemi's plays. He writes of post-millennial playwrights 'push[ing] theatre into being more experiential, more aggressively aimed at making audiences feel and respond' (Sierz 2008: 20). Harris Satkunananthan recites this label, reading Oyeyemi's and Sarah Kane's plays as exemplars of this contemporary theatre movement. She considers the 'near-contemporary norms' of in-yer-face theatre to have directly shaped the content and form of *Juniper's Whitening*, though she recognises Oyeyemi as subverting the 'paradigm' of the movement through her plays' cultural hybridity (Harris Satkunananthan 2015: 18, 19).

However, this clustering of plays and playwrights under a nominal category risks being content to classify rather than to comprehend their practices. Complementing the identification of this twenty-first-century British dramatic quality to Oyeyemi's work, I wish to illuminate it with reference to another cultural context. Turning away from Anglo-American comparator texts and Eurocentric critical categories, I invoke Yoruba epistemology to argue that the way Oyeyemi makes use of the theatre form consolidates her writerly efforts against colonial domination.[6]

Barry Hallen and J. Olubi Sodipo's comparative analysis of the English language and the Yoruba conceptual system – as articulated in conversation with the *onişẹgùn*, the Yoruba masters of medicine – finds an important distinction between English and Yoruba concepts of knowledge. In the English language, 'knowledge' designates that which is understood from a second-hand source, such as a testimony or text-book; its paradigmatic usage is in the sense of 'knowing that' (Hallen and Sodipo 1997: 46). This term abuts the concept of 'belief', describing that which is not verifiable: '"belief" begins where "knowledge" leaves off' (Hallen 1997: 6). In comparison, Yoruba culture situates the distinction between first-hand, personal, experiential and sensory comprehension, designated by the term *imọ̀*, and second-hand, propositional, received information, named as *ìgbàgbọ́*.[7] *Imọ́* requires witnessing something with one's eyes; *ìgbàgbọ́* depends on hearing a report from another (Hallen and Sodipo 1997: 60). To *mọ́* is to have experienced something oneself, while to *gbàgbo* is to learn something from a secondary source. *Imọ̀* can be said to yield *ooto*, truth or certainty; *ìgbàgbọ́* manifests *ogbon* – wisdom, sense – and *oye* – understanding or intelligence – but can only be said to show what is possible or what may be, not what is 'true.' The Yoruba conceptual system thus stresses personal experience, especially sight, as foundational to truth; testimony – whether spoken or read – must be verified empirically if it is to attain the status of *imọ̀*.[8]

This delineation of Yoruba and English epistemology enables me to argue that Oyeyemi's plays assert the importance of *imọ̀*, and are sceptical of 'knowledge.' Answering to the damaging Cartesian division of body from mind, Oyeyemi's plays emphasise sensory experience over sense-making explanation, aligning with Yoruba epistemology over its English-language equivalent. Without a narrator, there is no intermediary to facilitate *ìgbàgbọ́*. The audience is instead invited to *mọ̀*.

To validate this reading of Oyeyemi's use of the dramatic form, it is worth attending to the ways in which knowledge is thematised in her plays. The concepts of witnessing and testimony are addressed directly in the characters' dialogue. In *Juniper's Whitening*, Juniper first hears Aleph killing Beth, before seeing it for herself. According to

Aleph, the acquisition of this first-hand knowledge – *imọ̀* – burdens her with the responsibility to act:

> **Aleph** It was only when you saw it happen that you accepted that it was something that you had to handle. Guess what – now you own it! And you're trying to give it back, aren't you?
> (Oyeyemi 2005: 18)

Once possession of the knowledge has transferred to – or expanded to include – Juniper, she cannot revert to a posture of ignorance. Aleph makes it clear that knowledge has consequences.

The climactic revelation of the play also invokes the experiential quality of true knowledge. As Beth recounts the daughter's abuse, there is a suggestion that Juniper's understanding is not the kind produced by second-hand testimony but acquired by personal experience. Beth insists: 'You know the end, I think. You know the end' (Oyeyemi 2005: 31). The phrasing is not incidental: Beth claims in the first-person only to 'think', a propositional attitude flanked by the second-person interpellation of Juniper as the one who knows. For Juniper to *mọ̀* means that the experience is hers – not simply that the story has been told to her before. Beth's gentle revelation quickly becomes an accusation of Juniper's wilful denial: 'If I can't be dead, I want to be you [Juniper] [. . .] Because you think you don't know' (Oyeyemi 2005: 32). Aleph's murders of Beth thus become a projected attempt to suppress her testimony. But Juniper's forgetting is finally proven ineffective, as Beth insists: 'I'm the one who can remember, but you're the one who *knows*' (Oyeyemi 2005: 33, emphasis original).

Whereas prose fiction is mediated by a narrator, meaning its reader must *gbàgbo* the testimony of another, a theatre audience sees first-hand, enjoying empirical *imọ̀*. *Juniper's Whitening* and *Victimese* do not simply tell a story: they ask their spectators to inhabit an experience and participate in an empathic ritual. In Oyeyemi's onstage worlds, where the nightmare is real and the real is concealed, new kinds of truth and new ways of knowing are demanded of the audience. This includes, in Juniper's words, 'learn[ing] a different way to know myself' (Oyeyemi 2005: 26).

Notes

1 Names carry special significance in Juniper's Whitening. 'Aleph' is the first letter of the Hebrew alphabet, 'Beth' the second, and 'Gimel' the third. Juniper's name may allude to 'The Juniper Tree', a fairy tale by the Brothers Grimm adapted by Barbara Comyns for a 1985 novel of the same name.

2 Oyeyemi has referred to her own Catholic background in interviews (Hoggard 2014; Quinn 2014).
3 Self-harm features in Oyeyemi's *White Is for Witching*, too, where Miranda bites her own wrist in anticipation and deferral of a vampiric/succubus-like consumption of her fellow Cambridge student and Yoruba lover, Ore (2009: 191).
4 For a full study of tucker green's work and the concept of witnessing, see: Marissia Fragkou. 2013: Precarious Subjects: Ethics of Witnessing and Responsibility in the Plays of debbie tucker green. *Performing Ethos: An International Journal of Ethics in Theatre and Performance* 3 (1), 23–39.
5 Aristotle. 1996 [384–322 BC]. On the unity of time: 'Tragedy tries as far as possible to keep within a single day' (9); 'one must be able to take in the beginning and end in one view' (39). On place: 'it is not possible to imitate many parts of the action being carried on simultaneously, but only the one on stage involving the actors' (39). On action: 'A whole is that which has a beginning, a middle and an end' (13), 'If the presence or absence of something has no discernible effect, it is not a part of the whole' (15).
6 Extant criticism of Oyeyemi's work has already found an illuminating context in Yoruba mythology. Helen Cousins has identified the practice of *aje* – what she describes as 'a type of benevolent Yoruba witchcraft with aspects of symbolic maternal protection' – in *White Is for Witching* (2012: 50). Cousins also identifies the traces of Oyeyemi's Yoruba heritage in *The Icarus Girl*: the supernatural persistence of the ancestors into the present, the importance of twins, and the figure of the *abiku*, a possessing spirit who takes the food of the possessed child, leading to their death.
7 Hallen and Sodipo prefer the transliteration of the relevant terms to preserve the language's internal logic and admit the impossibility of 'single word equivalents in translation' (1997: 82). Their practice is adopted here to signal the same respect for the source context.
8 This is an important corrective to reductive accounts of oral cultures as uninterested in empirical information and lacking in the scientist's requisite scepticism. Here, by contrast, it is ìgbàgbọ́ which refers to that which is aurally received: 'agreeing to accept what one hears from someone' (Hallen and Sodipo 1997: 64).

Works Cited

Aristotle. 1996 [384–322 BC]: *Poetics*. Translated by Malcolm Heath. London: Penguin.

Bascom, W. 1969: *The Yoruba of Southwestern Nigeria*. New York: Holt, Rinehart and Winston.

Brontë, C. 1999 [1847]: *Jane Eyre*. Peterborough, Ontario: Broadview.

Cousins, H. 2012: Helen Oyeyemi and the Yoruba Gothic: *White is for Witching*. *The Journal of Commonwealth Literature* 47 (1), 47–58.

Eliot, T. S. 1980 [1917]: The Love Song of J. Alfred Prufrock. In *The complete poems and plays, 1909–1950*. London: Harcourt Brace Jovanovich, 3–7.

Fanon, F. 1986: *Black Skin, White Masks*. Translated by Charles Lam Markmann. London: Pluto.

Freud, S. 1919: The 'Uncanny'. *The Standard Edition of the Complete Psychological Works of Sigmund Freud* (XVII), 217–56.

Gabre-Medhin, T. 1977: *Collision of Altars*. London: Rex Collings.

Hallen, B. 2000: *The Good, the Bad, and the Beautiful: Discourse about values in Yoruba culture*. Bloomington: Indiana University Press.

Hallen, B. 1997: African Meanings, Western Words. *African Studies Review* 40 (1), 1–11.

Hallen, B. and Olubi Sodipo, J. 1997 [1986]: *Knowledge, Belief and Witchcraft: Analytic Experiments in African Philosophy.* Stanford, CA: Stanford University Press.

Harris Satkunananthan, A. 2011: Textual Transgressions and Consuming the Self in the Fiction of Helen Oyeyemi and Chimamanda Ngozi Adichie. *HECATE: An Interdisciplinary Journal of Women's Liberation*, 37 (2), 41–69.

Harris Satkunananthan, A. 2015: The Baby's Not for Burning: The Abject in Sarah Kane's *Blasted* and Helen Oyeyemi's *Juniper's Whitening*. *The Southeast Asian Journal of English Language Studies*, 21 (2), 17–29.

Hoggard, L. 2014: Meet the Author: Helen Oyeyemi. *Guardian*. https://www.theguardian.com/books/series/meet-the-author+helen-oyeyemi

Hron, M. 2008: 'Ora Na-Azu Nwa': The Figure of the Child in Third-Generation Nigerian Novels. *Research in African Literatures* 39 (2), 27–48.

Innes, C. L. 2007: Postcolonial issues in performance. In C. L. Innes (ed.) *The Cambridge Introduction to Postcolonial Literatures in English*. Cambridge: Cambridge University Press, 19–36.

Jeyifo, B. 1984: *The Yoruba popular travelling theatre of Nigeria*. Lagos: Dept. of Culture, Federal Ministry of Social Development, Youth, Sports & Culture.

Jeyifo, B. 1985: *The Truthful Lie: Essays in a Sociology of African Drama*. London: New Beacon Books.

Oyeyemi, H. 2005: *Juniper's Whitening and Victimese*. London: Methuen.

Oyeyemi, H. 2009: *White Is for Witching*. London: Picador.

Oyeyemi, H. 2016: What is Not Yours is not Yours. London: Picador.

Patmore, C. 1854: *The Angel in the House*. London: John W. Parker & Son.

Plath, S. 1981 [1962]: Lady Lazarus. In Ted Hughes (ed.), *Collected Poems*. London: Faber. 244–47.

Quinn, A. 2014: The Professionally Haunted Life of Helen Oyeyemi. *National Public Radio*. http://www.npr.org/2014/03/07/282065410/the-professionally-haunted-life-of-helen-oyeyemi

Quirke, K. 2007: Review of *The Icarus Girl*. *Theatre Record* 27 (8), 449.

Shakespeare, W. 1982 [1601]: *Hamlet*. Harold Jenkins (ed.). London: Methuen.

Sierz, A. 2001: *In-yer-face Theatre: British Drama Today.* London: Faber and Faber.

Soyinka, W. 1975: *Death and the King's Horseman*. Ibadan: Spectrum.

Woolf, V. 1995 [1931]: Professions for Women. In *Killing the Angel in the House: Seven Essays*. London: Penguin. 1–12.

CHAPTER

6

The Monsters in the Margins: Intersectionality in Oyeyemi's Works

Anita Harris Satkunananthan

Introduction

There are monsters in the margins in texts written from a place outside of the dominant discourse. These monsters exist in Helen Oyeyemi's novels and problematise the external expectations of the marginalised experience. My previous research on Oyeyemi has almost always been focused on the postcolonial (Harris Satkunananthan 2011) but this particular work is preoccupied with intersectionality, specifically because of the suspicion that over-relying on postcolonial reading strategies elides some of the nuances and differences found within the texts. Edna Aizenberg writes that many scholars have 'begun to step back and question postcolonialism's own anxieties and cracks' (1999: 461). More specifically, Aizenberg avers that the approach of post-colonialism may 'lack engagement with specific histories of suffering by specific classes, ethnicities, and genders, losing itself in a globalized mush of displaced and discontented subaltern identities' (1999: 462). Like Aizenberg, I am not suggesting we throw the analytical tools of postcolonial literary theory out with the bathwater. I do, however, very strongly feel that a reading of Oyeyemi's texts needs to consider the influence of visual and popular culture, and how this relates to the intersectional issues contained within her texts.

Rita Kaur Dhamoon avers that intersectionality 'opposes the idea that subject formation and identities are unified and autonomous' (2011: 231). Dhamoon's viewpoint highlights important facets of what intersectionality as a theory seeks to do. Following Dhamoon, I interrogate the ways in which the deployment of motifs from Alfred Hitchcock's *Vertigo* (1958) feeds into the intersectional aspects of Oyeyemi's novels that reference the motifs of the movie. The discourse of identity implicit within the Madeleine/Judy character and the function of the mirror within the diegesis of *Vertigo* are deployed more than once in Oyeyemi's novels through intertextual allusions in her literary exploration of identity. I propose an intersectional and Gothic approach to reading Oyeyemi's novels with full consideration of the fact that two of these novels directly allude to *Vertigo* (*The Opposite House* [2007] and *Boy, Snow, Bird* [2014]), while the third has complementing motifs both to the movie and to the other two novels (*White Is for Witching* [2009]). My study explores intersectionality in relation to the feminine, and to the myriad ways in which Oyeyemi's use of Gothic narrative explores the complexities of identity. Oyeyemi resists pinning down identity, whether gendered or cultural, by challenging the reader with mirrored perspectives that complicate Manichean considerations of the Other in the novels that reference *Vertigo*, whether directly or indirectly.

Hitchcock's *Vertigo*'s narrative centres upon the character of Scottie Ferguson, a police officer who retires from the force after an accident reveals that he has vertigo brought on by acrophobia, a mental condition that dictates the narrative of this tale. Scottie's 'fall' in this story from his prior position to one in which he becomes a voyeur and an unsuspecting accomplice is insidious and told not just through the eyes of the character but through the camera angles and deployment of light and mirrored/glass surfaces in the movie. Scottie is employed by his old college friend Gavin Elster to tail Elster's wife, Madeleine. According to Elster, Madeleine is supposedly either suffering from a mental ailment or possessed by the ghost of her ancestor, Carlotta Valdes. Unbeknownst to Scottie, Elster is capitalising on Scottie's vertigo to set the stage for the murder of the actual Madeleine, whom Scottie never sees, right up till the moment of her fateful descent to her death. In order to carry out his plans, Elster hires Judy to take on the role of Madeleine, to haunt and beguile Scottie into a paranoid landscape of the imagination tailored for Scottie's role as a witness and unwilling accomplice to a murder that he reports as a suicide.

The idea that Madeleine is haunted by her ancestor is seeded in Scottie's imagination by several staged visual cues. Gavin Elster tells him of a necklace that Madeleine/Judy wears that she has unknowingly inherited from Valdes; Madeleine appears and then disappears from a window in the McKittrick Hotel, which Scottie later learns is the old Valdes home; and Scottie sees Madeleine wander in an apparently somnambulistic state. However, Scottie is not just a victim in this story; he is also an aggressor. His actions towards Judy as both Madeleine and then Judy are often brutal and sexually predatory. The trauma experienced by Madeleine/Judy in *Vertigo* is that she must play the role of another woman, a woman who is about to be killed, a woman whose murder she witnesses. Even though *Vertigo* is a text mired in the dominant discourse of Caucasian and middle-class America, the film is still a visual text that provides multiple instances of the Other. These instances include Scottie's nervous condition and the gendered marginalisation suffered by Judy and Carlotta Valdes.

An intersectional reading of the Other cannot be separated from the monsters that lurk within the implied sepulchral depths of Otherness. Tabish Khair writes that the development of the Vampire, for example, 'coincided with growing and extravagant interest in "reports" of cannibalism from non-Europe' and asserts that the cannibal 'had to exist, for he was essential to a simplified "negative" notion of Otherness that finally justified colonial and evangelical missions' (2009: 54). The existence of the Vampire, the cannibal, and the monsters within the margins may be due to the various modes of silencing contained within the text that hinge upon demonising the Other. The mirrors in Oyeyemi's texts reveal these monsters to the protagonists, highlighting the Otherness that is contained within their façades. In *The Opposite House*, *White Is for Witching* and *Boy, Snow, Bird*, the mirror also works to elide those identities. In *White Is for Witching*, this elision is markedly xenophobic.

The active function of the mirror, as part of the *mise en abyme* of Hitchock's film and Oyeyemi's novels, complicates the reading of the narratives and ties them back to the overarching motifs with which this chapter is concerned. Brian McHale writes that the *mise en abyme* 'unsettles the structure of representation, opening up an epistemological "black hole" that swallows certainty' (2006: 177). McHale also refers to the *mise en abyme* as 'fiction at play' averring that it:

> proliferates uncontrollably, turning every text into a network of analogies where everything is mirrored, and finally no distinction is possible between the original and its double, the model and the thing modeled. (2006, 177)

This network of analogies is rife in *Vertigo*, in which the mirrors exacerbate the fractal effect of the diegesis. Scottie's vertigo stands as a metaphor for a more psychological descent into an abyss of problematic identities. This descent is foreshadowed through mirror-images, from Scottie's first glimpse of Madeleine through the mirror. This fractal effect may also be discerned within the three Oyeyemi novels discussed here, reinforcing the self-referential quality of the *mise en abyme*. McHale avers that the *mise en abyme* is an 'uncanny procedure', one which 'induces in the reader a sense of vertigo' as they gaze into said abyss (2006: 177). I read these vertiginous mirrored perspectives of Hitchcock's movies as a narrative strategy and deployment in three Oyeyemi novels: *The Opposite House*, *White Is For Witching*, and *Boy, Snow, Bird*. In all three novels, Oyeyemi connects the motifs of Hitchcock's *Vertigo* to mirrors, doubles, and identifications, marrying considerations of gender and sexuality with that of race and of class. These elements are inherently intersectional, and as such, intersectionality will be the main theoretical underpinning in this reading of her works.

The thresholds and enclosures of Oyeyemi's texts are sites for the destabilisation of identity from an intersectional perspective, undercutting lines of culture and of gender. Oyeyemi's heroines are liminal beings, struggling against multiple points of oppression, but not necessarily in the manner in which Gothic heroines are portrayed in Eurocentric Gothic texts. Diane Long Hoeveler writes that the tradition of the female Gothic is 'a coded system' through which female authors 'communicated to other women [. . .] their ambivalent rejection of and outward complicity with the dominant sexual ideologies of their culture' (1998: 5). Oyeyemi's subversive transformations of western Gothic tropes play with those communications found within what Long Hoeveler calls a 'coded system' (1998: 5). Aspects of Madeleine, the internally tortured Gothic heroine of *Vertigo*, may be discerned in the characters of Maja, Miranda, and Boy Novak but from an intersectional perspective. Oyeyemi's texts therefore do not focus merely on the interaction between the patriarch and the heroine. They shift between the identifications of gender, of race, of class.

Intersectionality provides an apparatus to examine the overlapping marginalisations which lead to the creation of monsters and to interrogate the ways in which multiple axes of marginalisation complicate our understanding of institutionalised oppression, toxic masculinity, and cultural hegemony. Intersectionality was coined by Kimberlé Crenshaw in order to examine the connection between overlapping axes of marginalisation and includes the consideration of different forms of disability, and issues of class (1991: 1242). Crenshaw writes that in relation to 'violence against women, this elision of difference in identity politics is problematic', because the 'violence that many women experience is often shaped by other dimensions of their identities, such as race and class' (1991: 1242). Crenshaw suggests that intersectionality provides a cartography of these differences for a more equitable negotiation of intersecting needs (1991: 1242). These 'crosshairs' or 'intersections' are constituent parts of all of Oyeyemi's novels, from Boy Novak's strategic marriage to the moneyed Whitman family in *Boy, Snow, Bird,* which takes her from the working class into a higher social bracket, to the liminal struggle experienced by the protagonist of *The Opposite House* as a Cuban immigrant in London.

Analogues to filmic depictions of torment in *Vertigo* appear in various guises and incarnations in Oyeyemi's novels, interrogating the ways in which trauma ruptures a sense of identity and selfhood. Oyeyemi's reframing of the motifs of *Vertigo* accords a form of problematic autonomy to the female characters within the fraught narratives in her novel, as may be seen in the novel with the most direct reference to *Vertigo*, *The Opposite House*. The novel opens with the pregnancy of the protagonist, Maja. Maja observes that *Vertigo* is a film that 'works to a plan that makes trauma speak itself out, speak itself to excess until it dies' (Oyeyemi 2007: 34). This excess takes the form of people sweating and licking 'their lips excessively and pound[ing] their chests and grab[bing] their hair and twist[ing] their heads from side to side' in order to perform 'this unspeakable torment' (Oyeyemi 2007: 34). It is significant that Oyeyemi presents this torment as performance, particularly because *The Opposite House* as a novel also works to this plan in order to unearth the hidden traumas and ruptures within Maja. Maja has experienced multiple traumas during her lifetime related to her family's migration from Cuba to London. Her pregnancy becomes a catalyst for her memories and her visions of an alternate embodiment of her own 'personal hysteric' (Oyeyemi 2007: 1). Maja says that this personal hysteric exists in every girl and she needs only to 'look up and a little to the right' to see 'the hysteria that belongs to me, the one that hangs on a hook like an empty jacket, and flutters with disappointment that I cannot wear her all the time' (Oyeyemi 2007: 29).

The revolt against patriarchal constructs may be discerned in all of the studied texts. I read the revolt as Oyeyemi's personal engagement with the gendered politics seen in *Vertigo*, as filtered through the split personas in her texts. For instance, by invoking the personal hysteric in Maja, as embodied by the mythical Yemaya in a somewherehouse filled with beings from the Yoruba and Afro-Caribbean pantheon, Oyeyemi re-creates the duality of the Madeleine/Judy construct in *Vertigo*. Maja says that Madeleine is 'doomed because she exists in a way that Scottie' does not (Oyeyemi 2007: 34). Madeleine, a mask worn by the vulnerable Judy, is in trouble because 'she's a vast wound in a landscape where wounds aren't allowed to stay open' (Oyeyemi 2007: 34). Rather, 'people have to shut up and heal up' (Oyeyemi 2007: 34). This is Maja's way of connecting the dual roles played by

Kim Novak to her own personal hysteric, created from her split self, due to the trauma of dislocation. She quotes the memorable scene in which Madeleine tells Scottie, 'there's someone inside of me, and she says I must die' (Oyeyemi 2007: 35). The vast wound within Madeleine is one that re-appears in both the visual text, and in the references to her in *The Opposite House*. Oyeyemi draws this ontological rupture out into a personal hysteric which Maja says is like a 'revelation that we refuse to be consoled for all this noise, for all this noise, for the attacks on our softnesses' (Oyeyemi 2007: 25). Maja's assertion is an indictment on the politics of silence, the ways in which women are required to suffer in silence, to be malleable and forgiving.

Split selves or problematic identifications appear in all three Oyeyemi novels discussed here, which explore *Vertigo*-like identities nesting within identities. This is the point of the mirrors that operate as a *mise en abyme*, creating a fractal effect of identity that reinforces the complexities of intersectionality and intersecting marginalisations. A fractal image that is so obviously a *mise en abyme* may be found in the beginning of *Boy, Snow, Bird* when Boy Novak speaks of the infinite possibilities of her reflection: 'when I stood between them I was infinitely reflected in either direction. Many, many me's' [sic] (Oyeyemi 2014: 3). Oyeyemi's elegant repurposing of plot points, structure and elements in *Vertigo* heightens the drama of her narratives and problematises traditional assumptions of identity. She appropriates the mirror motif of *Vertigo* in order to project the multiple and overlapping personas of her texts. Deborah Linderman writes that 'the dynamic of the whole textual system' of *Vertigo* 'struggles against the collapse of sexual difference, a collapse that the diegesis that limits and conditions this system essays to avert' (1991:52). Linderman's article offers an incisive reading of the gendered tensions in the text, and in her detailed analysis of the camera angles and perspectives of the ways in which John 'Scottie' Ferguson, the male protagonist of *Vertigo*, is present in the visual text as a male voyeur. Linderman reads in Scottie's gaze the desire for a sort of internalised femininity, which corresponds neatly with the revelation of Frank Novak's transmasculinity in *Boy, Snow, Bird* (1991: 52).

The hidden transmasculinity in *Boy, Snow, Bird* is foreshadowed by the various instances in which Frank's daughter Boy Novak peers at reflections of herself in the mirror and feels as though the image of herself in the reflection is a stranger. This sensation of dysmorphia is also felt by Frances Novak when he looks into the mirror and sees himself as Frank. By first visualising himself in the mirror as the man he was always going to be, Frank makes of the mirror a tool for the manifestation of his future self. Boy's form of dysmorphia is in turn connected to her traumatic upbringing, made even more complex when she realises that her parent is transmasculine.

Oyeyemi plays with different modes of 'passing' in *Boy, Snow, Bird*, depicting the layers beneath the façade people wear, sometimes obscuring from their own vision their complex identities. In so doing, Oyeyemi extends the conversation of identity inherent within the diegesis of *Vertigo*, an extension which directly connects to the mirror as part of the *mise en abyme*. Boy Novak is fascinated by mirrored surfaces and by the configurations of her own face, which she occasionally does not seem to recognise. Boy is constantly watching for herself in reflections, and sometimes does not know if she is upset by the sight of her own face (Oyeyemi 2014: 4). At other times, looking at herself in the mirror becomes an auto-erotic experience (Oyeyemi 2014: 40). The mirror is a site for desire, and these desires are connected to fears. In an explication of the mirror-stage, Jacques Lacan posits that the identification with the form in the mirror correlates with the 'ideal-I' or 'the agency known as the ego, prior to its social determination' (1949: 76). The monsters in the margin gaze at the mirror in a textual performance of the *mise en abyme* and the specular image in the mirror should correlate to the 'ideal-I.'

In the case of dysmorphia or the form of problematic identification implied by the *mise en abyme*, what the mirror reflects back to the observer may be a refraction of monstrosities or a carnival of intersectional differences. Of Madeleine as a specular image, Linderman writes:

> In the marked absence of any mediation by language or any meeting of eyes, it is plain that Madeleine is produced as a specular mirage. What this means is not simply that she is the support for Scottie's narcissism, but that a deeper specular transference, signaled by the overlaying of their gazes, is in question. (1991: 64)

I read the deeper specular transference as a manifestation of Scottie's desire as much as of his narcissism. It is obvious that the life he and Midge lead in their separate apartments is grounded in middle-class America, but it is still very different from the moneyed elegance of the Elsters' lifestyle. Through the mirror, one may discern Scottie's desire for an upper class life that is denied him and this desire is embodied in his attempt to transform Judy back into his vision of an elegant, moneyed, Madeleine. This aspect of Madeleine is reflected in the icy cool representation of Boy Novak in *Boy, Snow, Bird*. Scottie's attitude towards Madeleine changes when she is revealed to be the very down-to-earth and working class Judy. He becomes abusive, and forces Judy back up the clock tower, the scene of the real Madeleine's death. This leads to Judy's demise. *Boy, Snow, Bird* plays directly with what Linderman calls the 'overlaying' of the gaze in *Vertigo*. The 'fall' through the mirror occurs when Frances Novak sees a reflection of Frank, and when the half-sisters Snow and Bird cannot see themselves reflected on its surface (Oyeyemi 2014: 294, 207).

The representation of racial and gender identity in relation both to the mirror and to the male gaze in *Boy, Snow, Bird* is varied and complex. Boy Novak's past returns in the form of her memories of her abusive parent, who does eventually make an entrance into the new life she has constructed. Boy's reconstruction of her identity is a performance, one aimed at negating her childhood as the abused daughter of a rat-catcher who would punch her in the kidneys 'or from behind' and imprison her (Oyeyemi 2014: 6). The name Boy Novak is significant: Kim Novak is one of the principle actors of *Vertigo*, playing both Judy and Judy-as-Madeleine. Furthermore, Boy Novak has the blonde hair and classical lines of Judy/Madeleine. Like Judy/Madeleine, Boy recreates herself in order to have a new life. The difference is that she does it of her own free will, and this autonomy along with necessity guides her life-decisions in Flax Hill.

Oyeyemi's protagonists complicate and extend the complications of identification found in the character of Judy/Madeleine. Long Hoeveler writes that the ideology of the female Gothic 'positions women as innocent victims who deserve to be rewarded with the ancestral estate because they were unjustly persecuted', more often than not by a corrupt patriarch (1998: 6). It is undoubtedly true that Judy/Madeleine plays into this dialectic by using her emotions and her frailty to entice Scottie into Gavin's masterplan, which is to say, to witness the supposed death of Judy/Madeleine. Judy is seen in three guises in *Vertigo*, as Madeline, as Judy, and as Judy given a makeover by Scottie, pretending desperately that she is not the same woman. She achieves this in small rebellions, allowing small curls to escape from a rigid and patrician hairdo, not allowing her makeup to be precisely the way it was when she was Madeleine. The element of both mimicry and rebellion in Judy's performance of Madeleine is fraught. Scottie's controlling manoeuvres show that he is enacting his own specular transference, and so victimising the woman who has to act out his desires in forced simulation. This element of control may be discerned in the ways in which Luc controls his daughter by dictating what she eats and what she wears in *White Is for Witching*. In so doing, he dominates and victimises her.

Oyeyemi's novels take the reader beyond the binaries of gender and cultural identification, although the method through which these binaries are destabilised is far from unproblematic. Miranda's great grandmother, Anna Good may have been a heroine in another story, but because of her xenophobia she is a villain in *White Is for Witching*. Similarly, there is something chilling about *Boy, Snow, Bird*'s Boy Novak, as she is a means through which Oyeyemi undermines the cool, elegant blonde template of Hitchcock's heroines. Her father tells Mia, Boy's best friend, that Boy is 'evil' (Oyeyemi 2014: 261). What is singular about this proclamation is that neither Mia nor Boy's own daughter, Bird, automatically dismiss it. It is a possibility of evil, one that echoes Boy's earlier testimony that she had always been sure that she could commit murder (Oyeyemi 2014: 7). It is this potentiality for badness lodged within Boy Novak that makes her compelling, juxtaposed against her ice-cool beauty, and her acts of compassion and humanity.

The depictions of madness and oppression in *Vertigo* intersect with considerations of gender and class, but in Oyeyemi's intertextual references, elements of play (or costuming) may be discerned as non-verbal articulations of rebellion. These elements may be connected to the performative aspects of the 'gothic feminine' which Long Hoeveler writes about as a response to Naomi Wolf's labelling of a certain form of 'Western, white, middle-class' feminism as 'victim feminism' (1998: xi). Long Hoeveler connects this to the 'discourse system we now recognise as the female gothic novel', noting that female Gothic novelists created 'masculine spaces' that they attempted to 'rewrite into the literature more benignly' as being feminine (1998: xi, xii). Long Hoeveler asserts that the female Gothic author 'constructs female characters who masquerade as professional girl-women caught up in an elaborate game of playacting for the benefit of an obsessive and controlling male gaze' (1998: 4). In this she invokes Ellen Moers' perception of the Gothic (or Radcliffean) heroine as 'a young woman who is simultaneously a persecuted victim and courageous woman' (1976: 91). Long Hoeveler writes that such a woman is not male-identified but has learned to 'mime the mime' (1998: 11). Long Hoeveler further argues that the 'technique of masquerade' becomes an attempt to 'play the gender game' (1998: 1). This performative version of the feminine is a form of covert agency within a space seemingly reserved for masculine control and voyeurism. Both Judy in *Vertigo* and Miranda in *White Is for Witching* take on different identities through costumes and through a specular apprehending of their alternate selves in the mirror. There is an element of play-acting in Judy's performance, but for Miranda, the costuming lends her a form of non-verbal articulation and agency. Both lose themselves in a descent to the death in order to escape their fate in a patriarchal environment.

In both *Vertigo* and in *White Is for Witching*, mirrors act as a signifier for acts of conjuring and identification. In *White Is for Witching*, Luc Dufresne feels that his daughter is too thin and refuses to buy her new clothes, as an incentive to make her eat. Luc controls Miranda's dressing in much the same way in which Scottie refuses outfit after outfit brought out to Judy in the clothing store because it does not match the grey suit that Madeleine was wearing when she died. Luc comments that:

> 'You are not all right. None of these dresses will do. They will not do at all. Nothing that fits you now will do, do you understand?'
> 'I suppose so, but what am I going to do about clothes, then?'
> He looked around. Was his cue written on the walls?
> 'You will have to eat. You will wear your other clothes until they fit. It will be good for you.'
> Miranda nodded and her reflection nodded, so that was twice.
> (Oyeyemi 2009: 39–40)

Luc's seemingly benign action is aimed at forcing Miranda to eat more as a means of overcoming her eating disorder, pica. However, his controlling behaviour leads to Miranda's decision to make her own coat, which results in her buying a mannequin from the fifties 'for only ten pounds' (Oyeyemi 2009: 123). The mannequin becomes the site for a manifestation of the 'goodlady' (Oyeyemi 2009: 137). The goodlady uses the mannequin to be physically present within the household, and to become a silencing agent of xenophobia and racism.

For the purposes of this chapter I define silencing as the patriarchal and imperialistic imperatives towards silencing any dissent or hint of discontent amongst those whom are considered Other. Silencing may be observed in the complicating of the patriarchal gaze through mirrored surfaces in the *mise en scène* and *mise en abyme* of *Vertigo*, as well as in the frames of narration set up in Oyeyemi's fictions. For instance, the quiet horror and the mental torment expressed in Kim Novak's depiction of Madeleine/Judy, coupled with the mirrors and the exploration of madness, exemplify the many instances of silencing and control. In short, Judy seems to move from one oppressive partnership with a controlling patriarch to another. An example of rebellion against these politics may be seen in the act of costuming and of making in *White Is for Witching*. Sade and Ore, the Yoruba players in this Gothic mystery, are the grounding forces aiding Miranda in her efforts at extricating herself from the xenophobic 'goodlady.' The dressmaking scenes and the inclusion of the mannequin are both empowering and horrifying because the mannequin slowly comes to life (Oyeyemi 2009: 139). It is of some significance that the mannequin's awakening may be connected to Miranda's rebellion in costuming herself. In so doing, Miranda is participating in what Long Hoeveler refers to as a 'masquerade' (1998:11). Miranda is aided in her endeavours by Sade, the Yoruba housekeeper. They later visit Petticoat Lane in London for fabric (Oyeyemi 2009:122). Miranda buys 'purple thread and some unassuming polyester-and-viscose mix that fell well and warmly when she held a sample length of it up against herself' and then 'some black petticoat gauze' so that she could make a full overcoat (Oyeyemi 2009: 122–23). This scene is an act both of solidarity and of rebellion against Luc's paternalistic sanctions, a method of articulation against the silencing.

Intersectionality acknowledges that there are overlapping modes of identification, and multiple ways in which a person may be Othered. In *Vertigo*, Madeleine's supposed ancestor, Carlotta Valdes, is marginalised as an impoverished and cast-off mistress, left to wander the streets of San Francisco in search of the child that is taken from her. The ways in which Carlotta is ostracised become a sinister subtext in the movie, indexing all of the people cast aside, left in doubt because of their differences: Carlotta, for her gender, class and race (the hidden subtext here is that Carlotta is Hispanic); Judy, for her gender and her class; Scottie, for his mental disability and his class; and the absent and specular Madeleine for her gender. The most marginalised character is still one who is not visually present in the film, except as a portrait. Carlotta, a cabaret girl and mistress, provides a more insidious narrative on the privilege of class. Although the simulacra of Madeleine that is represented by Judy is a mere fiction, the retelling of 'sad Carlotta's tale is given some veracity by the owner of a bookstore who is also Midge's friend. Given Midge's role in this film as someone outside of Elster's wicked carnival of untruth, this eye into the past reveals that in Carlotta's story at least there is some diegetic truth. This diegetic truth has an analogue in the ways in which the malign entity who controls 29 Barton Road in *White Is for Witching* is also connected to Miranda's ancestry.

Linderman writes that the 'axis of falls' in *Vertigo* is significant because it captures the latent 'ambivalence of the text' (1991: 69). Scottie's 'falls' are metaphorical, whereas the women do actually plunge to their deaths (Linderman 1991: 69). Linderman's reading of Scottie's metaphorical descents as a 'transsexual substitution' suggests a link to the transition of Frances into Frank in *Boy, Snow, Bird* (Linderman 1991: 69). The transsexual substitution Linderman identifies is evident in Scottie's obsession with Judy's transformation into

Madeleine, and with the minute details of what she wears and the exact placement of the fringe on her forehead. Linderman writes:

> Where 'falling' registers transsexual substitution, the text thus both avows and disavows difference. In this sense, the 'accidents' of the policeman and Judy that inaugurate and close the narrative and by which its end answers to its beginning are both exhibitions of the same problematic. (1991: 69)

This motif of falling may be connected to the desire of what is seen in the mirror and the ways in which this complicates the modes of silencing endured by the monsters in the margin.

The connection between the mirrored surfaces of the house in *White Is for Witching* and the descent of Miranda within the text is exemplified in the scene in which Miranda descends through the trap-door into a grotesque dining scene with Miranda's mother, grandmother and great-grandmother seated naked except for tightly-laced corsets around their waists and padlocks upon their mouths (Oyeyemi 2009: 127). The padlocks offer a visual metaphor for the politics of silencing that are both racial and gendered, rendering mute the literal monsters in the margin. The malignant spirit of the house serves as an imperial and patriarchal mechanism as much as it is also spectral. All three of the studied novels contain monstrous mothers or female ancestors. They are connected to the mental and emotional traumas and illnesses of the main characters. I argue that this may be connected to the spectral presence of Carlotta in *Vertigo*.

In *The Opposite House*, the ancestor is made manifest in the malignant Mama Proserpine, an alter-ego of Maja's mother Chabella in the physical reality of both Cuba and London. The connection between Mama Proserpine and the events of *Vertigo* is clearly signposted in *The Opposite House*. Aya is warned in the somewherehouse about Mama Proserpine 'since she is the murder that walked from my heart' (Oyeyemi 2007: 27). This statement from Aya's mother suggests that Proserpine is a spectre who came into being when Aya's mother was pregnant with Aya. The tale of sad and mad Carlotta also finds an analogue in the narrative of Anna Good in *White Is for Witching*. Anna Good, Miranda's grandmother, is positioned as a white woman who would have been a heroine of her own Gothic novel, were she not trapped in 29 Barton Road, eaten alive by her hatred and xenophobia because of her husband's death in the Second World War. This hatred is expressed in overtly racist terms when Anna Good rails against 'Blackies, Germans, killers, dirty . . . dirty killers' (Oyeyemi 2009: 118). By positioning Anna Good as a recurring and malignant ancestral entity, Oyeyemi deploys an intersectional perspective to the family drama, alluding to the class- and gender-related tensions in *Vertigo* from a multicultural point of view. Oyeyemi offers the perspective of the refugee, the immigrant, and of the multicultural workers and visitors of 29 Barton Road on the haunting presence of Anna Good.

Mirrors and Fraught Identification

The monster in the mirror may be read as the different parts of a character's identity. *White Is for Witching* contains a powerful instance of the splitting of a character's identity, as seen by the colonising and subsequent splitting of Miranda's identity by the goodlady. The metaphor is extended in *Boy, Snow, Bird*, which begins as a narrative of the androgynously-named Boy on the run from an abusive parent, starting a new life in Flax Hill as an ingénue. The opening passage of the novel foreshadows the ambiguous identifications in this book when Boy Novak avers that nobody had warned her about mirrors, and so she 'believed them to be trustworthy' (Oyeyemi 2014: 3). She continues: 'I'd hide myself away inside them, setting two mirrors up to face each other so that when I stood between them I was infinitely reflected in either direction' (Oyeyemi 2014: 3). Here, the mirror-image is deployed to depict doubling which becomes monstrous. Boy sees a girl with a 'white-blond pigtail', eyebrows and eyelashes (Oyeyemi 2014: 3). Her detached way of observing her reflection is indicative of dysmorphia, a coy nod to what will later be the revelation that Boy's parent is transmasculine. It speaks not just of passing, but of the inherently performative nature of gender. The depiction of that abuse is in itself problematic, as the transparent is belatedly outed by the text, an action that on the face of it problematises the entire narrative because it demonises the transparent and seems to hint that transsexualism happens due to trauma or mental dysfunction. The revelation of Frank/Frances's identity includes the mirror as a narrative device in keeping with the function of the mirror in *Boy, Snow, Bird*. Frank Novak was originally Frances Novak, a brilliant woman who was a lesbian and had a promising career before her rape by an acquaintance (Oyeyemi 2014: 290–92).

> You know how Frank says he became Frank? He says he looked in the mirror one morning when he was still Frances, and this man she'd never seen before was just standing there, looking back. Frances washed her face and fixed her hair and looked again, and the man was still there, wearing an exact copy of her skirt and sweater. He said

> one word to her to announce his arrival. What he did was, he flicked the surface of his side of the mirror with finger and thumb and he said: 'Hi.' After that he acted just like a normal reflection. (Oyeyemi 2014: 294–95)

The active nature of the reflection of the man in the mirror is very suggestive, inverting the male gaze and internalising it. It is a deeply provocative passage, one that may be connected to Oyeyemi's playful approach towards depicting the problematics of intersectional identity. Alix E. Harrow writes that the representation of Frank Novak 'delved dangerously into the old trans-people-are-the-products-of-trauma trope' but concludes that this is 'another story about passing, and about fooling the mirror into showing you someone else' (2014: par. 9). Harrow writes that passing

> has always had a special magic that simultaneously reveals the power of racial hierarchies to [mould] lives, and the deeper absurdity of racial classification. The very nature of passing makes it painfully clear that race is a vicious mask of our own making, a distorted reflection in a mirror, which has nothing to do with the arrangement of our DNA. (2014: par. 7)

The mirror becomes an agent for the transformation, evolution, and complication of identity. In *Vertigo*, Madeleine tells Scottie that during her episodes she cannot remember specifics, but she can remember mirrors that point her towards a dark corridor that she is sure leads to her death. The camera angles and lighting in *Vertigo* suggest mirrors and alternate worlds of darkness and light, that perspective heightened by the position of Scottie as saviour and voyeur. In a sense, we are voyeurs into Madeleine's internal trauma, in the same way that Oyeyemi's texts turn us into voyeurs of the traumas experienced by Maja, by Miranda, and by Boy Novak, Snow, and Boy's daughter, Bird.

The ending of *Boy, Snow, Bird* reveals an under-layer of trauma experienced by Boy's parent and is consistent with the ways in which Oyeyemi has played with identity and identification in previous novels. Even the inimical relationship between generations is consistent. The relationship between Boy and Frank also fits within the various ways Oyeyemi depicts the body in different texts. The violence perpetuated upon the bodies in Oyeyemi's texts evidence the various systematic forms of oppression imposed upon the multiply marginalised. Violence occurs in *Boy, Snow, Bird* when Boy's parent abuses her, threatening to scar her so that her lover will no longer find her attractive (Oyeyemi 2014: 122). This scene of psychological terror also shows the rat-catcher Frank threatening to use a blind rat to scar Boy's flawless face. 'There is no exquisite beauty without strangeness in proportion,' Frank says as he taunts his daughter, 'Let's fix it so that Charlie is truly mesmerized by you. Let's fix it so he stares. Seven scars should do it' (Oyeyemi 2014: 122). Once the reader discovers that Frank used to be a woman, the scene becomes suggestive in a different manner, implying that Frank is passing on a coded secret to his daughter, the intimate understanding of how the male gaze scars and mutates. However, Frank cannot go through with his plan of torture, and instead ends up crying (Oyeyemi 2014: 123). Boy examines her face but she has not been scarred.

The mirror is a powerful element in problematising or highlighting complications of identity. This scene in *Boy, Snow, Bird* is particularly significant because it is the prelude to a lengthy exposition about the mirror by Oyeyemi:

> 1. A surface capable of reflecting sufficient diffused light to form an image of an object placed in front of it.
> 2. Such a reflecting surface set in a frame. In a household setting this surface adopts an inscrutable personality (possibly impish and/or amoral), presenting convincing and yet conflicting images of the same object, thereby leading onlookers astray. (Oyeyemi 2014: 124)

This description of the mirror offers a clue that the preceding scene of abuse is not heteronormative in the least; the code that Frank is passing to his daughter is that of being trapped within the margins of gender identity and of the performative nature of that identity. The dysmorphia felt by Boy Novak as she gazes at mirrored surfaces provides a clue that her cold, pristine femininity is a role thrust upon her, augmented by the change in her personality after she puts on the serpent bracelet that Arturo Whitman makes for her. The mirror is as puckish as the narrator, and the images foreshadow the revelation of Frank's previous identity as a woman.

Monsters, Horror, and the Body

Body horror, monstrosity and the Other are all present in Oyeyemi's texts in a dislocating manner, inducing the second-guessing of textual identifications in relation to hybridity and the narrative of passing. Metaphors of opening and consumption may be read as being part and parcel of the body horror in *White Is for Witching*. The novel focuses on the disappearance of Miranda Silver after she succumbs to pica and, seemingly, to possession by the house itself, animated by Miranda's inimical ancestor Anna Good. Possession is thus connected to intergenerational conflict and women driven mad due to confinement and patriarchal oppression. An example of this is found in the following compelling narrative in *White Is for Witching*, concerning a distant ancestor of Anna Good:

> This woman was thought an animal. Her way was to slash at her flesh with the blind, frenzied concentration that a starved person might use to get at food that is buried. Her way was to drink off her blood, then bite and suck at the bobbled stubs of her meat. Her appetite was only for herself. This woman was deemed mad and then turned out and after that she was not spoken of. I do not know the year, or even how I know this. (Oyeyemi 2009: 24)

This passage suggests that the madness that infects Anna Good is transmitted through blood inheritance, finding itself in the veins of Miranda Silver much in the same way that Bird cannot run away from the problematised racial and gender inheritance of both of her parents. What I find very suggestive in this passage is the fact that the woman 'was thought an animal' (Oyeyemi 2009: 24). Africans have been depicted as being animalistic and cannibalistic in the narratives of white supremacists. This suggests that the ancestor referred to by the house is not white, but possibly African. This is not implausible, given the history of slavery within Great Britain. For instance, Nicholas Draper writes that up till 1833 when the British government decided to abolish slavery, thousands of British citizens owned slaves (2010: 278). Draper's book and other historical documents in relation to the period of British slaveholders offer a context for the history of Miranda's family, and makes a strong case for the possibility of passing as a hidden motif for the violence of the house. Anna Good's xenophobia may thus be read as a form internalised racism.

The Whitmans in *Boy, Snow, Bird* also harbour an internalised racism, even as they 'pass' for a respectable, white family. The entire novel is a narrative of passing, including passing as an act of social mobility. The novel charts Boy's rise in society, from her jobless, near-homeless status when she arrives in Flax Hill to her marriage to Arturo Whitman, an affluent man from a family with a hidden African-American heritage. Boy has a makeover and changes her identity to fit into her new life away from her abusive parent. The layers of identification reflected back to the reader connect back to the various levels of identification and mirrors found in Hitchcock's *Vertigo*. The narrative of passing becomes a code that is transmitted from generation to generation, of hiding in plain sight against a dominant narrative. The monsters that lurk within the blood may be identified with the fear of discovery and what that discovery brings: racial persecution and violence.

Instances of body horror exist in all three of the texts, from the stripping of skin from Ore in *White Is for Witching* to the abuse suffered by Boy Novak at the hands of her parent in *Boy, Snow, Bird*. There are abusive parents in all of Oyeyemi's texts, the only difference in the latter text is that the trauma and abuse is passed on by a transman. The antagonistic relationship between abusive parent and daughter exists in more than one text, from Maja's traumatic relationship with her mother in *The Opposite House* – mirrored by the relationship Aya has with Mama Proserpine in the somewherehouse – to the relationship Miranda Silver has with previous generations of the Duchesne-Silver family in *White Is for Witching*. The connection between fraught identifications, xenophobia and the mirror is also a consistent motif:

> I saw my face in the glass of the shower door and I concentrated on it as if it was a talisman or charm. A tune came unbidden, it was '*Frère Jacques*' so I was clearly terrified. Hello monster, hello, monster, I sang, *dormez-vouz? Dormez-vous?* (Oyeyemi 2009: 214)

The reflection of Ore's face in the shower door of 29 Barton Road prefaces a scene of acute body horror which heightens the realisation that the house is sentient and deeply malignant (Oyeyemi 2009: 214). The *mise en abyme* in this scene leads towards the visual metaphor of Ore's skin being stripped off by the towels. As Ore observes her reflection in the mirror using the towel after the shower, she notices that the colour from her skin is being stripped off as 'black liquid, as dense as paint' (Oyeyemi 2009: 214). The stripping of colour is suggestive of the identity and personhood of blackness being stripped by that bastion of British society, the bed-and-breakfast. Vampirism and possession in *White Is for Witching* may thus be connected to xenophobia – what animates the house is a vengeful being that reflects the growing xenophobia in Dover as is evidenced by the British National Party leaflets that appear in the text (Oyeyemi 2009: 227). The function of the reflection as a *mise en abyme* that leads into a vertigo of displaced cultural identity may be seen as an analogue to the events of *Vertigo*.

Conclusion

I am continuously fascinated by the ways in which the imagery from *Vertigo* is incorporated in Oyeyemi's novels in a purposeful way, transmuted and reflecting back to the observer their own perceptions and conjectures. The monsters in the margins of Oyeyemi's texts are unapologetic, and sometimes almost gleeful. The monsters in the looking glass may very well be a reflection of the spectator. This relationship is suggested when Boy Novak stares entranced at a portrait, only to realise that what displeases her is really her own reflection in a mirror, which seems artificial and painted on. The mirrors in *Boy, Snow, Bird* extend the mirror metaphor found in *White Is for Witching* and it is clear that Oyeyemi is not done in her fictive exploration of whiteness, identity and the uneasy liminal place in-between cultural identities. Always challenging, Oyeyemi's novels toy with our traditional assumptions about identity. This identity is not only racial or gendered, but composed from a myriad of fragments and associations: books, madness, movies, and hysterics. Her characters are unapologetically flawed. In Oyeyemi's narratives there is no need of redemption for madness, and that, in itself, is an intersectional triumph.

Acknowledgements

Work on this article is funded by the following grant for early career researchers: Geran Galakan Penyelidik Muda (Project Code: GGPM-2013-020), awarded by The Centre for Research and Instrumentation (CRIM), National University of Malaysia (UKM).

Works Cited

Aizenberg, E. 199: 'I Walked with a Zombie': The Pleasures and Perils of Postcolonial Hybridity. *World Literature Today* 73 (3), 461–66.

Bellour, R. 1979: Psychosis, Neurosis, Perversion. *Camera Obscura*, 3–4, 104–34.

Crenshaw, K. 1991: Mapping the Margins: Intersectionality, Identity Politics, and Violence against Women of Colour. *Stanford Law Review*, 43 (6), 1241–99.

Draper, N. Capitalism and Slave Ownership: A Response. *Small Axe* 16 (1), 168–77.

Harris Satkunananthan, A. 2011: Textual Transgressions and Consuming the Self in the Fiction of Helen Oyeyemi and Chimamanda Ngozi Adichie. *Hecate: An Interdisciplinary Journal of Women's Liberation*, 37 (2), 41–69.

Harrow, A. E. 2014: *Boy, Snow, Bird* by Helen Oyeyemi. *Strange Horizons*. http://www.strangehorizons.com/reviews/2014/07/boy_snow_bird_b.shtml.

Hills Collins, P. 2012: Social Inequality, Power, and Politics: Intersectionality and American Pragmatism in Dialogue. *The Journal of Speculative Philosophy*, 26 (2), 442–57.

Hitchcock, A (dir.)1958: *Vertigo*. Paramount Pictures.

Kaur Dhamoon, R. 2011: Considerations on Mainstreaming Intersectionality. *Political Research Quarterly* 64(1), 230–43.

Khair, T. 2009: *The Gothic, Postcolonialism and Otherness: Ghosts from Elsewhere*. Basingstoke: Palgrave Macmillan.

Lacan, J. 2006: *Ecrits*. New York: W.W. Norton & Co.

Lee, K. 2012: Rethinking with Patricia Hill Collins: A Note toward Intersectionality as Interlocutory Interstitiality. *The Journal of Speculative Philosophy*, 26 (2), 466–73.

Linderman, D. 1991: The Mise-en-Abîme in Hitchcock's *Vertigo*. *Cinema Journal*, 30(4), 51–74.

Long Hoeveler, D. 1998: *Gothic Feminism: The Professionalization of Gender from Charlotte Smith to the_Brontës*. Pennsylvania: Pennsylvania State UP.

McHale, B. 2006: Cognition En Abyme: Models, Manuals, Maps. *Partial Answers: Journal of Literature and the History of Ideas*, 4 (2), 175–89.

Moers, E. 1976: *Literary Women*. London: The Women's Press.

Nash, J. C. 2008: Re-thinking intersectionality. *Feminist Review* 89, 1–15.

Oyeyemi, H. 2007: *The Opposite House*. London: Bloomsbury.

Oyeyemi, H. 2009: *White Is for Witching*. London: Pan Macmillan.

Oyeyemi, H. 2014: *Boy, Snow, Bird*. London: Pan Macmillan.

CHAPTER

7

'The genesis of woman goes through the mouth': Consumption, Oral Pleasure, and Voice in *The Opposite House* and *White Is for Witching*

Sarah Ilott[1]

The relationship between eating and power has long been a concern of Western feminist criticism, which has established a connection between appetite and voice. In their introduction to *Scenes of the Apple*, Tamar Heller and Patricia Moran draw some of these debates together, focusing on Hélène Cixous' essay 'Extreme Fidelity' to explore the subject of food in women's writing as symbolising 'bodily and sexual experience, drawing on the 'dual association of the mouth with both eating and speaking' (2003: 2). In the vein of Susie Orbach's work, which identified that 'Food is a metaphor through which women speak of their inner experience' (cited in Heller and Moran 2003: 26), they argue that 'appetite can function as a form of voice' (2003: 26). Following in their footsteps, I argue that the disordered eating habits displayed by Helen Oyeyemi's female protagonists can be read as indexes of protest, dissent, transgressive desire, or the reclamation of power and authority absent in speech that is silenced through patriarchal or imperialist systems.

This extension into addressing imperialist as well as patriarchal systems through the motif of appetite takes into account recent work that has explored the broader application of analysing acts of consumption by critics such as Njeri Githire, who states in *Cannibal Writes*, that 'as significant sites for reproduction, contestation, and negotiation of power and its implications, food and (non)eating provide the frame of reference for analyzing social systems where power is manifest' (2014: 6). With this in mind, I read acts of consumption (and within this I include its opposite – vomiting, or refusing to eat) as ways of illustrating female identity formation and highlighting lingering imperialist and patriarchal hierarchies in the context of a Britain still haunted by its colonial legacies, through close analysis of Oyeyemi's *The Opposite House* (2008 [2007]) and *White Is for Witching* (2009).

The feminist writing of Hélène Cixous is key to my readings of Oyeyemi's work. In many ways, Oyeyemi's writing embodies what Cixous describes as 'l'écriture féminine.' Oyeyemi's novels are feminine textual bodies, frequently characterised by their lack of closure, unpredictability, concerns with beginnings but not origins, the 'voice of the mother', feminine desire that is not organised around the phallus, and an 'exploration of woman's powers' (Cixous 1981: 52–54). Oyeyemi's writing is concerned with the overflowing and transgression of borders, with 'vomiting as opposed to masculine incorporation' (Cixous 1981: 54). For Cixous, vomiting and incorporation are opposed and gendered, as the former is deemed to represent an openness and crossing of borders that is not withholding and is linked to a feminine unconscious that 'does not resign herself to loss', whilst the masculine unconscious is associated with an attempt to 'bring the outside in' in order to 'resign himself to loss' (1981: 54).

Furthermore, Oyeyemi's novels are concerned with what Cixous terms a 'feminine economy' or mode of behaviour embodied by her female characters (1981: 42). Cixous' assertion that 'the genesis of woman goes through the mouth' is taken from 'Extreme Fidelity' and focuses on Eve's response to prohibition in the biblical myth in which she eats the forbidden fruit; this 'genesis' operates 'through a certain oral pleasure, and through a non-fear of the outside' (1994: 133). This quotation is integral to my exploration of the various ways in which the formation (or genesis) of Oyeyemi's characters is frequently linked to the functions of the mouth as the site of oral pleasure (both sexual and gastronomic), speech, and the border between internal and external worlds, particularly when faced with prohibitive structures. It would do a disservice to both Oyeyemi and Cixous if I were to attempt to impose a pattern on the texts, to suggest that such works could be 'theorized, enclosed, coded' (Cixous 1976: 883). Instead, I aim to open up two of Oyeyemi's British-based novels to diverse and sometimes conflicting readings that indicate the possibilities and limitations of Cixous' work as made evident in Oyeyemi's literature.

Oyeyemi's literature addresses some of the charges of biological essentialism, universalism, and removal from the political sphere frequently launched at Cixous and French feminism. By situating her novels in the magic realist genre, Oyeyemi is able to bring together the distinct political realities of decolonisation, xenophobia, and racism of clearly identified places and moments with the symbolic realities evident in other-worldly or fantastic spaces. Furthermore, contrary to claims that the highly theoretical terrain of French feminism is 'irrelevant to the lives of black, poor, and third-world women' (criticisms summarised by Dallery 1992: 60),[2] Oyeyemi's literature is concerned with self-definition and with relationships between women of many different backgrounds: old and young, black and white, British, Cuban and Nigerian, entitled Oxbridge elites and disenfranchised Kosovan refugees. Indeed, my readings of Oyeyemi's work indicate ways in which discourses of race and gender intersect, as protagonists' gendered and raced identities are both explored through motifs of consumption, abjection, and the workings of the mouth. In so doing, I suggest that Oyeyemi foregrounds the imperialist as well as the patriarchal structures to which women – both black and white – are subjected.[3] However, I suggest that the novels also go some way towards offering a critique of feminist formulations of pleasure in light of the postcolonial context of the novels, in which relationships between black and white women (romantic and otherwise) are frequently thwarted as racist and nationalist structures create barriers.

Through the Mouth

Eating disorders are frequently the unhappy lot of Oyeyemi's female protagonists, particularly in her first three novels, all of which feature black or mixed-race characters that feel caught between points of identification or affiliation in the overtly racist context of a Britain in which blackness is made Other. The theme of eating as a means of negotiating a contested identity is central to *The Opposite House*, in which protagonist Maja cannot hold food down as a result of morning sickness whilst pregnant with a son who challenges her relationship with the past, as she realises that she has no reliable memories of Cuba to pass on to him. In *White Is for Witching*, there is a mirroring of psycho-corporeal and nationalist processes of identification, as the contested borders of Britishness (as constructed by a nationalist rhetoric hostile to immigrants and their descendants) are paralleled in protagonist Miri's increasingly emaciated body as she pursues a lesbian relationship with black Ore against the wishes of her racist foremothers. Through analysis of these novels I suggest that the physical workings of the mouth in taking in (and sometimes vomiting out or avoiding) food are frequently used to symbolise the formation of Oyeyemi's protagonists, as the mouth functions as border between inside and out and involves processes of identification, internalisation, and assimilation, or abjection, dissociation, and disgust.

For Cixous, the biblical myth of Eve's consumption of the forbidden fruit – the 'scene of the apple' – is an analogy for 'libidinal education' in which 'knowledge and taste go together' (1994: 133). Rather than responding to a meaningless prohibition (the prohibition is 'absolutely incomprehensible [. . .] since for Eve "you will die" does not mean anything' [1994: 133]), Eve opts for the knowledge represented by the apple. This sensory acquisition of knowledge is the 'genesis of woman' (Cixous 1994: 133). I read Oyeyemi's work as building on the connection constructed by Cixous between knowledge and taste, as food becomes a link to national cultures otherwise repressed or forgotten. This is particularly apparent through Oyeyemi's use of the dinner table as a site of national belonging and tradition in *The Opposite House*. Readers are presented with a smorgasbord of cuisines: Maja's parents originate from Cuba, and at their house the family sits down to Cuban stew; at Cypriot Amy Eleni's house, Maja is served a Mediterranean feast featuring lamb cooked in three different ways; at Maja and Aaron's house they share a love of fufu, a staple dish in both of their countries of origin (Aaron is Ghanaian).

However, it is at this site of belonging and identification represented by shared food that breakdowns begin to occur. Cuban fufu is not the same as Ghanaian fufu, and Aaron accuses his partner of being incapable of making it properly, whilst Amy Eleni's family meals are disrupted by her mother's refusal to eat, which leaves Maja and Amy Eleni self-conscious and ultimately hungry, as they feel too awkward to glut themselves. Chabella is hostile to Amy Eleni's enjoyment of their family's Cuban stew, leaning towards her 'as if she wanted to snatch the food out of [her] jaws, as if she didn't think Amy Eleni should ever know what a good Cuban stew tasted like' (Oyeyemi 2008: 106). In this scene, Chabella adopts the role of prohibiting agent exemplified by God in the Genesis myth, denying the possibility of the intimacy of her daughter and her best friend implied through shared enjoyment of the food. This signifies the close link between taste and cultural knowledge explored throughout the novel.

Most disruptive is Maja's younger brother Tomás's condition – reflux – which means that he is unable to keep his food down. If eating signifies assimilation and a shared identity (shared cultural knowledge), then *The Opposite House* is more concerned with the failure to ingest, whether this is through anorexia, reflux, or morning sickness. Tomás's family despairs of his condition, particularly his father, who questions why this is happening to his son. His wife Chabella's reply is as follows: 'Juan, he'll grow out of it. He's so small now. And he's the London baby' (Oyeyemi 2008: 152). Tomás's reflux is linked to his national identity: unlike Maja and their parents, he was born in the UK after the family's migration. Like Oyeyemi's *Icarus Girl* protagonist, Jessy, Tomás is presented as having a disrupted sense of identity – British, yet the wrong colour – causing him at one point to cover his face with edible white face paint in order to become invisible and run faster. His disrupted sense of identity is signified through the involuntary motions of his stomach. It is notable, perhaps, that Tomás is gendered female through an eating disorder that is culturally coded as feminine and otherwise the sole lot of Oyeyemi's female characters, while his mother adopts a patriarchal role as (with)holder of cultural knowledge that leads to her son's emptying out. This is consistent with Oyeyemi's foregrounding of the damage inflicted by women: her exploration of the possibilities offered by a feminine economy do not mean that she uncritically celebrates women.

White Is for Witching is also concerned with the relationship between knowledge, taste, and identity, which in this case takes the form of a xenophobic nationalism hungry only for itself and hostile to the intrusion of the external world. I have explored elsewhere the figure of 29 Barton Road, the animate guest-house that 'becomes a microcosm for British border politics' by expelling foreign bodies and ensnaring the maternal female line of the Silver family in its walls in a manner reminiscent of the alimentary processes of absorption and elimination (Ilott 2015: 62). This self-consumption is reflected in the actions of protagonist Miri, who suffers from a condition called pica, 'an appetite for non-food items, things that don't nourish', particularly the chalk on which her home town of Dover is built (Oyeyemi 2009: 22). A distant relation of Anna Good (who is Miri's great grandmother), is the figure through whom this tendency to self-cannibalism is explicitly made monstrous. She is described as being:

> Thought an animal. Her way was to slash at her flesh with the blind, frenzied concentration that a starved person might use to get at food that is buried. Her way was to drink off her blood, then bite and suck at the bobbled stubs of her meat. Her appetite was only for herself. (Oyeyemi 2009: 24)

The language is explicitly linked to vampirism, and the abject reference to 'food that is buried' coupled with human ingestion conjures up images of consuming the dead. The self-cannibalism portrayed in *White Is for Witching* that represents a desire for knowledge only of the self is implicitly linked to the damaging and insular nationalist structures that the novel highlights.

The genesis of woman 'through the mouth' also occurs at the site of language in Oyeyemi's fiction. Her female characters often find themselves silenced, or their voices under threat, signifying the historical '*suppression*' of women's voices of which we hardly need Cixous' reminder (1976: 880). Acknowledging this suppression coming from phallocentric discourses, Maja first recognises the need to 'protect my throat, my voice' after her mother tries to strangle her (Oyeyemi 2008: 149). This attack follows from Chabella's inability to speak English well enough to report a rape that she has witnessed alongside her daughter, and from her daughter's subsequent offer to help by talking to the police on her behalf. There are three acts of silencing staged here: Chabella is figuratively silenced as she cannot speak in the language of the British law; Maja is literally silenced through her mother's strangulation that leaves her croaking and vomiting; and the unnamed rape victim is effectively (systemically) silenced, able to speak only the word 'rape' – useless without a witness to take action – and through 'involuntary sounds' as she loses control of her body (Oyeyemi 2008: 148). This scene conveys the many means of silencing, but also importantly points to the power imbalance between these three women, as they do not have equal access to a language that will be heard. This is not the 'universal woman subject' imagined by Cixous (1976: 875), but a group of women divided by background and circumstance. The struggle for each of them to find a voice that will render their experiences audible is different. As such, Oyeyemi's female characters must find a new mode of articulation to overcome the actual, ideological and systemic prohibitions that render them voiceless. This occurs in different ways, through things like singing (Maja) and disordered eating (Miri) that repurpose the mouth to speak otherwise, eat otherwise.

Through a Certain Oral Pleasure

Not only does the genesis of Oyeyemi's female characters 'go through the mouth' as a form of individual and cultural knowledge gained through acts of consumption and voice, but characters also come to identify through erotic desires – often constructed as transgressive –

that focus on the mouth. There are many moments of erotic pleasure in Oyeyemi's novels, between women, and between women and men, yet all such references to sexual desire and fulfilment are described orally (through kissing, biting, and the contemplation of cunnilingus), without a single reference to the penis or penetrative sex.

The main plot of *The Opposite House* follows the heterosexual relationship between Maja and her partner Aaron, and Maja's burgeoning relationship with the child that they are expecting together. Disregarding the obvious product of their intercourse, Maja and Aaron's relationship is described in largely sexless terms. When Aaron himself, or their relationship, is presented in eroticised terms, it is in relation to their mouths. Listening to Aaron singing in a choir, Maja describes his voice in intimate terms as 'soar[ing], naked, clear, but unsure of its strength' (Oyeyemi 2008: 134). This is a sensual moment for Maja, who hugs him and finds him 'more beautiful to me for having raised his voice alone' (Oyeyemi 2008: 135).

The most intimate relationship in *The Opposite House* is undoubtedly between Maja and her openly lesbian friend, Amy Eleni, and the most sensual moment of the novel that in which they share a kiss. After lying under the covers together in bed – reading, sharing food, and breathing the same air – Maja recounts the following:

> Amy Eleni paused at the door, turned, studied me, came back to me. She stood over me, sweetly serious, and I hauled myself up by degrees, matching her look for look; the inches between our faces grew warmer as they fell away. She dipped her head to kiss my mouth, and whispered against my lips, 'Happy graduation.' Her eyes were closed, and mine were wide open. (Oyeyemi 2008: 241)

The gently sibilant language leading up to the kiss creates a soothing atmosphere and the kiss is represented as welcome and a natural outgrowth of the intimacy of their relationship, despite the surprise signified by Maja's open eyes. Though the overt meaning of Amy Eleni's greeting – 'Happy graduation' – is a reference to Maja's completion of her degree, coming where it does in the narrative it implicitly gestures towards Maja's sexual awakening to a different kind of erotic pleasure and relationship.

White Is for Witching develops the theme of erotic embodiment beginning with the mouth, particularly through the relationship between Miri and Ore, which is described almost entirely in terms of consumption, whether it be of shared food, or of each other's bodies as food. Reading a chapter by Chris Foss in which he discusses the trope of cannibalism in Cixous' fictional *Book of Promethea*, I was struck by the parallels to Oyeyemi's *White Is for Witching*. Like Cixous' text, Oyeyemi also mobilises the trope of cannibalism, interpolating the oral pleasure of love making between women and the consumption of food. Scenes that bear a particular resemblance depict the opening up of the body to the sexual partner. In *The Book of Promethea*:

> She is incomprehensible. Inexplicable. Why at night does this sudden desire, a great black shiny violent foal carry her away, cry out 'I want you to split open my breast, I want you to set my heart free,' want to offer her life to be drunk, want the knife in her breast, eat my heart, I want to be good things for you, your rice, your food, I want to be the apple between your teeth, take my life. (Cixous 1991: 154)

Here, the 'scene of the apple' is explicitly referenced as the characters share this moment of erotic pleasure that is not afraid of the inside, the opening up of the body to another. During a comparable scene in *White Is for Witching*:

> Ore's smell was raw and fungal as it tangled in the hair between her legs. It turned into a blandly sweet smell, like milk, at her navel, melted into spice in the creases of her elbows, then cocoa at her neck. Miranda had needed Ore open. Her head had spun with the desire to taste. She lay her head against Ore's chest and heard Ore's heart. The beat was ponderous. Like an oyster, living quietly in its serving-dish shell, this heart barely moved. Miranda could have taken it, she knew she could. Ore would hardly have felt it. (Oyeyemi 2009: 191)

Gastronomic and sexual desires run together, with an undercurrent of violence. Indeed, Oyeyemi's Miri recognises the potential monstrosity of her desire for Ore's body, reminding herself that '*Ore is not food*', ordering herself to '*Manage your consumption*', and confessing '*I think I am a monster*' (Oyeyemi 2009: 191–92). For Foss 'Cixous [. . .] drains [the] figural power [of violence] by blurring the very distinction between such violence and feminine lovemaking, by going so far as to incorporate it into and subsume it within such lovemaking' (2003: 157). Such a manoeuvre refuses a naïve 'fairy tale vision of an untainted love' (Foss 2003: 160). Similarly, Miri and Ore's relationship is constructed as taboo and must operate in a less than ideal situation, far removed from the 'happily ever after' of its Snow White intertext (that is signified by the frequent appearance of apples with the tell-tale red and white bifurcation).

Yet I would suggest that Oyeyemi's novel goes further in working against the construction of Miri's desires for Ore as monstrous, as their mutual consumption is juxtaposed with the self-cannibalism of the guesthouse (29 Barton Road) and Anna Good. According to Foss's reading of Cixous' *Book of Promethea*, there is a 'revolutionary re-visioning of the self-other relation', characterised by an 'ethic of generosity' that emphasises '"taking in" rather than "taking over"' (2003: 149). The distinction between the modes of consumption are marked through the workings of the guesthouse that prioritises a more 'masculine' economy of incorporation, taking the Silver family in, and ejecting those marked as other by virtue of nationality or ethnicity. This works as a shoring up of borders that mimics the workings of nationalist discourses. However, Miri's consumption of Ore is different, marked instead by a process of 'continuous transformation and "self"-dissolution in which the very boundaries of self and other are intentionally blurred', effectively working against the xenophobic nationalism that characterises the Britain evoked through the guesthouse (Foss 2003: 153). Unlike 29 Barton Road, which fails to recognise the subjectivity of foreigners and non-white Britons, Miri's consumption of Ore effectively functions to 'acknowledge one's need for the other in a way that accepts the other as a legitimate self in its own right (a self worthy of learning from)' (Foss 2003: 161). Tracing the parallels between the genesis of women's identity through feminine patterns of consumption in Cixous' work, and acts of consumption in *White Is for Witching* indicates the potential of Cixous' deconstructive work to intersect with discourses of race, through her dismantling of binaries that are to be found in post/colonial power structures as they are in gendered hierarchies.

Through a Non-fear of the Outside

A loving form of consumption that blurs the boundaries between self and other also links to the 'non fear of the outside' that ends Cixous' statement regarding the genesis of woman. I further read this 'non-fear of the outside' as playing out in Oyeyemi's fiction through the mockery of mouths that remain closed in fear of the intrusion of the Other. This plays out through the potential threat of broken borders that is indexed through a focus on starving or anorexic bodies. Cixous' Eve is not self-denying; she is hungry, curious for the knowledge represented by the apple. I would argue that Oyeyemi plays with this trope by mocking characters who adopt hunger as a form of self-preservation.

The attraction of the anorexic body (and it is important to remember that Oyeyemi's protagonists are in constant battle with imperialist and patriarchal structures that have idealised the female body in particular ways) is signalled through its celebration as beautiful. This is most evident in the Orisha strand of *The Opposite House*, which reflects the realist strand of the narrative in a non-realist and richly symbolic manner. Aya, or Yemaya – the mother god who is nominally linked to the novel's protagonist Maja – goes to hospital to visit a girl called Amy who she had previously found rocking and calling her name on the pavement near the London door of the Somewherehouse. Whilst there, she sees a girl in a nearby bed and describes her in terms that clearly denote anorexia:

> She has a sharp little face, like a baby bird's, and she cannot walk because her spirit does not want her body and bids it disappear. Beneath the girl's covers, atrophied muscles make her legs lithe and kneeless [. . .] the girl sleeps even though the blankets are too heavy for her, even though her mother's sad hand on her pillow is too heavy for her. (Oyeyemi 2008: 172–73)

Despite the fact that this girl is evidently close to death, Aya finds her gaze repeatedly drawn towards her, and refers to her as 'the beautiful bird girl', making a virtue of the features pinched and sharpened by weight loss (Oyeyemi 2008: 173).

Hunger as a weapon in a global context in which many do not have the luxury of such a choice is made apparent through references to malnutrition, experienced by Maja's Papi amongst others (Oyeyemi 2008: 155). As well as flagging up the lived realities of hunger that is not a choice, the metaphorical implications of denying food as a mode of protecting the boundaries of the self are also made ironic. In the fantastical strand of *The Opposite House*, the Kayodes live in the somewherehouse with Aya. Aya, on one hand, 'overflows with *ache*, or power', *ache* being a Yoruba word described in the novel as denoting 'blood', or 'energy', it 'is is is' (Oyeyemi 2008: 3). On the other hand, the Kayodes 'do not eat' the feasts she prepares and speak only in mutters amongst themselves, defined as such by their sealed mouths (Oyeyemi 2008: 3). However, they become increasingly isolated as the Nigerian door of the somewherehouse is sealed. Doubly displaced, from West Africa, to the Caribbean, to London, these gods that refuse the change implied by eating and entry of the Other find themselves incapable of return or of survival in a new environment. As they starve, they weaken and eventually die, not knowing 'that the ache meant "eat"' (Oyeyemi 2008: 245). Unitalicised here, the use of 'ache' plays on the double meaning of the word, which in English might refer to a physical pain associated with hunger, whilst the Yoruba designation refers to an openness of the body and spirit to others. Closing the mouth as a means of protecting the identity of the self signifies a refusal to change that ultimately leads to stagnation and death, and the body itself is undone in the process of trying to save it.

An openness to the outside is played out in both novels through fantastic and symbolic entities that link female characters (and only female characters) together. The hysteric in *The Opposite House* and the soucouyant in *White Is for Witching* are entities that transcend bodily borders and move between characters, occupying multiple characters simultaneously. Both of these figures are linked to foreignness and to the mouth. Though primarily associated with the white British characters of the female Silver line, the soucouyant is a mythical creature derived from Caribbean folklore, whilst Maja and Amy Eleni's hysteric in *The Opposite House* 'smells foreign' (Oyeyemi 2008: 30). As such, these figures can be read allegorically as signifying an openness to the outside that pushes against the xenophobic nationalism and racism otherwise experienced by the characters in a Britain defined by chants of 'Rule, Britannia' and British National Party pamphleteering (Oyeyemi 2009: 214, 200).

The soucouyant is an ambivalently monstrous creature in *White Is for Witching*, and one whose workings are associated with a consumption that is constructed as transgressive. As described by Ore, the soucouyant is a monster, 'the wicked old woman who flies from her body and at night consumes her food, the souls of others – soul food! – in a ball of flame' (Oyeyemi 2009: 147). However, when Ore tells Miri a story about the soucouyant it becomes apparent that the latter interprets the figure differently. Having requested 'a story about a girl who gets away', Ore responds with a story 'about the girl who killed the soucouyant' (Oyeyemi 2009: 165). Defeated by the girl who 'Treat[s] her skin with salt and pepper', the soucouyant has no option but to 'join her flame with that of the rising sun' (Oyeyemi 2009: 166). Miri responds with thanks, having interpreted the soucouyant as a girl who gets away, much to Ore's horror. Ore replies firmly: 'No [. . .]. She is a monster. She dies. [. . .] All monsters deserve to die' (Oyeyemi 2009: 166). Miri's sympathy with the soucouyant is related to her identification with it: she comes to believe that her GrandAnna is the soucouyant, and that she has been possessed by her female ancestor.

Yet things become more confused in a narrative that persistently refuses the patriarchal closing down of meaning. After spending a period of time together at 29 Barton Road, Ore and Miri come to suspect each other of being (or being possessed by) the soucouyant. Just a page later, the soucouyant is also identified with the house itself. Miri whispers to Ore: 'Please understand. We are the goodlady. [. . .] The house and I' (Oyeyemi 2009: 218). For Ore, this is a perversion:

> I told myself that no matter what Miranda said, the soucouyant was the old lady. That was the rule. It was the young girl that defeated the soucouyant. The two did not enter the story in each other's bodies; the two did not share one body, such a thing was a great violation. Of what? I didn't know. (Oyeyemi 2009: 219)

The question at the end of this quotation marks Oyeyemi's challenge to such a framework that insists on seeing individuals in isolation. Instead, the soucouyant creates connections between characters, and the monstrosity of the soucouyant is never confirmed, as the novel's ending remains ambivalent.

The endings of *White Is for Witching* (recounted at the beginning) are key to reading the ambivalent monstrosity of the soucouyant. One of the three possible endings sees Miri trapped under the ground 'Her throat blocked with a slice of apple' as 'the only way to fight the soucouyant' (Oyeyemi 2009: 1). But whether the soucouyant represents the xenophobia embodied by her female ancestors and the racist guesthouse, or a force that unites Ore and Miri in a way that is only *constructed* as monstrous by such racist discourse, remains unresolved. Equally, whether the apple represents knowledge and the overcoming of patriarchal prohibitions, or whether it is a Snow White's apple, one of 'the poisoned apples her culture offers her' as Sandra Gilbert and Susan Gubar would have it, and which Miri has henceforth resolutely avoided, equally remains ambiguous (1979: 58). It is significant that the soucouyant is ambivalently monstrous, but resolutely female. As critic Giselle Anatol has observed, the monstrous figure has recently been appropriated by feminist authors, who 'reclaim this folkloric figure as a paragon of female agency', pointing in particular to Caribbean authors Edwidge Danticat and Jamaica Kincaid, who celebrate the soucouyant 'for her ability to transform herself and fly' (2000: 52). Following these feminist readings of the soucouyant, I suggest that Oyeyemi's soucouyant is purposefully ambivalent. On the one hand, the soucouyant is unequivocally feminine in its capacity for flight and the transgression of boundaries in a way that is pitched against 29 Barton Road, which alternatively prioritises a masculine incorporation that retrenches rather than undermines self-other relationships based on nationalist ideals. The soucouyant represents cohabitation and the elision of self-other boundaries that is monstrous only when the merging of bodies in a lesbian, interracial relationship such as Ore's and Miri's is constructed as taboo. On the other hand, Oyeyemi does not shy away from the violence visited upon women by other women (and particularly by mothers upon their daughters). This highlights the fact that in a racist or neo-colonialist context not all women are held equal.

Oyeyemi appropriates the figure of the hysteric, often 'taken to epitomize a universal female oppression' and repurposes the figure in this feminine text (Showalter 1993: 286). In *The Opposite House*, both Maja and Amy Eleni claim to possess a hysteric, an embodiment of hysteria that is personal to each of them but simultaneously unites them. The hysteric is associated with the voice, manifesting itself through songs and screams, and with emotions that overwhelm. Maja and Amy Eleni support each other to 'beat' their personal hysterics by mimicking Madeleine Elster from Alfred Hitchcock's *Vertigo* (1958) and claiming 'I'm not mad! I'm not mad! I don't want to die!', laughing at it to reduce its seriousness and capacity to induce fear (Oyeyemi 2008: 35). However, the women also recognise the benefit of the hysteric:

> Our hysteric is the revelation that we refuse to be consoled for all this noise, for all this noise, for the attacks on our softness, the loss of sensitivity on my scalp with every batch of box-braids. Sometimes we cannot see or hear or breathe because of our fright that this is all our bodies will know. We're scared by the happy, hollow discipline that lines our brains and stomachs if we manage to stop at one biscuit. We need some kind of answer. We need to know what biscuit-tin discipline is, where it comes from. We need to know whether it's a sign that our bones are turning against the rest of us, whether anyone will help us if our bones win out, or whether the people that should help 's will say 'You look wonderful!' instead. (Oyeyemi 2008: 35)

The hysteric is an assertion of an undisciplined femininity that refuses to be controlled by losing weight or taming unruly hair in a context in which other women cannot be relied upon to warn against the danger of burgeoning eating disorders. It is constructed as a rebellious feminine spirit, one that unites women and spills forth in denial of social constraints.

Contrary to Western medical and psychological institutions that have worked together to associate hysteria with *disorders* of the womb (cf. Gilman *et. al* 1993), *The Opposite House* associates it with the healthy functioning of the womb through motherhood; Maja is quite clear that 'Hysteria has got nothing to do with an empty womb' (Oyeyemi 2008: 223). Indeed, after the initial introduction to the hysteric, its appearance in the text most frequently coincides with discussions of maternity, whether it be Amy Eleni's choice to donate her eggs, or Maja's anxieties about the child that she bears. The following scene is particularly telling: 'Later I examined myself from four different angles in the mirror and thought, *Why? Am I dangerous? Does the hysteric show?*' (Oyeyemi 2008: 131–32). When this scene occurs, Maja is during the early stages of pregnancy, and the question as to whether it 'shows' mimics questions asked by/of newly pregnant women as to the visibility of the bump; yet her concerns are directed towards the hysteric. As Maja's fears and feelings of repulsion to her unborn child develop – indexed not only through her thoughts, but through abject moments of vomiting and vaginal bleeding – it becomes increasingly identified with the hysteric, and Madeleine Elster's refrain '*There's someone inside of me, and she says I must die*' becomes ever more sinister (Oyeyemi 2008: 120). The foetus (identified by Maja but never confirmed as male) represents a threat to Maja's sense of identity and her fears are directed at self-expulsion through admittance of the other, which the hysteric pushes against by opening Maja up to others through an affiliation with Amy Eleni and a child with Aaron.

As feminist critics such as Elaine Showalter have noted, however, there has been scepticism about 'the ultimate power of hysteria as a form of feminine subversion'; 'the hysteric is unable to communicate because she is outside of reality and culture – [. . .] in Lacanian terms, her expression remains in the Imaginary, outside the Symbolic' (1993: 332). Such a claim is pertinent to Oyeyemi's work, where characters seem to become trapped in the Imaginary, and any realist reading of the endings of Oyeyemi's novels see her characters as dead, overtaken by madness, or both. Whilst it is possible to read utopian promise into the 'body language' of characters' endings (in which *The Icarus Girl*'s Jessy's spirit flies out of her body, or Miri's sacrifice protects Ore from the soucouyant, for example), it is impossible to see the endings as anything but bleak when framed by the realist rather than the magical work of the novels. However, one might read Oyeyemi's use of the pre-linguistic hysteric as a deliberate means of demonstrating the social situations that render certain voices unheard; as Showalter suggests, 'Anger that has social causes is converted to a language of the body' (1993: 335). Though less widely discussed, hysteria has historically been raced, as well as gendered, and as Showalter describes, 'Black activists and radicals have also been stigmatized as hysterics and neurotics, leading to distrust of psychotherapy in the 1960s and 1970s among African-Americans' (Showalter 1993: 334). As such, there is a tension within Oyeyemi's fiction between an openness to the outside, or the other, and a need to retreat inwards or protect the self in the context of a sexist or racist society in which an openness leaves characters vulnerable.

And yet . . .

It is on this note that I want to shift the discussion away from Cixous as I draw to a close, so as to focus on a different reading of the mouth. I want to suggest in conclusion that although the rich symbolism of Oyeyemi's novel points to ways of eating otherwise, speaking otherwise, being otherwise, these moments of possibility in which the body talks are also always thwarted, becoming moments of potential or actual threat to the self. This leads to a dual impulse in the novels. On the one hand, the symbolism and the writing push outwards, constructing new self-other relationships that are generous and loving, determined by 'taking in rather than taking over' and promising the genesis of a new woman to offer hope and promise to contemporary multicultural Britain. Yet on the other hand, the mouth is treacherous, rendering the self vulnerable to unsolicited intrusions.

Indeed, consumption is often associated with violence in the novels in question. In *The Opposite House*, Aaron begins force feeding Maja when she feels unable to eat due to the nausea brought on by morning sickness:

> 'You have got to eat,' he says. His voice is very hard. It hurts. He stands over me and drags my wrist so that I have to put soup into my mouth. [. . .] He jams the sloppy spoon into my mouth. (Oyeyemi 2008: 231)

The language used here has uncomfortable parallels with rape: his instructing voice is 'very hard' and 'hurts' Maja, whilst the spoon is 'jammed' into her mouth without consent. Aaron's cruelty at this point is depicted as the result of seeing the foetus rather than his girlfriend Maja as the subject: 'In his eyes I am a throat working down red juice, I am a shaking hand and a spoon and beyond that his baby' (Oyeyemi 2008: 231). Maja's pregnancy causes her to experience a shift from subject to object; her son is the consumer and she is the consumed, as she imagines herself to be a 'gourd, bound in crisp servility to [her] insides' (Oyeyemi 2008: 169). Maja's maternity causes her to experience an excavation of her sense of self identity, which is paralleled in the morning sickness that causes her to vomit up 'far more food than [she] could have eaten' (Oyeyemi 2008: 5). As such, the ambivalent motif of consumption in the novel depicts a scenario in which it is necessary to allow the other in and create connections – as starvation is associated with silence and death – yet in which these connections are often violent or cause the expulsion of the self.

The mouth also functions as a site of historical memory in *The Opposite House*. This is foregrounded early on, when it is revealed that 'Sugar makes Chabella cry. She hints at other memories, other sugar horrors, ancestral' (Oyeyemi 2008: 9). From the outset, food is constructed as a link to the past, through which traumatic memories haunt the present day (and here both the plantation work undertaken by the enslaved Africans of Chabella's ancestry and the nationalisation of the Cuban sugar industry that led to severe rationing in order to meet export requirements are referenced).[5] The mouth as the sensory organ through which historical trauma is revisited is significant in relation to the novel's primary trauma: that Maja's only memory of Cuba is proven false. What Maja describes as 'my Cuba' is 'a hut with a tabletop for a roof, wall-less and unmoored by strange music and feet and fruit juice', as she remembers sitting under a table with another child at a party (Oyeyemi 2008: 45). In this solitary memory, she witnesses the other girl (Magalys) having a fit, and the focus is on the uncontrolled workings of the mouth: 'she slurped and dribbled and winced as she bit her tongue over and over' (Oyeyemi 2008: 45). As another moment of disrupted consumption, the girl simultaneously consumes herself and lets herself dribble out. Yet when Maja is reunited with Magalys many years later in the UK, she finds that it was in fact herself not the other girl who had suffered the fit. It becomes apparent that Maja's real trauma, experienced at a temporal and spatial remove, is not the realisation that she had a fit, but that she has no reliable memory from Cuba to function as 'food for my son, for me' (Oyeyemi 2008: 169).

In *White is for Witching* the mouth is similarly constructed as a site of damage as well as one of possibility. In Eliot's description of Miri's disappearance, he suggests that she has left due to an argument started by her refusal to eat a pie filled with poisonous winter apples that he made her.[6] For Eliot, the argument 'was a stupid one that opened up a murky little mouth to take in other things' (Oyeyemi 2009: 2). The opening of the mouth in response to this moment of trauma has parallels with the body's opening through an act of wounding, whilst the sinister description of the 'murky little mouth' ensures that this openness to 'other things' is not conceived – at least by Eliot – in a positive light.

I have suggested that the mouth functions as the wound, through which trauma speaks via oral and gustatory hauntings of sound and taste. However, *The Opposite House* provides intertextual clues that a healing of this trauma would not be desirable, through Maja's description of *Vertigo*'s Madeleine Elster. She describes the tragic heroine of her favourite movie as:

> A vast wound in a landscape where wounds aren't allowed to stay open – people have to shut up and heal up. She's in trouble because the film works to a plan that makes trauma speak itself out – speak itself to excess until it dies. (Oyeyemi 2008: 34)

Maja is critical of a situation in which trauma needs to be overcome, forgotten, and smoothed over – the 'healthy' process of grieving loss that is identified in Freudian terms as 'mourning' through contrast to its pathological counterpart: 'melancholia' (Freud 1917). Maja's implicit critique of the possibility of closure represented by mourning has resonances with Ranjana Khanna's concept of 'critical melancholia', which alternatively sees the productive capacity of keeping the wound open, in an article that is particularly concerned with the processing of the traumas visited through colonialism (Khanna 2006). Khanna's theorisation of critical melancholia highlights the impossibility of fully narrating the past:

> Melancholia as symptom and reading practice [. . .] offer[s] a way of gauging how critical agency functions constantly to undo injustices performed in the name of justice and novelty. The impossibility of completed digestion of the past, and its calm production of novelty, manifests itself in constant critique. (Khanna 2006: n.p.)

This encourages a critical engagement with the traumas of colonisation, suggesting that to imply that wounds have been fully healed would be to damage their real and lasting impact. Diverging from a model of trauma therapy that accords cathartic power to narrative reclamation through speech (cf. Brison 1999), Khanna sees the potential in a state of permanent mourning, or melancholia, where the loss cannot be overcome but must always be critically evaluated.

In Oyeyemi's fiction, then, the mouth is the open wound, reminding of the perpetual incompleteness of identity construction and the impossibility of assimilation for migrants for whom a series of displacements preclude return and an atomised multicultural society thwarts new affiliations or modes of belonging. The possibility of new self-other relationships are gestured towards through acts of loving consumption and oral pleasure, and the significance of the mouth in the (perennially incomplete) construction of identity in Oyeyemi's work is undeniable. However, by foregrounding the postcolonial context of a Britain in which racist and nationalist structures create barriers between female relationships – both novels can be understood in the simplest of terms as thwarted romantic relationships between white and black women – the somewhat utopian possibility of Cixous' imagining of the genesis of 'woman' is challenged. For Oyeyemi the possibility of writing the body is problematised, as language causes alienation from the skin due to the displacements encountered through migration and the racist rhetoric that associates Britishness solely with whiteness:

> There is skin, yes. And then, inside that, there is your language, the casual, inherited magic spells that make your skin real. It's too late now – even if we could say "Shut up" or "Where's my dinner?" in the first language, the real language, the words weren't born in us. And unless your skin and your language touch each other without interruption, there is no word strong enough to make you understand that it matters that you live. (Oyeyemi 2008: 185)

Despite their efforts to escape, transcend, or go beyond, Oyeyemi's female characters are confronted with and frustrated by the persistence of patriarchal and (neo)colonial structures, which means that her work does not retain the level of optimism regarding the transformative power of writing or eating otherwise that is evident in Cixous' work.

Notes

1 Thanks go to Leanne Bibby, Rachel Carroll, and Helen Davies, for their comments on early drafts of this chapter.

2 Such criticisms pay little heed to the Cixous' own situation as a French Jew growing up in the imperialist and anti-Semitic culture of colonial Algeria, and the ways in which her own writing draws on this experience (Cixous in Lecoq 2008, 92).

3 In *White Is for Witching* both black Ore and white Miri are adversely affected by the nationalist, xenophobic, and racist structures that combine to cast blackness as other to British identity and to mark their relationship as transgressive. This is not to suggest that Oyeyemi posits a 'Universal' woman that is undifferentiated in her relationship to imperialist structures that breed contemporary xenophobia and racism – far from it – but to indicate that Oyeyemi recognises the damaging effects that this can also have on white women. A similar manoeuvre has recently been made by feminists such as Chimamanda Ngozi Adichie and Emma Watson, who have highlighted the ways in which men are also damaged by gender inequality and a patriarchal system in which masculinity is defined 'in a very narrow way'

(Adichie 2014, 26; see also Emma Watson's 2014 speech on gender equality delivered to the UN, transcribed at http://sociology.about.com/od/Current-Events-in-Sociological-Context/fl/Full-Transcript-of-Emma-Watsons-Speech-on-Gender-Equality-at-the-UN.htm).

4 I began to explore these ideas in my monograph, though they have developed since then (Ilott 2015, 74–75).

5 Thanks go to Jenni Ramone for the latter insight into the nationalisation of the Cuban sugar industry. See further http://faculty.mdc.edu/tpedraza/MMF-Ten%20Million%20Ton%20Harvest.htm.

6 As an aside, I would suggest that the apples of this scene can be read not in the hopeful light presented by Cixous in which the apple symbolises possibility and a moment of knowledge and becoming, but from the other angle as posited by Gilbert and Gubar in which to overcome the prohibitive intervention of the patriarchal law women must 'Reject[] the poisoned apples her culture offers her' (Gilbert and Gubar 1979, 58).

Works Cited

Adichie, C. N. 2014: *We Should All Be Feminists*. London: Fourth Estate.

Anatol, G. 2000: Transforming the Skin-Shedding Soucouyant: Using Folklore to Reclaim Female Agency in Caribbean Literature. *Small Axe* 7, 44–59.

Brison, S. 1999: Trauma Narratives and the Remaking of the Self. In M. Bla, J. Crewe, and L. Spitzer (eds.), *Acts of Memory: Cultural Recall in the Present*. Hanover, NH: University of New England Press, 39–54.

Cixous, H. 1976: The Laugh of the Medusa. Translated by K. Cohen and P. Cohen. *Signs* 1 (4), 875–93.

Cixous, H. 1981: Castration or Decapitation? Translated by A. Kuhn. *Signs* 7 (1), 41–55.

Cixous, H. 1991: *The Book of Promethea*. Translated by B. Wing. Lincoln, NE: University of Nebraska Press.

Cixous, H. 1994 [1984]: Extreme Fidelity. In S. Sellers (ed.), *The Hélène Cixous Reader*, New York, NY: Routledge, 131–37.

Dallery, A. B. 1992: The Politics of Writing (The) Body: Écriture Féminine. In A. J. Holt (ed.), *Gender/Body/Knowledge: Feminist Reconstructions of Being and Knowing*. New Brunswick, NJ: Rutgers University Press, 52–67.

Foss, C. 2003: 'There Is No God Who Can Keep Us From Tasting': Good Cannibalism in Hélène Cixous's *The Book of Promethea*. In T. Heller and P. Moran (ed.) *Scenes of the Apple: Food and the Female Body in Nineteenth- and Twentieth-Century Women's Writing*. Albany: State University of New York Press, 149–66.

Freud, S. 1917: Mourning and Melancholia. In James Strachey (ed.), *The Standard Edition of the Complete Psychological Works of Sigmund Freud: On the History of the Psycho-analytic Movement, Papers on Metapsychology, and Other Works*, vol. XIV. London: Hogarth, 243–58.

Gilbert, S. M., and Gubar, S. 1979: *The Madwoman in the Attic: The Woman Writer and the Nineteenth-Century Literary Imagination*. New Haven: Yale University Press.

Gilman, S. L., King, H., Porter, R., Rousseau, G. S., and Showalter, E. 1993: *Hysteria Beyond Freud*. Berkeley: University of California Press.

Githire, N. 2014: *Cannibal Writes: Eating Others in Caribbean and Indian Ocean Women's Writing*. Champaign: University of Illinois Press.

Heller, T. and Moran, P. 2003: Introduction. In T. Heller and P. Moran (ed.), *Scenes of the Apple: Food and the Female Body in Nineteenth- and Twentieth-Century Women's Writing*. Albany, NY: State University of New York Press, 1–42.

Ilott, S. 2015: *New Postcolonial British Genres: Shifting the Boundaries*. Basingstoke: Palgrave.

Khanna, R. 2006: Post-Palliative: Coloniality's Affective Dissonance. *Postcolonial Text*, 2 (1) http://journals.sfu.ca/pocol/index.php/pct/article/view/385/815.

Lecoq, D. 2008: Against the emotion of history (interview). Translated by J. Benson. In S. Sellers (ed.) *White Ink: Interviews on Sex, Text and Politics*. Stocksfield: Acumen, 88–94.

Oyeyemi, H. 2006 [2005]: *The Icarus Girl*, London: Bloomsbury.

Oyeyemi, H. 2008 [2007]: *The Opposite House*, London: Bloomsbury.

Oyeyemi, H. 2009: *White Is for Witching*, London: Picador.

Showalter, E. 1993: Hysteria, Feminism, and Gender. In S. L. Gilman, H. King, R. Porter, G. S. Rousseau and E. Showalter, *Hysteria Beyond Freud*, Berkeley: University of California Press, 286–344.

CHAPTER

8

'People can smile and smile and still be villains': Villains and Victims in *Mr Fox* and *Boy, Snow, Bird*

Jo Ormond

Fairy tales and villains go together like Beauty and the Beast. The European fairy tale is structured around an opposition between antagonist and protagonist, between villain and hero. Snow White must face the Evil Queen, Sleeping Beauty is tricked by Maleficent, and the young wife defies her murderous husband, Bluebeard. Oyeyemi manipulates this classic oppositional fairy tale structure to complicate the idea of villains and victims in her novels *Mr Fox* (2011) and *Boy, Snow, Bird* (2014), inverting and blurring their positions within the narrative. Both texts are based on fairy tales with well-known villains: *Boy, Snow, Bird* is a retelling of 'Snow White' (Grimm 1812) and *Mr Fox* retells 'Bluebeard' (Perrault 1697). Oyeyemi calls *Boy, Snow, Bird* her 'wicked stepmother story' in acknowledgement of the wicked stepmothers of Snow White and other Perrault and Grimm fairy tales such as 'Cinderella' (Perrault 1697; Grimm 1812) and 'Hansel and Gretel' (1812) (Oyeyemi in Hoggard 2014: n.p.). The monstrous bridegroom found in Bluebeard appears in other fairy tales, too – such as the Grimms' 'The Robber Bridegroom' (1884) and 'Fitcher's Bird' (1843). The most well known contemporary 'Bluebeard' retelling is, of course, Angela Carter's 'The Bloody Chamber' (1979).

The fairy tale structure works well for Oyeyemi's purpose because the plots and characters are so familiar to readers who are likely to know who the villains and the victims are supposed to be. By mixing this structure with other narrative forms, Oyeyemi turns this familiarity on its head, leaving the reader to question pre-conceived notions of what a villain or victim is and how they should behave. Using the fairy tale genre in this way, Oyeyemi asks readers to consider the construction of the villain while at the same time shedding light on issues such as trauma, identity, race and gender-based violence. Oyeyemi refuses easy answers; her villains are often victims of trauma, and while she does not allow their trauma to excuse their actions, the way her villains are constructed does imply evil is a social construction and not inherent.

At the end of *Mr Fox*, Oyeyemi acknowledges the influence that fairy tale writings by Margaret Atwood, Marina Warner and Anne Sexton have had on her novel. Through acknowledging these writers, Oyeyemi places herself firmly within a tradition of feminist retellings of fairy tales. As Andrew Teverson argues, Carter is the pioneer of feminist retellings of fairy tales, simultaneously exposing the original tales as complicit with patriarchal ideologies and harnessing them as a new form of creative expression, subverting such ideologies (Teverson 2013: 134–37). In 'The Bloody Chamber' Carter creates a feminist heroine in the form of the mother hunting down the Marquis and saving her daughter; however, many of Carter's retellings are more complicated and she does not subvert patriarchal ideologies by simply switching the roles of male aggressor and female victim. Likewise, Oyeyemi complicates the fairy tale characters, making them difficult to define as purely 'villain' or 'victim.'

Atwood's essay, 'Running with the Tigers', argues that Carter's *The Bloody Chamber* counters a view expressed by Marquis de Sade that there is only the predator or victim, the tiger or the lamb. Atwood's comments are pertinent also to Oyeyemi's *Mr Fox* and *Boy, Snow, Bird:*

> *The Bloody Chamber* may be read as a 'writing against' de Sade, a talking-back to him; and, above all, as an exploration of the possibilities for the kind of synthesis de Sade himself could never find because he wasn't even looking for it. Predator and prey, master and slave, are the only two categories [. . .] that he can acknowledge. [. . .] Carter [. . .] is looking for ways in which the tiger and the lamb parts of the psyche, can reach some sort of accommodation. (1994: 136)

This is also a fitting description for Oyeyemi's *Mr Fox*, which has the heroine Mary Foxe 'talking back' against the excuses that are made when women are abused, telling St John 'You simply have to change. You're a villain' (2011: 3). Carter's work also appears to have influenced Oyeyemi's subversion of the gendered positions of passive female victim and active male villain in both *Mr Fox* and *Boy, Snow, Bird*. My readings of these two novels thus follow Atwood's comments, and link Oyeyemi to the explicitly feminist project of Angela Carter's work, though Oyeyemi herself does not acknowledge this connection. Carter has been criticised by the likes of Patricia Duncker and Avis Lewallen for reversing the position of the aggressive male and passive female by making her female characters predatory (Makinen 1992: 4). As Merja Makinen explains, feminist critics have suggested that Carter is 're-writing the tales within the strait-jacket of their original structures' and that her 'attempts at constructing an active female erotic are badly compromised – if not a reproduction of male pornography' (1992: 4). However, Atwood argues that what Carter is doing is far more complex by creating characters who hold both the tiger and the lamb within themselves. Similarly, Oyeyemi uses strategies to blur and complicate narrative lines, unsettling the reader's grasp of victims and villains. Where Oyeyemi differs from Carter is in the construction of the villain; while Carter explores the possibility of synthesis between the tiger and the lamb through her characters, I will argue that Oyeyemi complicates her characters in order to demonstrate that evil, and therefore the villain, is a social construct.

Mr Fox

In *Mr Fox*, Oyeyemi uses the character of a 1930s American novelist to retell the 'monstrous bridegroom' story of fairy tales such as 'Bluebeard' (Perrault 1697), 'Fitcher's Bird' (Grimm 1843) and 'The Robber Bridegroom' (Grimm 1884), as well as the lesser known English fairy tale 'Mr Fox' (Joseph Jacobs 1890) from which Oyeyemi takes her lead characters' names: Mr Fox and Mary. In Oyeyemi's novel, St John Fox (the novelist) is visited by his fictional creation, Mary Foxe, who accuses him of being a serial killer for consistently killing off his female characters and challenges him to change his ways. What follows is a series of stories within stories, weaving together myth, folklore and fairy tale in a battle of wits between St John and Mary. To begin with, it is clear who is telling which story: St John begins by telling the story of a man who cuts off his wife's head; this story results in Mary losing her head back in St John's study. When St John asks how his story could impact on Mary in 'real life', Mary responds with 'It's all very technical [. . .] You couldn't possibly understand' (Oyeyemi 2011: 9). Oyeyemi appears to be making a point about how violence against women in art can impact in real life, while at the same time mocking the idea that it can have an impact with such a ridiculous situation. St John pleads that 'that's just the way the story went. I didn't know that was us' (Oyeyemi 2011: 9). The 'synthesis' between victim and villain referred to by Atwood takes place in *Mr Fox* when the stories within stories become so complex that readers lose track of who is telling the story, St John or Mary. One would expect a Bluebeard retelling to have an obvious villain and victim; however, Oyeyemi undermines this assumption by having the villain and victim as facets of the same character.

The voice who rebukes St John Fox for his ways, Mary, is St John Fox himself. When St John explains that he did not know how his stories would impact Mary (such as causing her to lose her head), he is really acknowledging the impact that the stories he tells have on himself. In interview, Oyeyemi said that this 'battle of words' between Mary and her creator was what she found most enjoyable about writing the novel and that 'the sparks between Mary and Mr. Fox over the necessity of the "death and the maiden" trope' are the most interesting part (Crispin 2011: n.p.). Mary challenges St John Fox on the treatment of women in his work and points out the danger in what Mr Fox does:

> What you're doing is building a horrible kind of logic. People read what you write and they say, 'Yes, he is talking about things that really happen,' and they keep reading and it makes sense to them. You're explaining things that can't be defended [. . .]. It was because he needed to let off steam [. . .] it was because she was irritating and stupid, it was because she lied to him, made a fool of him, [. . .] it was because 'nothing is more poetic than the death of a beautiful woman', it was because of this it was because of that. It's obscene to make such things reasonable. (Oyeyemi 2011: 120)

Mary Foxe challenges this contempt for women, which has taken the form of glamorisation of the murder and torture of women in film, literature and art. Mary argues that violence against women cannot be justified simply because it is used in art or as a form of entertainment such as in the novels of St John Fox. However, in an interview Oyeyemi states that she does not feel *Mr Fox* argues one way or another regarding the depiction of violence against women in art, but that she would 'be thrilled if it adds to the fund of narratives that question the legitimacy of such a centerpiece' (Oyeyemi in Crispin 2011: n.p.).

There are strong ties between 'The Bloody Chamber' and *Mr Fox*.

Carter describes the Marquis in 'The Bloody Chamber' watching his 'dolls' break free of their strings (Carter 1979: 40). St John also watches as first Mary and then his wife Daphne fight back against the roles he has ordained for them. In the opening paragraphs of *Mr Fox* St John is quick to describe the control he has over his wife, boasting that:

> She doesn't complain about anything I do; she is physically unable to. That's because I fixed her early. I told her in heartfelt tones that one of the reasons I love her is because she never complains. So now of course she doesn't dare complain. (Oyeyemi 2011: 1)

From the opening of the novel, St John is closely aligned with Carter's Marquis as a 'puppet master' controlling the women in his life. Whilst Oyeyemi's St John 'fixed' Daphne early, Carter's Marquis ordained rituals for his wives 'since time began' (Carter 1979: 40). Carter's feminist strategy is to overturn the patriarchal society that demands women remain passive while men are active, creating feminist heroines and deconstructing patriarchal roles by having the Marquis killed by his mother-in-law. At first glance Oyeyemi appears to be using the same strategy; however, the fact that Mary and St John are one and the same prevents the reader from seeing a clear feminist standpoint on the issues raised in the novel. This is a deliberate manoeuvre on the part of Oyeyemi who has stated that she does not have a clear standpoint for or against the violent deaths of women in entertainment (Crispin 2011: n.p.). Indeed, as with the earlier scene in which St John's story results in Mary losing her head, Oyeyemi treats it in a humorous way: Mary doesn't want St John to see her without her head and asks him to keep his eyes closed so she can retain some dignity while she tidies herself up. It is more reminiscent of a woman wanting to fix her make-up so no one can tell she has been crying than a woman who has had her head cut off by her husband.

Oyeyemi alludes to other Bluebeard retellings within *Mr Fox* including in the story 'What happens next' (Oyeyemi 2011: 123–71), which is reminiscent of Daphne Du Maurier's *Rebecca* (1938). 'What happens next' tells the story of a younger woman enthralled by a mysterious older man who may or may not have murdered his wife. The young woman is drawn to the man in part because he may be a murderer, not in spite of it. As Joseph Crawford writes of the Gothic Romance genre: 'Precisely because of its lower cultural status, genre fiction is sometimes less rigorously policed than more prestigious literary forms, allowing it to directly address themes that such forms can explore only indirectly' (2014: 2). Likewise, Oyeyemi is able to do the same thing with the fairy tale genre. By allowing the Bluebeard character of St John to argue with himself, Oyeyemi puts what he does into context: when Mary loses her head as a result of St John's story he sees the impact his story can have. What he writes – crime fiction centred upon the murder of young female characters – sells. Thus it is not St John who is at fault here, but the society that popularises the type of entertainment that romanticises violence against women, to the point that women themselves think of such violence as 'normal.' Therefore St John is only a villain because society demands it of him. Oyeyemi has said herself that:

> As a reader and film watcher, I find the death and the maiden trope spectacular when it's properly done – for example, when it feels organic to the story and doesn't participate in a dodgy aesthetic. [. . .] All I ask of a story about the murder of a woman, or the murder of several women, is that it doesn't imply that her death was beautiful, or that the murdered woman is in some way more beautiful or potent or interesting in death. (Oyeyemi in Crispin 2011: n.p.)

As Anne Cranny-Francis argues, the most important role of feminist discourse is to make the 'naturalised' role of women visible and to challenge it (1990: 2). Oyeyemi does this through the fairy tale genre not only by inverting the passive female / active male role, but by blurring those roles entirely.

The separation between victim and villain is further confused by the attraction of the female character to the villain. Warner writes in *Once Upon a Time* that fairy tales such as 'Bluebeard' or 'Beauty and the Beast' with a monster bridegroom are as 'entangled with the bride and with questions of female desire as they are with male drives. [. . .] Bluebeard [is] [. . .] an enemy, a sadist, and a rapist – who can also be irresistibly alluring' (2014: 92). This 'attractive villain' has become rooted in popular culture and is explored by Crawford in *Twilight of the Gothic*, in which he notes that the villain and the romantic hero have become one and same:

> By the late 1980s [. . .] the heroes of popular romance had been growing steadily darker [. . .] carried from respectability to criminality, and from self-control to physical and sexual aggression. [. . .] the villains [. . .] had been growing increasingly sympathetic [. . .] capable of love and aching for redemption. (2014: 58)

Like the traditional Gothic villain, St John is presented as conflicted, challenging his own villainous behaviour and presenting alternative pathways, through Mary's intervention. As Cranny-Francis points out, genre fiction 'foregrounds its conventions, rather than stitching them seamlessly into the fabric of the text and so its ideological framework may be, or may appear to be, self-evident' (1990: 2). Whilst genre fiction has tended to draw on sexist tropes and reproduce patriarchal ideology, Cranny-Francis argues that genre fiction also provides a self-awareness about these tropes that lends itself to feminist revision (1990: 2). Likewise, Cranny-Francis's argument can be applied to fairy tale retellings: as a genre, the European fairy tale structure has the same recognisable tropes that have been used by feminist writers, such as Carter, for the pointedly political project of opening up the naturalisation of sexist discourse to scrutiny. Oyeyemi's use of these tropes enables her to explore the idea of the sympathetic villain in a new way, to unsettle the idea of a traditional villain and to explore whether such a thing actually exists, an issue she continues to explore in *Boy, Snow, Bird*.

Boy, Snow, Bird

Boy, Snow, Bird retells the story of 'Snow White', with the story narrated in part by each of the title characters. The novel examines the relationship between the female characters, drawing on the fairy tale tropes of the wicked stepmother and the beautiful fairy tale heroine who is her victim. The first voice we hear is that of Boy Novak, a beautiful blond who escapes from her violent rat-catcher father in New York to the town of Flax Hill. As the title of her book, *From the Beast to the Blonde,* suggests, Warner has a lot to say about how hair is significant in fairy tales, particularly blonde hair: 'Golden hair tumbles through the stories in impossible quantities' (1995: 365). Warner points out that among the fairy tale heroines only Snow White is traditionally dark, based on her mother's wish to have a child with hair 'as black as the wood of the window-frame' or in some versions 'the colour of a raven's wing' (1995: 365). Boy's blondeness sets up an interesting contrast to Snow's dark-haired beauty later in the novel, but more immediately identifies her as a traditional fairy tale heroine, beautiful and blonde, and fleeing the clutches of an evil villain.

In Flax Hill, Boy meets the widowed Arturo and his beautiful young daughter Snow, upon whom the whole family dotes. At first, Boy is equally smitten by Snow, although she finds the adoration of the rest of the family unsettling:

> I watched the women watching Snow. Their reverence was over the top. Sure, she was an extraordinary-looking kid. A medieval swan maiden, only with the darkest hair and the pinkest lips, every shade at its utmost. She was like a girl in a Technicolor tapestry, sure, sure, but . . . they'd had a while to get used to her, and acting like that every time they laid eyes on her seemed to me like the fastest way to build an insufferable brat. (Oyeyemi 2014: 78)

Oyeyemi's description of Snow is typical of the fairy tale 'Snow White' with 'every shade at its utmost', lips as red as blood, skin as white as snow and hair as black as a raven's wing, as in the Grimms' telling of the story (Oyeyemi 2014: 78). Unknown to Boy, much of the admiration the family has for Snow's 'Technicolor' beauty comes from Snow being the child of black parents and grandparents who have been 'passing' as white. Like the Snow White of the Grimm fairy tale, Oyeyemi's Snow is the product of wish fulfilment; Snow is 'the fairest of them all' in terms of her racial heritage. When Boy gives birth to Arturo's child she discovers that Arturo's family are actually black and have been passing as white:

> then there was Bird in my arms, safe and well, and dark. No. It wasn't just her shade of gold [. . .], it was her facial features too. As that nurse said when she thought I was too wiped out to hear: 'That little girl is a Negro.'
>
> I didn't want to show her to anybody. [. . .] The doctor thought I'd gone to bed with a colored man, and I had. He was my husband. (Oyeyemi 2014: 131–32)

Boy sends Snow away to live with Arturo's sister, Clara, who was sent away by her mother for having dark skin. Here, Oyeyemi subverts the meaning of the 'fairest of them all' trope to contrast beauty and lightness of skin. As Warner points out, the Old English meaning of 'fair' was 'beautiful, or pleasing', developed by the thirteenth century into 'free from imperfections or blemish' and, by the sixteenth, carried explicit connotations of 'a light hue; clear in colour' (1995: 363). Oyeyemi's subversion of the traditional fairy tale trope of 'fairest' meaning 'most beautiful' to 'palest' exemplifies Warner's statement in *From the Beast to the Blonde* that 'evidence of conditions from past social and economic arrangements [can] co-exist in the tale with the narrator's innovations' (1995: xix). The treatment of African Americans in the 1950s as inferior citizens lends itself well to the retelling of a fairy tale where an African American girl not only passes as white, but is also admired for her beauty by white people. Boy does send Snow away because she is the fairest of them all, but this is because it threatens the wellbeing of her dark skinned daughter, Bird, rather than Boy's vanity.

While Snow clearly fills the role of Snow White, the identity of Oyeyemi's 'wicked stepmother' or other such villain is less clear. Boy Novak, Olivia Whitman and Frank Novak are all contenders, but each character is complicated, unlike the two-dimensional villains of traditional fairy tales. Boy Novak at first seems to be the most likely villain, mainly because she is Snow's stepmother and sends her away. However, the reader first meets Boy as the victim of abuse at the hands of her father and she initially appears to be our golden-haired, fairytale heroine. Through the character of Boy, and the way that other characters react to her, Oyeyemi shows how assumptions are made about what a woman is like based on her looks. At a party Boy finds herself transfixed by a 'god-awful' portrait, which it turns out is actually her own reflection in the mirror. Arturo sees her and mistakes it for vanity, growing cold towards her. Believing her to be shallow, he dismisses her ability to bring anything of worth to Flax Hill, asking if her previous job in New York was as a dress-maker's model and thereby dismissing her as a beautiful dumb object (Oyeyemi 2014: 23).

Readers' views of Boy have been complicated, as has Arturo's, but even Boy does not have a clear idea of who or what she is, as demonstrated by her complex relationship with mirrors. When Boy begins to feel resentful towards Snow she also acknowledges that 'Snow was blameless' (Oyeyemi 2014: 132), but that she still found herself hating her:

> Snow's daintiness grew day by day, to menacing proportions. I would've hit her and decided it was self-defense. I wouldn't have seen the rat catcher (or the snake bracelet) in my actions until much later. [. . .] Maybe there is no Snow, but only smoke and mirrors. The Whitmans need someone to love, and have found too much to hate in each other, and so this lifelike little projection walks around and around a reel, untouchable. (Oyeyemi 2014: 142)

The snake bracelet Boy refers to is the engagement gift Arturo gives her that she feels screams 'wicked stepmother', and the rat catcher is Boy's abusive father (Oyeyemi 2014: 105). The fact that Boy recognises her 'wicked stepmother' tendencies and the effect of her childhood abuse, and is able to stop herself from physically abusing Snow, makes her an unlikely villain. The first person narrative also complicates readers' views of Boy as a villain: hearing her voice prevents the reader from othering her and readers are instead inclined to see her point of view and even sympathise with her reasoning.

Again, this points to Oyeyemi's socially constructed villain: putting the behaviour of the character in context can stop the behaviour appearing villainous. It is the action that can be labelled 'villainous' rather than the character themselves.

Far less sympathetic is the character of Olivia Whitman, who rejects Bird based on the colour of her skin:

> It was Olivia Whitman I could not forgive. When Bird came home, she was our first visitor, and she took one look at Bird, a cold, thorough look, then turned her gaze away. [. . .] I said: 'You think I won't slap you, Olivia, but I will. Keep going and you'll see.'
>
> [. . .] 'The last person who threatened to slap me was a white woman. Blonde, like you. No Southern belle, either. Just trash.'
>
> I told myself, *Stop it. Whatever else she says don't rise to it.* I wanted a grandmother for Bird. Olivia wasn't the one I would have chosen, but she was a generous grandmother to Snow and if she put her mind to it, she could do it again. (Oyeyemi 2014: 133–34)

Olivia's continued coldness towards Bird, and the fact that she sent away one of her daughters, Clara, for having dark skin, also makes her a likely candidate for villain of the piece. Boy certainly sees her as a villain and describes herself physically recoiling from her 'to keep us from catching what was in her, what was there in her voice and her eyes. [. . .] Olivia was terrible, just the worst' (Oyeyemi 2014: 135). But like Boy, Olivia is also the victim of abuse, in this case racial abuse. She recounts how she was threatened with a slap by a white woman when working in a shop and that she would have lost her job if she had argued with her. Instead, she pleaded stupidity and silently wished:

> *If I have a daughter I don't want anyone talking to her like that. I don't ever want to hear my daughter wheedling at anyone the way I do every working day. I thought: If I do, if I ever hear that in the voice of a child of mine, I'll make her sorry all right. I'll wring her damn neck.* (Oyeyemi 2014: 135)

Oyeyemi again subverts a common fairy tale trope, that of wishing. Unlike Snow White's mother who wishes for beauty for her child after seeing drops of her blood on snow, Olivia's language is aggressive; she would be violent towards her child if she behaved the way a black woman is forced to behave by a white society. This closely aligns her with Boy: both send away children and both do it to prevent themselves becoming violent towards the child. It is possible to have sympathy with Olivia's actions, which makes it difficult to see her as a villain, although she does not have the same self-awareness of her potential villainy as Boy. Snow is the ultimate wish fulfilment for Olivia, and by sending Snow away Boy is able to punish Olivia indirectly.

Mother figures sending children away is a common fairy tale trope, although motivation of the mother or stepmother varies from jealousy ('Snow White', 'Hansel and Gretel'), marriage ('The Goose Girl' [Grimm 1815]), payment of a debt ('Rapunzel' [Grimm 1812]) and errands ('Red Riding Hood' [Perrault 1697] and 'Jack and the Beanstalk' [Jacobs 1890]). Oyeyemi uses it in a far more complex way by embedding it in a social context and showing us the repercussions, not just on the child but also on those who stay behind. This is unusual, as readers do not usually get to see what happens to the characters 'left behind' in fairy tales; this is another device Oyeyemi employs to complicate the idea of the villain. The awareness that Boy has of these repercussions makes her actions far more sympathetic than those of Olivia, who persists in believing she did the right thing.

Frank Novak is the first villain introduced in the book. The way he kills rats is described in graphic detail: 'he goes to the basement, selects a cage, and pulls its inhabitant's eyes out. The rats that are blind and starving are the best at bringing death to all the other rats, that's your father's claim' (Oyeyemi 2014: 6). He is also violent towards his partners and to Boy. Boy describes occasions when her father would punch her in the kidneys, thump the back of her head and hold her facedown in a sink of water until she fainted (Oyeyemi 2014: 6–7). There is a particularly disturbing scene where Frank drugs Boy, ties her to a chair and holds a starving rat up to her face to gnaw at her cheek.

> 'Why are you shaking like that?' my father asked, tenderly. 'Do you think that if I scar you no one will love you? You've got the wrong idea, girl. This will help your true love find you. He'll really have to fight for you now.' There was a thickness to his voice; I cracked one eye open. He was crying. (Oyeyemi 2014: 122)

Frank's use of fairy-tale language while he tortures his daughter further reinforces his role in this scene as the fairy-tale villain and Boy as the damsel in distress; he refers to Boy's 'true love' having to fight for her, rather like a prince in a fairy tale saving the beautiful princess. However, at the same time Oyeyemi complicates our view of Frank by having him cry as he tortures his daughter, showing that there is more at play here and hinting at Frank's own secret trauma. Frank's job as a rat catcher aligns him with another fairy-tale character, the Grimms' 'Pied Piper of Hamelin' (1816), who is a slightly more sympathetic fairy tale villain. While he does commit the terrible act of stealing all the children from the village of Hamelin, it is only in retribution for the villagers denying him fair payment for his work in ridding the town of rats.

The Pied Piper differs from many other fairy-tale villains in that we see the motivation for his actions, and this parallel can be drawn with the character of Frank. Later in the novel we find out that Frank was Boy's birth mother Frances, who became pregnant with Boy after being raped when she was a college student. While this does not excuse Frank's abuse of Boy, it allows the reader to revise their reading retrospectively. Frank, formerly Frances, is also the victim of abuse. Boy's friend Mia tells her about what happened to Frank:

> Frank told me this himself. Frances was raped. It was an acquaintance of hers [. . .]. He was an undergrad at Columbia who thought that all lesbianism meant was that you were holding out for the man who really got you excited. Frances had warned him to stop airing this view. Frances had issued her warning to this guy in front of other people and I guess that had humiliated him and – don't let me rationalize what he did anymore, Boy. (Oyeyemi 2014: 293)

Since Frank is the victim of rape, his gender change can be read as a reaction to the trauma of his abuse. Like Olivia, Frank uses 'passing' as a form of survival, in this case passing as a man. This quote also closely echoes Mary's critique of St John Fox in *Mr Fox*. Both list excuses that are given for committing violence against women and both decry the attempt to make such excuses; Mary calls it 'obscene' (Oyeyemi 2011: 120). And yet, while Mary is disgusted by the idea of 'nothing being as poetic as the death of a beautiful woman' (Oyeyemi 2011: 120), Frances is described as being attractive with a 'knock-out smile', 'hair as long as Lady Godiva's' and a 'twinkle in [her] eye' (Oyeyemi 2014: 292). When Mia shows Boy photos of her mother she says 'Look at her. [. . .] I know she's your mother, but you get the appeal, right?' (Oyeyemi 2014: 292). Frank's attempt to mutilate Boy's face could be read as a misguided way of protecting her from rape, justified by Frank's logic that men will not want Boy if she is no longer beautiful. In linking this back to the earlier discussion around the death and the maiden trope and violence against women in art, this shows a change in direction for Oyeyemi. A stronger statement against violence against women is being made here, although the circumstances are different: in *Mr Fox* Oyeyemi writes about the depiction of violence against women as entertainment, although she also touches on how this can translate into real life.

In *Boy, Snow, Bird*, Oyeyemi explores the social impact of this trauma and how it perpetuates further abuse of women, even abuse committed by other women. Frank, like Olivia and Boy, all justify the abuse or abandonment of their children as being for the greater good. In the essay '"Nobody's Meat": Revisiting Rape and Sexual Trauma through Angela Carter', Charley Baker argues that Angela Carter's writing displaces the myths which are held about rape victims by using her characters' responses to rape and sexual violence to emphasise the differences and individuality of trauma (2011: 66). At first Frank appears to be the embodiment of de Sade's predatory aggressor who has 'adopted tigerhood', as Mia describes how Frances became Frank after being asked to leave a women's shelter:

> She was . . . uh, demoralizing the other women who 'had suffered their own violations but were determined to continue their lives as women in spite of them' [. . .]. Frances understood and admired that, but it wasn't her way. Her distress had hardened. You know how Frank says he became Frank? He says he looked in the mirror one morning when he was still Frances, and this man she'd never seen before was just standing there, looking back. (Oyeyemi 2014: 294)

Oyeyemi provides complex characters who are both victims and inflictors of trauma; she makes it uncomfortable for the reader, who is unable either to sympathise fully, or to find the villain of the fairy tale. Indeed, Oyeyemi has said that *Boy, Snow, Bird* is about the troubling relationships between women and that 'Every wicked stepmother story is to do with the way women disappoint each other [. . .] across generations. A lot of terrible things can come out of that disappointment' (Oyeyemi in Hoggard 2014: n.p.). Through the complicated character of Frank / Frances, Oyeyemi demonstrates how the burden of the trauma can passed from one woman to another.

The influence of earlier feminist retellings on Oyeyemi's writing can also be seen in her conflation of victim and villain: Sharon Rose Wilson writes that all the characters in Atwood's *The Robber Bride* are both the Robber and the Robber's victims: 'Despite differing intentions and illusions all are "children" of the violence that has characterized human history' (2008: 19). Likewise, Olivia, Frank and Boy are all children of the violence of racism, homophobia and misogyny; they are both the Robber and the Robber's victims. Oyeyemi is clearly signifying that there are no real villains, only the social systems that construct them.

Conclusion

Oyeyemi's work continues in the feminist tradition of Angela Carter and Margaret Atwood by using the fairy tale genre to highlight issues such as misogyny and racism. Oyeyemi does not reverse the traditional gendered positions of villain and victim, but instead she unsettles them. In *Mr Fox*, Oyeyemi is wary of making a clear statement for or against the depiction of violence against women in writing and film; as a writer she acknowledges that such things happen and will be portrayed. Through the mouthpiece of Mary Fox she expresses her disgust at the way violence against women can be glorified; however, as Mary Fox is the creation of St John, the 'Bluebeard' of the tale, the lines between villain and victim are blurred, making them one and the same. In *Boy, Snow, Bird*, Oyeyemi critiques the technique of inversion through the character of Frank, and explores the difficult relationships between women and the way they disappoint one another. Oyeyemi portrays Frank as an example of de Sade's 'tiger': a woman who, as a result of sexual abuse, becomes the abuser, destroying his relationships with other women with violence. Boy, who is initially set up as the golden-haired fairy tale heroine, becomes the wicked stepmother. Unlike the traditional fairy tales she retells, Oyeyemi does not allow villains or heroines to be easily identified and she does not allow trauma to be an excuse for violence. Oyeyemi shows that society can make a villain of anyone, a woman such as Frances becomes the abuser of her daughter; while her Bluebeard character St John Fox, voices disgust at the depiction of violence against women as entertainment. This marks Oyeyemi out as a rebellious new voice in the feminist tradition of rewriting fairy tales.

Works Cited

Atwood, M. 2007: Running with the Tigers. In L. Sage (ed.) *Flesh and the Mirror: Essays on the Art of Angela Carter.* London: Virago Press, 133–50.

Baker, C. 2011: 'Nobody's Meat': Revisiting Rape and Sexual Trauma through Angela Carter. In S. Onega and J. Ganteau (eds.) *Ethics and Trauma in Contemporary British Fiction.* Amsterdam: Rodopi, 61–84.

Carter, A. 2007 [1979]: *The Bloody Chamber.* London: Vintage.

Cranny-Francis, A. 1990: *Feminist Fiction.* Cambridge: Polity Press.

Crawford, J. 2014: *The Twilight of the Gothic? Vampire Fiction and the Rise of the Paranormal Romance, 1991–2012.* Cardiff: University of Wales Press.

Crispin, J. 2011: Sex, Love and Murder in *Mr Fox. Kirkus Reviews.* www.kirkusreviews.com/features/sex-love-and-murder-mr-fox/

Grimm, J. and Grimm, W. 2002 [1843]: Fitcher's Bird. *University of Pittsburgh.* http://www.pitt.edu/~dash/grimm046.html

Grimm, J. and Grimm W. 2001 [1884]: The Robber Bridegroom. *University of Pittsburgh*. http://www.pitt.edu/~dash/grimm040.html

Hoggard, L. 2014: Helen Oyeyemi: 'I'm interested in the way women disappoint each other'. *Guardian*. www.theguardian.com/books/2014/mar/02/helen-oyeyemi-women-disappoint-one-another

Jacobs, J. 2003 [1890]: Mr Fox. *Authorama: Public Domain Books*. http://www.authorama.com/english-fairy-tales-29.html

Makinen, M. 1992: *The Bloody Chamber* and the Decolonization of Feminine Sexuality. *Feminist Review* 42 (1), 2–15.

Oyeyemi, H. 2012 [2011]: *Mr Fox*. London: Picador.

Oyeyemi, H. 2014: *Boy, Snow, Bird*. London: Picador.

Perrault, C. 2003 [1697]: Bluebeard. *University of Pittsburgh*. http://www.pitt.edu/~dash/perrault03.html

Teverson, A. 2013: *Fairy Tale: The New Critical Idiom*. Oxon: Routledge.

Warner, M. 1995: *From the Beast to the Blonde*. Cambridge: Vintage.

Warner, M. 2014: *Once Upon a Time: A Short History of Fairy Tale*. Oxford: Oxford University Press.

Wilson, S. R. 2012: *Myths and Fairy Tales in Contemporary Women's Fiction: From Atwood to Morrison*. New York: Palgrave Macmillan.

CHAPTER

9

'As white as red as black as . . . ': Beauty, Race and Gender in the Tales of Helen Oyeyemi, Angela Carter and Barbara Comyns

HELEN COUSINS

'It must be great being a blonde' says Webster to Boy (Oyeyemi 2014: 27). Boy certainly has a Nordic beauty: 'near-black eyes', 'fine-boned' features and 'white-blonde' hair preserved with peroxide when it darkens with age (Oyeyemi 2014: 3, 5). But Boy is not entitled to be the heroine of this tale. *Boy, Snow, Bird* (2014), as a retelling of 'Snow White' (Perrault 1697; Brothers Grimm 1823), is concerned primarily with another ideal of beauty: that of 'the darkest hair and the pinkest lips' found in the fairy tale heroines who are 'as white as that snow, as red as that blood, and as black as that ebony' (Oyeyemi 2014: 78; Brothers Grimm 1823). Oyeyemi's version of this fairy tale allows her to pay attention to both race and gender through the trope of racial 'passing', a very particular type of mimicry, and key to this trope is the notion of beauty.

A productive way to explore the notion of beauty in *Boy, Snow, Bird*, is to put the text in dialogue with Angela Carter and Barbara Comyns, two other contemporary writers who retell fairy tales, as this also has been a consistent feature of Oyeyemi's work. It is particularly explicit in her last two novels where she rewrites, like those other authors, the staples of European fairy stories. Such writers are often referred to as 'revisionist mythmakers' who, as Alice Ostriker explains, retell myths to 'offer us [women] one significant means of redefining ourselves and consequently our culture' (1982: 71). A striking feature of these retellings for Ostriker is that they are multivoiced, something also noted by Cristina Bacchilega. For Bacchilega, feminist retellings seek to 'expose, bring out, what the institutionalization of such tales for children has forgotten or left unexploited. This kind of rereading [. . .] listens for the many "voices" of fairy tales' (1997: 50). *Boy, Snow, Bird* is itself multi-vocal with its two narrators, and in drawing on two different fairy tales: 'Snow White' and 'The Juniper Tree.'[1] The dialogue between the tales allows for discussion of both race and gender, in relation to beauty, and the particular versions being considered here are Carter's version of 'Snow White', entitled 'The Snow Child' (1979); and Comyns's novel *The Juniper Tree* (1985).

Carter's version of 'Snow White' derives from a variant recounted to the Grimms but not published in their final tales, as noted by Maria Tatar (2012). In this version, the wish for a child as white as snow, as red as blood, and as black as a raven, is expressed by the Count rather than his wife. The Count has 'tender feelings' for the girl who subsequently appears, but the Countess either drops a glove or in another version, asks for a rose, then orders the coachman to drive off leaving the girl behind (Tatar 2012: n.p.). In Carter's alternative ending, a red rose thorn pricks the girl, killing her, whereupon the Count gives rein to his 'tender feelings', weeping whilst copulating with the corpse of the Snow Child who then vanishes (1979: 92).

Carter's pared down tale of only around six hundred words provides a response to Susan Sellers' question of whether feminist rewriting is possible given how 'embedded' the *logos* is in our 'culture and language' (2001: 25). Can women writers only mimic, as Irigaray proposes (Sellers 2001: 24)? Or only 'operate from inside the systems of representation', as Kristeva suggests, meaning that 'women's writing will repeat the way we have been taught to see' (Sellers 2001: 24)? Carter's answer is to use mimicry as described by Homi Bhabha in relation to colonial contexts, although it is somewhat reversed. From a feminist perspective, the 'desire for a reformed, recognizable Other, *as a subject of difference that is almost the same*, but not quite', can be applied to Carter's depiction of the Count (Bhabha 1994: 86). Here, the female writer uses her power of representation to offer readers a monstrous version of male desire which mimics the character function of the Prince. The distilled writing of the first line, which sets the scene in three words, is also found in the description of the sexual act: 'the count [. . .] unfastened his breeches and thrust his virile member into the dead girl' (Carter 1979: 92). This draws the narrative beyond the usual closure point of fairy tales, which traditionally close with the marriage and an assertion that they 'lived happily ever after'; in Carter's tale the consummation is enacted within the narrative to make explicit the male function within a fairy tale – consummation with the heroine. Here, it is stripped bare of all the usual discourse of rescue and romance so that the mimicry produces 'its slippage, its excess, its difference' in order to expose male desire explicitly (Bhabha 1994: 86). Sandra M. Gilbert and Susan Gubar note how in the better known version of 'Snow White', the King is absent from the story because his presence is 'the voice of the looking glass, the patriarchal voice of judgement that rules [. . .] every woman's [. . .] self-evaluation' (1984: 38). There is no need for the King to appear 'because, having assimilated the meaning of her own sexuality [. . .] the woman has internalized the King's rules' (Gilbert and Gubar 1984: 38). In Carter's version the male figure is present, which allows her to reveal the raw effect of that male judgement on female sexuality rather than eliding it through the focus on female rivalry. The male Other is appropriated by the female gaze in Carter's version, which visualises its power but not quite as it would wish to be represented, creating an ambivalence typical of mimicry. The mockery and menace in this condensed variant shows us male desire stripped of romance.

Carter's decision to use a little known variant, which unusually gives the Count this sexual role, is indicative of her interest in using the 'latent content of those traditional stories [. . .] [which] is violently sexual' (Simpson 2006, n.p.). However, she also preserves the conflict between the Queen and her stepdaughter whereby 'women almost inevitably turn against women because the voice of the looking glass sets them against each other' (Gilbert and Gubar 1984: 38). In Carter's tale the icy stillness of the snowy scene emphasises even more strongly the coldly murderous intentions of the Queen/stepmother (named the Countess in 'The Snow Child'); less a character 'maddened, rebellious [and] witchlike' than one who enacts 'the stifling intensity' and 'intense desperation' of female rivalry (Gilbert and Gubar 1984: 38, 37, 38). Carter's tale might be interpreted either as an interrogation of women in conflict or as an exposé of the violence of male desire – or as both. However, by putting 'The Snow Child' in dialogue with *Boy, Snow, Bird*, I want to draw attention to an implicit racial division between the women in Carter's text, which brings a different dimension to being 'as white' or 'as black as' – the colour scheme so commonly used in fairy tales.

Francisco Vaz da Silva offers a chromatic analysis of these three colours in relation to fairy tales.[2] He notes that for fairy tale heroines, white is significant as tinted with red so that white – the purity and innocence of a child born of supernatural intervention – is a 'precondition for red' (2007: 245, 246). Red itself symbolises the fertility associated with female bleeding: '"Red as blood," then, sets the dynamic frame of a shared destiny in which related women interact, both for good and evil' (Vaz da Silva 2007: 245). In Carter's story red is one of the shared elements between the women. The Countess has 'boots with scarlet heels' whilst the girl has a 'red mouth' (Carter 1979: 91, 92). Red also connects them through the rose that the Countess asks the girl to fetch for her, which pricks her and kills her, and which is then given to the Countess by the Count. The Countess lacks the white element of virginal purity that the girl has, and which is so attractive to the Count. When white is 'tinged' with red via the 'prick' that kills the girl, she melts away whilst the Countess survives predominantly in black: 'she on a black [horse], she wrapped in the glittering pelts of black foxes; and she wore high, black, shining boots' (Carter 1979: 91).

In Vaz da Silva's analysis, black relates to death and the otherworld. Usually, he notes, black is a barely discernible element, associated with enchantment, and manifests, for example, in the death-like coma of Snow White. It is also temporary as 'Enchantment is something like reversible death, and death itself appears in tones of enchantment' (Vaz da Silva 2007: 247). The black element vanishes with the rescue of the princess and the death of the villain who is often the enchanter – the evil stepmother in the case of 'Snow White.' Carter's version reverses that fairy tale ideal whereby the pure white heroine survives whilst the evil enchanter is destroyed; the black queen is not in this case 'replaced by [the] angelically innocent and dutiful daughter' (Gilbert and Gubar 1984: 38). When putting Carter's variant of 'Snow White' side by side with Oyeyemi's variant, *Boy, Snow, Bird*, however, the possibility of a racial division between the two women is raised. We know the Snow Child has white skin but whether or not the Countess is racially Black or just dressed in black is uncertain. The alignment in Carter's tale of white as supernatural purity and black as evil, death-bringing enchantment matches that of the traditional fairy tale as discussed by Vaz da Silva. It suggests that although Carter has used what we might interpret as mimicry (from a postcolonial perspective) effectively to challenge gender, the usual attention to race and the 'function of colonial power' is absent (Bhabha 1994: 86). Oyeyemi is able to interrogate both gender and race in relation to beauty by inflecting the notion of being 'the fairest of them all' with racial and gendered 'passing.'

In his analysis, Vaz da Silva uses the tale of 'The Three Citrons' to illustrate his point that black is associated with the death of the heroine. In this tale the princess is killed by a Black slave whose ugliness stands in stark contrast to the superlatively beautiful princess: 'a delicate maiden, white as a junket with red streaks, – a thing never before seen in the world, with a beauty beyond compare, a fairness beyond the beyonds' (Basile 1911: n.p.). In contrast, the slave is 'a black crow', a 'great blot of ink', and like a house 'hung with mourning', reinforcing the association with death (Basile 1911: n.p.). Yet it is not the case that black and white have to correlate with ugliness and beauty in fairy tales. Many examples of enchantresses, evil queens and wicked stepmothers are beautiful, as Gilbert and Gubar point out in relation to 'Snow White.' In this story the contrast is between two women, 'one fair, young, pale, the other just as fair, but older fiercer [. . .] the one sweet, ignorant, passive, the other both artful and active; the one a sort of angel, the other an undeniable witch' (Gilbert and Gubar 1984: 36). I would further add that one is clearly White (with skin as white as snow) and one is indeterminately 'black.' In *Boy, Snow, Bird*, Oyeyemi explores the associations of beauty with race and it is helpful to recognise that for her too, there is not a simple notion of what it might mean to be 'fair.' In fact, Oyeyemi is interested to explore the order of beauty associated with 'white', which, as Vaz da Silva points out, is not just pure and innocent but also related to the supernatural.

In order to explore this further, I turn now to the other intertext; the specific variant of 'The Juniper Tree' written by Barbara Comyns. 'The Juniper Tree' is possibly less well known than 'Snow White' although it shares with 'Snow White' the wish for a child as white as snow and as red as blood (omitting the black element). In the Grimms' version, the mother dies soon after bearing her white-and-red son. When the father remarries, his new wife has a daughter but she becomes increasingly jealous of her stepson because he will eventually inherit everything at the expense of her own daughter: she 'loved her daughter very much, and when she looked at her and then looked at the boy, it pierced her heart to think that he would always stand in the way of her own child' (Brothers Grimm 1823). This is a matter of financial inheritance and the stepmother eventually kills the boy, attempting to make her daughter the sole heir.

The presence of stepsiblings in *Boy, Snow, Bird* suggests that Oyeyemi has drawn on more than one fairy tale in her rewriting. In fact, she directly acknowledges her debt to Comyns' *The Juniper Tree* in an online interview:

> This book is my wicked stepmother story – I'd read Barbara Comyns' *The Juniper Tree*, also told from the perspective of a stepmother, and I'd been wondering and wondering how Comyns managed to find

> such a different (and yet wholly true) story within the original fairy tale [. . .]. I found my own way into Snow White by looking more closely at the 'fairest of them all' angle of the story. (Shiny New Books: n.p.)

The rivalry between the stepchildren in Comyns' novel is reconceptualised as one of race. In Comyns' version, the stepmother – Bella Winter – already has a mixed race daughter, Marline, when she marries. Bella understands the preference, shown by her husband, towards his own son in racial terms:

> when the children played together and Johnny cried because he couldn't have his own way, Bernard would appear from nowhere and accuse Marline of being rough with him [. . .]. When I looked at my daughter I loved her so much, and when I looked at my stepson, with his fairy-story red and white cheeks, it cut me to the heart and I'd think: 'He'll always come first with his father. Marline and I are nothing'. (Comyns 1985: loc. 2268)

Bella knows on one level that Marline's Blackness is of little significance to Bernard but she filters his favouritism through the prejudices of others. Bella identifies her daughter as 'beautiful' but even she finds it a 'bitter rapture' to love her dark child (Comyns 1985: loc. 304, 307). Bella's mother claims that she 'would have enjoyed a grandchild if it had been a normal one but illegitimacy combined with colour is too much' (Comyns 1985: loc. 863); and the nanny engaged to look after the baby son refuses to take Marline out on walks with her stepbrother, or to let them bathe together as if 'the darkness of [. . .] [her] skin might contaminate the water' (Comyns 1985: loc. 1364). In order to counter such prejudice, the 'red and white' favoured child has to die – accidentally killed by Bella in Comyns' version. In Comyns' tale, Vaz da Silva's chromatic analysis is realised as he explains it in terms of 'The Three Citrons.' The Black slave is 'the black aspect of the white-and-red heroine that appeared to be missing' and brings death just as Marline unwittingly does in *The Juniper Tree* (Vaz da Silva 2007: 247). Further, in parallel with Carter's 'The Snow Child', the 'black' element remains whilst it is the 'white' that vanishes from the text.

Oyeyemi may then have derived her interest in the conjunction of race within one family unit from Comyns. Similarly, it is the 'fairness' of Snow, set against Bird's darkness, which seals her fate. Boy is incensed by Snow's apparent show of affection to the baby Bird, which she interprets as malicious: 'She pressed the side of her face against the side of her sister's face as if showcasing the contrast between their features' (Oyeyemi 2014: 141). It is not at all certain in the book that Snow is aware of the power she holds because of her beauty; later in the book, a teenaged Bird wonders 'Does she know that she does this to people?', impressed by the gifts people bring Snow when she finally returns to Flax Hill (Oyeyemi 2014: 266). However, just like the other 'fair' children in 'Juniper Tree' variants, Snow has to be removed. In Boy's mind this will negate the comparative effect that is to the detriment of her own child. With the 'Snow White' cross-over in evidence, Snow is banished rather than killed, but the banishment has a fundamentally destructive effect on Snow's identity as she realises for the first time that she is not the White person she thought she was. It is in her interest in the visible (or not) differences of race, where Oyeyemi develops Comyns' premise; what is the effect of 'fairness' when both its meanings are considered: beautiful and light-skinned?

An answer can be approached via another parallel between Comyns' and Oyeyemi's novels. At first, Bella is the white-red-black heroine of *The Juniper Tree*: 'My black hair is [. . .] thick and glossy [. . .] My skin is fine and white, a healthy white, and my lips are red even without lipstick' (Comyns 1985: loc. 207): but then her face is scarred in a car accident (Comyns 1985: loc. 203). Bella is acutely conscious of this mar on her beauty, finding it a 'fearful disfigurement' even after two operations to diminish its effects (Comyns 1985: loc. 270). She still sees herself as she was reflected in the mirror at the hospital: 'the purple seam decorated with stitch marks, the half sneering mouth and leering eye' (Comyns 1985: loc. 256). It seems that the image in the mirror retains more power than the reality; when she overhears her co-workers discussing how 'She must have been beautiful before the accident' there is the distinct possibility that this only occurs in her imagination (Comyns 1985: loc. 263). This scar, rather than Bella's marriage, marks the beginning of her transformation from the heroine into stepmother as she might still be 'fair' (the injury is barely noticeable in reality (Comyns 1985: loc. 211; 269)) but can no longer claim to be the 'fairest.'

At the time of the accident, Bella has a boyfriend whose 'handsome face' identifies him as her Prince Charming. When he sees Bella's scar in the hospital he cries and Bella notes: 'I think he really did love me then. He took me back to the flat and loved me for at least a month' (Comyns 1985: loc. 262). Despite the fact that their relationship has been deteriorating, now he buys Bella 'beautiful scarves' to drape over her damaged face and becomes devoted to her care (Comyns 1985: loc. 262). This may be because, as the driver, he blames himself for the accident; but setting the text against Oyeyemi's version offers us another explanation – that there is an awful fascination with damaged beauty that goes beyond admiration of the unimpaired loveliness. Oyeyemi's Boy, too, has her equivalent of a handsome prince in Charlie Vacic. When he tells Boy's father, Frank, that he thinks Boy is 'beautiful', Frank's impulse is to damage that beauty. He drugs Boy and ties her up in the basement; when she regains consciousness, her face is numb and Frank is holding one of his starving rats to her face, apparently letting it chew her flesh in order to scar her. He tells her: 'There is no exquisite beauty without strangeness in the proportion [. . .]. Let's fix it so Charlie is truly mesmerized by you. Let's fix it so that he stares' (Oyeyemi 2014: 122). Frank asks: 'Do you think that if I scar you no one will love you?' asserting that: 'This will help you find your true love': true, if Charlie behaves as Bella's boyfriend does (Oyeyemi 2014: 122). Boy is actually untouched by the rat but ironically in preserving her 'ordinary' beauty, she cannot compete with Snow whose beauty is 'extraordinary' (Oyeyemi 2014: 78). Therefore, it is not only that Boy sends Snow away to protect her own daughter (referencing 'The Juniper Tree') but also an allusion to the wicked stepmother's jealously in 'Snow White.' After Bird's birth, Boy describes herself as 'grey-skinned with exhaustion, fat around the middle, my eyes were smaller than the bags beneath them, and Snow's daintiness grew day by day to menacing proportions' (Oyeyemi 2014: 142). Snow is sent away to show her that she 'is not the fairest of them all' (Oyeyemi 2014: 144).

Snow's beauty is not, of course, what it seems. It is as if she enchants those around her, provoking a universal adoration (Oyeyemi 2014: 139). This is the 'supernatural' beauty that Vaz da Silva associates with the colour white. Boy describes Snow as 'so abundantly beautiful that it feels contagious' and that excess appears to be the effect of Snow not being White at all (Oyeyemi 2014: 140). The fascination is produced through an equal capacity to attract and repel, like Bella's scarring in *The Juniper Tree*. It is the excess of mimicry produced by Snow – along with the rest of her family – pretending to be racially White when socially (and legally in the Southern States of America at this time) they are racially Black, a phenomenon known as 'passing.' For Snow's grandmother, Olivia Whitman, this is the only response to a segregated society. In the South, as she describes it to Boy, Black people are 'being kept down' (Oyeyemi 2014: 135). Even worse, Black people become only pale imitations of Whites:

> All the high-class places we were allowed to go to, they were imitations of the places we were kept out of [. . .] sitting at the bar or at the candlelit table you'd try to imagine what dinnertime remarks the real people were making [. . .] the white folks we were shadows of,

> and you'd try to talk about whatever you imagined they were talking about, and your food turned to sawdust in your mouth. (Oyeyemi 2014: 135–36)

In feeling that her whole life is fake, Olivia's choice is to take her whole family and, as she says, 'go north, let people take us how they take us' (Oyeyemi 2014: 136). She finds, though, in the North, the 'Same thing, only no signs' so that rather than being themselves, the family ironically are forced to enact their mimicry even more convincingly (Oyeyemi 2014: 136): to work at 'passing' all the time in order to be equal to the White families and not just, for example, when using a 'Whites Only' restroom.

What Snow represents then, is a defective beauty with a scarring that is more than skin deep; it is a consequence not of an individual deception, but of a sickness within society. As the adult Snow points out to teenaged Bird: 'you can't feel nauseated by the Whitmans [. . .] without feeling nauseated by the kind of world that's rewarded them for adapting to it like this' (Oyeyemi 2014: 218). However, it is not merely Whiteness that is valued in this 'kind of world', but beauty as well; to pass convincingly it is necessary to dazzle the White gaze. In literary representations of passing, it is not enough for women to have the features associated with being White (such as light skin, smooth hair, a high-bridged nose); they also have to be notable for their beauty. For example, in Nella Larsen's classic story, *Passing* (1929), Clare, who is passing for White, is 'incredibly beautiful' (Larsen 2014: 79), much like Snow being 'extraordinary-looking' (Oyeyemi 2014: 78). It is not just Snow but also her two grandparents who share those exquisite looks: 'Agnes [. . .] and Olivia were pretty good examples of lasting beauty [. . .] [and] clearly intended for Snow to be part of [the] long-lasting beauty club' (Oyeyemi 2014: 79). It could be argued that this is an enchantment, to dazzle and enrapture the Whites with an excess of what they expect beauty to be, which aligns with Vaz da Silva's associating black with enchantment.

Yet passing is not an enchantment, but a trick. As Boy sees it: 'Snow's beauty is all the more precious to Olivia [. . .] because it's a trick. When whites look at her [. . .] we don't see a coloured girl standing there. The joke's on us' (Oyeyemi 2014: 139). Snow, reflected in the White gaze, is not beautiful because she is 'white' (or fair) but rather, must be racially White because she is beautiful. The joke is not so much that Whites think Snow is White when she is in fact Black, but that Whites are oblivious to how enraptured they are by their own veneration of Whiteness. Black cannot be, is not, beautiful; they are sure of that. In fact, Vaz da Silva's use of 'The Three

Citrons' to illustrate the association of enchantments with blackness fails to be explicit regarding the actual actions of the Black slave. It is the princess who enchants herself to escape death by transforming into a dove, whilst the slave's claim to be the princess enchanted to look Black is just a trick.

There is, of course, a tradition of the trickster as a positive association with Blackness, deriving from Eshu, the Yoruba trickster and discussed, for example, in Henry Louis Gates Jr.'s signifyin(g) monkey figure, Br'er Rabbit, and Anansi the Spider, the Caribbean trickster (1988). In *Boy, Snow, Bird*, Bird recounts her conversations with the spiders in her room in which they are quite affronted that she knows stories about Anansi, who always gets the better of his enemies by his tricks (Oyeyemi 2014: 221). Like Anansi's victims, Boy has been entirely fooled by the Whitmans' 'confidence tricks' and feels hurt and bewildered by them (Oyeyemi 2014: 213). This illustrates the 'effect of mimicry on the authority of colonial discourse as profound and disturbing' (Bhabha 1994: 86). Bhabha suggests that the effect is to throw into relief the 'normalizing' nature of colonial discourse in a way that alienates 'its own language of liberty and produces another knowledge of its norms' (1994: 86). How true this is for Boy. She would like to think of herself as liberal and non-prejudiced (for example in her friendship with the Black teenager, Sidonie, who frequents the bookstore where Boy works). Yet, after Bird's birth when Arturo asks her if she would have married him if she had known he was Black she 'couldn't honestly answer yes or no' (Oyeyemi 2014: 133). The trick interpellates Boy as one of Them when she thought that she was one of Us, and through this Boy understands the inevitable outcome of her relationship with Bird. Although Boy claims that she stands 'with Bird in any Them versus Us situation', in fact 'all [Bird] hears is mumbling' aligning with Olivia's interpellation of Boy as actually one of Them (Oyeyemi 2014: 275, 274). Boy resists that interpellation by sending Snow away. It is hardly conscious as a response: when Bird asks her 'what Snow had ever done to her' all Boy can say is 'it was a good question', but it looks like an aggressive reassertion of White authority against the show of Black power enacted by Olivia adopting a position as trickster (Oyeyemi 2014: 240).

Boy, Snow, Bird does not clearly endorse mimicry as a positive strategy, though. Bhabha notes that 'the *menace* of mimicry is its *double vision* which in disclosing the ambivalence of colonial discourse also disrupts its authority' (1994: 88). Yet, Olivia's strategy, now it is overt, gives Snow a double vision of herself too. She explains to Bird: '*I was only eight years old [. . .] and nobody had ever told me to my face that I'm colored, so I knew it and didn't know it at the same time*' (Oyeyemi 2014: 211). She refuses Clara's interpellation of her as Black: '*don't say that about me. That's awful. It can't be true*' (Oyeyemi 2014: 211). It seems that both Boy and Snow suspect that they have misperceived themselves. By sending Snow away, Boy cannot make her life as it was before Bird was born; neither is Snow made more 'real' by having to accept a Black identity. Snow's capability to mimic a White ideal of beauty which is now exposed publically, has the greater effect of revealing that both beauty and race are merely constructs and not at all 'real'.

Bhabha's insistence that 'Mimicry conceals no presence or identity behind its mask' (1994: 88) would fit with Baudrillard's view of the hyperreal. Snow's ability to mimic White beauty is not a 'distorted truth' – Baudrillard notes that 'one can live with [that]' (1994: 5) – but induces 'metaphysical despair' because of the realisation that:

> the image didn't conceal anything at all, and that these images were in essence not images, such as an original model would have made them, but perfect simulacra, forever radiant with their own fascination. (Baudrillard 1994: 5)

Aptly, for retellings of 'Snow White', Baudrillard explains that ideas of 'abstraction' no longer operate in relation to representation such as the 'double, the mirror' (1994: 1). These rely on reflecting some original 'real'; rather simulation is 'the generation of models of a real without origin or reality: a hyperreal' (1994: 1). Boy describes Snow variously as 'a girl in Technicolor' and as a 'replica' (Oyeyemi 2014: 78, 195). There is no original or real model that Snow is replicating, only that fantasy of an ideal White beauty. Hence, passing exposes both Snow's and Boy's claims to be the 'fairest of them all' as empty posturing. As Baudrillard suggests, 'present day simulators attempt to make the real, all of the real, coincide with their models of simulation' (1994: 2). The simulation modelled by the colonial powers was of a racial difference that allowed a hierarchy to be drawn hence creating an idea of race that now is popularly assumed to be a biological reality.

Discussing 'Snow White', Gilbert and Gubar note that, 'the conflict between these two women [Snow White and her stepmother] is fought out largely in the transparent enclosures into which [. . .] both have been locked: a magic looking glass' for example (1984: 36). They differentiate between the first Queen (Snow's birth mother) and the next one in terms of the framing devices used in the narrative: 'To be caught and trapped in a mirror rather than a window [like the first Queen] [. . .] is to be driven inward, obsessively studying self-images as if seeking a viable self' (Gilbert and Gubar 1984: 37). This is not a description of a reflective process so much as the system according to Baudrillard:

> The whole system becomes weightless, it is no longer anything but a gigantic simulacrum – not unreal, but a simulacrum, that is to say never exchanged for the real, but exchanged for itself, in an uninterrupted circuit without reference or circumference. (1994: 5–6)

Boy, Snow, Bird suggests that both beauty and race are weightless systems of circulating simulacra. For example, the first description of Boy rehearses that image:

> I was fond of [mirrors], and believed them to be trustworthy. I'd hide myself away inside them, setting two mirrors up to face each other so that when I stood between them I was infinitely reflected in either direction. Many, many me's [sic] [. . .]. The effect was dizzying, a vast pulse, not quite alive, more like the working of an automaton. (Oyeyemi 2014: 3)

Right from the beginning of the novel, then, Boy's own presence as a replica is signalled. The warning about mirrors that nobody ever reveals to Boy, allowing her to be entrapped, is that mirrors also play tricks.

Mirrors pretend to be merely reflective of the self but, in fact, they only have the capability to generate simulacra. The self is not hidden but absent in the proliferation of simulacra produced by replication. In a review of *Boy, Snow, Bird*, Alex Clarke notes the allusion to Hitchcock's film *Vertigo*:

> Early on, Boy tells us about her white-blonde hair, her black eyes and her high forehead – put it together with her surname and you come up with Vertigo, that terrifying exploration of disguise and duplicity, in which Kim Novak plays twin roles. Like Hitchcock, Oyeyemi is interested not merely in what happens when you attempt to pass for someone else, but in the porous boundaries between one self and another. (Clark 2014: n.p.)

The mirror signifies such a border in the novel, but I suggest that its function is to question whether there is a possibility of recognising something called the self in a postmodern world. The possibility that the answer might be 'no' is what causes the 'panic' and despair identified by Baudrillard (1994: 7). When Boy marries Arturo, officially becoming a stepmother, the mirror simply reproduces another artifice:

> When I stood in front of the mirror, the icy blonde was there, but I couldn't swear to the fact of her being me. She was no clearer to me than my shadow was. I came to prefer my shadow. She came into the shower cubicle with me and stood stark against the bathroom tiles, so much taller than I was that when I began to get backaches, I could find shelter crouched under her. (Oyeyemi 2014: 128)

This function of mirrors is alluded to in Comyns' *The Juniper Tree*, when the disfigurement Bella sees in the mirror becomes the 'viable self' despite the reality of operations and time that reduces the scars actual effects and visibility. Other objects also have the power to generate models. Boy has a suspicion about the snake bracelet Arturo makes her when they get engaged: it coils around her arm from wrist to elbow, and prompts Boy's friend Mia to observe, 'could that scream "wicked stepmother" any louder?' (Oyeyemi 2014: 105). Boy muses: 'I can't discount the possibility that the [snake] bracelet's been moulding me into the wearer it wants' (Oyeyemi 2014: 141).

A similar reflective transformation happens to turn Frances into Frank. As Mia reports:

> [Frank] looked in the mirror one morning when he was still Frances, and this man she'd never seen before was just standing there, looking back [. . .] he flicked the surface of his side of the mirror [. . .] he said: 'Hi.' After that he acted just like a normal reflection. (Oyeyemi 2014: 294)

Frank 'passes' for a man because being a woman is as unbearably oppressive for him as being Black is for Olivia. Oyeyemi is not a writer who seeks to flatten out complexities so the two ways of passing are recognised as different although both are rooted in the concept of beauty. Frances's beauty is not an asset to be used in passing but a female jeopardy. Frances is a lesbian but for a 'male friend's younger brother' (Oyeyemi 2014: 293) her beauty is a consumable object for men, so he rapes her (as does the Count in 'The Snow Child'). One consequence of that rape is Boy. The other is Frances's fear of female beauty, solved by vanishing (much as the Snow Child dissolves in Carter's story) and being replaced by a male replica.

However, like racial passing, the creation of Frank appears to accept what are, after all, only social constructs, as inevitable or natural orders of being. They are absorbed into the weightless, 'gigantic simulacrum' (Baudrillard 1994: 7). It is true that the power of beauty and Whiteness is their naturalization. This seems to be the message of the story about the Magician co-written by Boy and Mia; in this, the Magician only has to suggest to live objects (trees, animals, people) what they should be and they transform (Oyeyemi 2014: 52–57). His most lucrative work is in making women more beautiful: 'He'd look into women's eyes and say: "You are a beauty," and she heard the words and believed them so deeply that her features fell into either lush, soft harmony, or heartbreakingly strict symmetry' (Oyeyemi 2014: 53). Frank's efforts to challenge the system of Beauty are a miserable failure; he abuses Boy and then tries to disfigure her. If he stops short at this point, it is perhaps because of his recognition that the cultural embeddedness of beauty is such that one violent act (or even the multiple violences he enacts on Boy's body) is not going to undermine its power. Beauty holds such sway that even non-beauty (the allure of the disfigured beauty or ugliness for example) cannot circumvent it.

What, then, is the solution? Or what challenge can be raised against beauty? Oyeyemi suggests that her interest in the wicked stepmother is to 'explore the way women disappoint each other' and the 'terrible things [that] can come out of that disappointment' (Hoggard 2014: n.p.). We could conclude then that the ending of *Boy, Snow, Bird* offers a triumphal solution of solidarity as that car-ful of women go to save Frances; a united group representing the blonde, the brunette, the dark and fair, Black and White, the daughter, the stepdaughter and the stepmother. That is a seductively neat conclusion with which Oyeyemi tempts us; of course the operations of power are not so easily overcome. Can Frances be found or, as Boy asks Mia: 'Do you think Frances is gone forever?' (Oyeyemi 2014: 297). If the hyperreal is operating then all that can be found is more artifice. Boy tells Mia to stop calling Frank 'him' but Mia argues: 'It's gone beyond alter egos [. . .] you have to ask if becoming someone else is more than some delusion or some dysfunction of the mind' (Oyeyemi 2014: 296). There is no authentic self to be found in hyper-reality, as Mia points out, because the model generates 'a real with no origin or reality' (Baudrillard 1994: 1).

It might be too late for Frank but perhaps Snow was, after all, saved by Boy. In sending Snow away Boy inadvertently saved her from Olivia, who would have chained Snow to her beauty, as Snow's mother might have done too. Snow asks: '*Would she have very delicately led me to believe that there's something about us Whitmans that isn't quite nice, something we've got to keep under control?*' (Oyeyemi 2014: 217). As it is, Snow now manages sometimes to elude mirrors and their simulating power. She explains to Bird in one of her letters: '*I don't always show up in mirrors [. . .]. It's a relief to be able to forget about what I might or might not be mistaken for. My reflection can't be counted on, she's not always there but I am so maybe she's not really me*' (Oyeyemi 2014: 207). This is in response to Bird's confession that mirrors sometimes do not reflect her either (Oyeyemi 2014: 156). In Bird's description, the mirror is almost maliciously searching for her and she has to elude it. The escape is not perfect; when she is caught in Boy's mirror helping her choose earrings by holding them up behind her she sees what the mirror makes of her: 'In the mirror I looked like her maid, and that made me want to throw the earrings at her head and run' (Oyeyemi 2014: 185). Like Snow, though, the absence of her reflection allows an eruption of the 'real' person into the text as opposed to those shadowy simulacra.

Bird has been protected by Boy in order to let her be real. When Bird agitates for Snow to visit, Boy wonders aloud, 'Bird, what would you have to say to a replica? You're so much yourself. Whatever else happens, don't let her mess that up' (Oyeyemi 2014: 196). By sending Snow away, Boy allows Bird to be herself and not the apparently racial inferior to Snow (who is, at best, a favoured light-skinned black girl, at worst a fake). Arturo is also far from dismayed at having a dark-skinned daughter. When Bird is born, Arturo:

> felt Bird was more [theirs], in a way he hadn't felt with Snow. He said for a long time he'd looked at Snow and seen her as Julia's child. Snow's beauty had seemed so strange to him for a while, so blank, like a brand-new slate (Oyeyemi 2014: 133).

She has a realness for Arturo and for Boy, 'Bird was beautiful too, with her close curls and bottomless eyes' – a real beauty perhaps because it is seen with a gaze of love rather than bedazzled adoration (Oyeyemi 2014: 134).

Oyeyemi's novel does not suggest that it is easy to find the real. When Snow instructs Boy in how to be a mother, one of her stipulations is: 'You have to come and find me if I get lost' (Oyeyemi 2014: 91). Boy replies: 'Let me think about that one. It's a big job' (Oyeyemi 2014: 92). Boy, of course is instrumental in Snow getting 'lost' in one way – by sending her away from home – but the text suggests that Snow is lost already long before Boy arrives, because of Olivia's choices to make her a replica. Frances too may not be able to be found. Retaining the fairy tale feel, Boy imagines Frances as under an enchantment. The bookshop owner for whom Boy works advises her on how to break a spell:

> magic spells only work until the person under the spell is really and honestly tired of it [. . .] Pester this person [. . .]. Make the enchantment inconvenient for them, find myriad ways to expose their contentment as false, show them that the contentment is part of the spell, engineered to make it last longer. (Oyeyemi 2014: 300)

This can perhaps be interpreted as a call for action. Snow has learnt an alternative and better way to counter White hegemony through direct action. Rather than trying to 'invent advantage – some of them have marched or staged sit-ins, others have just lived with their heads held high' (Oyeyemi 2014: 217). Yet Snow is not so 'found' or disenchanted that she is never tempted to be 'a deceiver' (Oyeyemi 2014: 231). When an altercation in a queue for a nightclub starts and a White man questions her associating with a group of Black people, assuming she is White, Snow does not challenge him: 'I felt as if I were standing over on the other side of a room, watching as a big lie was being told about me' (Oyeyemi 2014: 232). Allowing White people to assume she is White (re)incurs her unreality, but it is the easier option.

Oyeyemi's greatest challenge to the unreal, lies perhaps in the book itself. Ironically, the story (a fiction) is what allows egress into the real. As Ostriker notes, in revisionist mythmaking, 'the old stories are changed, changed utterly, by female knowledge of female experience, so that they can no longer stand as foundations of collective male fantasy' (1982: 73). Similarly, *Boy, Snow, Bird* changes our awareness of how race is encoded in many fairy tales through the construction of Whiteness through beauty's association with being the 'fairest of them all.' The texts embed race as a 'collective' social 'fantasy' as effectively as Ostriker suggests that they encode female sexuality. No reader of this text will ever be able to watch Disney's cartoon, or the film *Enchanted*, or pick up a children's book of fairy tales, or encounter any of the myriad other versions of this tale that exist without seeing the shadow of Snow, Bird and Boy standing behind the characters projected therein. Proliferation of objects may have alarmed Baudrillard, but when we retell stories 'each teller should add a little something of their own' so that we can see the world through a different lens (Oyeyemi 2014: 223).

Notes

1 There are many variants of both these tales and the analysis presented here should make sense to readers who have a familiarity with the main events and characters in the stories. Many of the versions in circulation are based on the tales originally written by The Brothers Grimm, hence if readers wish

to familiarise themselves with a starting point for either tale, they might refer to these variants. These are available on Project Gutenberg at http://www.gutenberg.org/files/2591/2591-h/2591-h.htm (NB 'Snow White' in this text is entitled 'Snowdrop'). These versions are apt for a discussion of gender as the Brothers Grimm versions are popularly interpreted as variants shaped by the patriarchal norms of eighteenth-century Europe.

2 There is much discussion over whether or not to use a capital when using 'black' as a racial designation. With the development of studies in whiteness, this debate is also beginning to encompass the use of 'white' to designate race. In this chapter, the further complication is that I want to make a connection between black and white as used in fairy tales to describe elements in setting, dress and so on, and the symbolic meanings that they take on (white for purity; black for evil, for example). Therefore, in this chapter, I am using Black and White with capitals to designate when the terms are being used to indicate race; and with lower case for colour. Where I want to indicate ambiguity in the term or a blurring of race and colour, I will use quotation marks.

Works Cited

Bacchilega, C. 1987: *Postmodern fairy tales: gender and narrative strategies.* Philadelphia: University of Pennsylvania Press.

Basile, G. 1911: *Stories from the Pentamerone.* London: Macmillan & Co. Translated by J. E. Talyor. http://www.surlalunefairytales.com/pentamerone/31threecitrons1911.html.

Baudrillard, J. 1994: *Simulacra and Simulation.* Translated by S. F. Glaser. Ann Arbor: University of Michigan Press.

Bhabha, H. 1994: *The Location of Culture.* London and New York: Routledge.

Brothers Grimm, 1823: *Grimms' Fairy Tales.* Translated by E. Taylor and M. Edwardes. Project Gutenberg. Available at: http://www.gutenberg.org/files/2591/2591-h/2591-h.htm.

Carter, A. 1979: *Tales from the Bloody Chamber and other stories.* London: Virago.

Comyns, B. 1985: *The Juniper Tree.* London: Methuen.

Diamond, J. 2014: Flavorwire Interview: *Boy, Snow, Bird* author Helen Oyeyemi on Fairy Tales and Feminists with Flawless Prose. *Flavorwire.* http://flavorwire.com/443678/flavorwire-interview-boy-snow-bird-author-helen-oyeyemi-on-fairy-tales-and-feminists-with-flawless-prose.

Gates, H.L. 1988: *The Signifying Monkey.* New York: Oxford University Press.

Gilbert, S. and Gubar, S. 1984: *The Madwoman in the Attic: The Woman Writer and the Nineteenth-Century Literary Imagination.* New Haven and London: Yale University Press.

Haase, D. 2004: Feminist Fairy-Tale Scholarship. In D. Haase (ed.), *Fairy Tales and Feminism: new approaches.* Detroit: Wayne State University Press, 1–36.

Hoggard, L. 2014: Helen Oyeyemi: 'I'm interested in the way women disappoint one another'. *Guardian.* http://www.theguardian.com/books/2014/mar/02/helen-oyeyemi-women-disappoint-one-another.

Ostriker, A. 1982: The Thieves of Language: Women Poets and Revisionist

Mythmaking. *Signs: Journal of Women in Culture and Society* 8 (1), 68–90.
Oyeyemi, H. 2014: *Boy, Snow, Bird*. London: Picador.
Sellers, S. 2001: *Myth and Fairy Tale in Contemporary Women's Fiction*. Houndmills, Basingstoke: Palgrave.
Shiny New Books. n.d.: Q & A with Helen Oyeyemi, Author of *Boy, Snow, Bird*. http://shinynewbooks.co.uk/bookbuzz01/q-and-a-with-helen-oyeyemi.

Simpson, H. 2006: Femme Fatale. *Guardian*. http://www.theguardian.com/books/2006/jun/24/classics.angelacarter.
Tatar, M. 2012: Snow White and the Huntsman. *Breezes from Wonderland*. http://blogs.law.harvard.edu/tatar/2012/06/08/snow-white-and-the-huntsman/.
Vaz da Silva, F. 2007: Red as Blood, White as Snow, Black as Crow: Chromatic Symbolism of Womanhood in Fairy Tales. *Marvels & Tales* 21 (2), 240–52.

Conclusions

Chloé Buckley and Sarah Ilott

This volume of essays has identified and explored a range of approaches to Oyeyemi's fiction in order to open up this important contemporary author's work to further academic discussion. As we maintained in our introduction, Oyeyemi's work eludes closure and cannot be made to serve one theoretical reading or political ideology in isolation. In this conclusion, we read Oyeyemi's recent collection of short stories, *what is not yours is not yours* (2016), as further revealing the elusive and unclassifiable nature of her fiction. Our reading of Oyeyemi's latest work suggests that the collection simultaneously supports readings of Oyeyemi's work already identified within this collection and opens up trajectories to new locations and ideas that suggest further avenues for critical exploration. We propose, further, that the collection typifies Oyeyemi's oeuvre in the way it produces a tension between the promise suggested by reading and writing as the site of shifting identifications and representations, and real political and social realities that always form the backdrop of deeply entrenched power divisions and resist such utopianism. In the spaces created in these fictions, Oyeyemi imagines new locations for identity production, but always offers a reminder of continuing real world barriers such as sexism, poverty, and racism.

In multiple ways, *what is not yours is not yours* is testament to the intangible, metaphorical power of writing as a revolutionary space of transformation. The collection presents many imaginary spaces that expand the territories of identity politics in Oyeyemi's ongoing project of writing subjectivities that have elsewhere been silenced, marginalised or othered. This opening up of imaginary territory for the writing of identity occurs through the rhizomatic structure of *what is not yours is not yours*, in many ways exemplifying the multiplicity and openness of the model of the book as rhizome offered by Gilles Deleuze and Félix Guattari. In *A Thousand Plateaus* (1980), the image of the rhizome counters the 'vapid idea' that the book offers an image of the world and the traditional linguistic model of tree and root: a static and hierarchical explanation of the process of signification (Deleuze and Guattari 1987: 6). They assert that the book produces multiple meanings through its various convergences and connections with other objects, discourses, organizations of power, and semiotic chains ((Deleuze and Guattari 1987: 4, 7). Oyeyemi's collection of short stories, like the body of work that it follows, exemplifies the multiplicity of the book as rhizome in the many tangents and interconnections it initiates, all of which combine to refuse an overarching or totalising reading.

Oyeyemi creates new worlds that suggest the hope contingent upon new beginnings and new affiliations through a complex network of characters. The connections between the stories in *what is not yours is not yours* produce a crisscrossing map of interconnections between characters and their histories. The technique Oyeyemi employs, effected through having characters appear in each other's stories, is also used by contemporary British novelist, David Mitchell, and, on a smaller scale, in the unsettling short fiction of American writer Shirley Jackson. Mitchell's novels thematically and formally explore the concept of interconnectedness, suggesting an expansive fictional universe whilst also focusing on detailed individual character studies (Clark 2015: n.p.). In contrast, the recurring names of characters in the short fiction of Jackson, such as *The Lottery and Other Stories* (1949), disrupt a novelistic impulse towards character psychology and development. Though names recur, character histories and identities are not developed, resulting in a sense of disconnection and fragmentation within and between stories. Oyeyemi employs both stratagems. The rhizomatic connections in *what is not yours is not yours* suggest an expansive interconnectedness that locates characters within a community beyond the story, and so within wider social relations. However, Oyeyemi also echoes the fragmentary nature of Jackson's loosely connected short stories. She gestures to lines of interconnection, but stops short of giving an overarching rationale. It is never clear when, in the narrative timeline, the interconnections and crossings between characters take place. The map the stories produce is not genealogical, producing a clear 'family tree'; nor is it teleological, since each subsequent story refers back and outwards to previous and forthcoming stories simultaneously. This creative cartography produces new territories of being and new possibilities for subjectivity through non-linear interconnection.

This rhizomatic structural map of the collection *in totum* is reproduced in miniature within each story. 'Books and Roses', for example, tells the story of the orphan Montse, but also that of the lovers Lucy and Safiye, and of Lucy's relationship with the gambler (and, by extension, the gambler's wife), of the intrigues between Safiye and Señora Fausta del Omo, and, tangentially, of the infidelities between Señor Artiga and Señora Valdes. These separate stories are loosely interconnected along multiple threads that lead not to a central tale, but fold back in on themselves as the story reaches its climax. Likewise, 'is your blood as red as this' begins as though it will tell the story of a blossoming love affair between two young women. However, when the protagonist is persuaded to join a school of puppetry, new characters enter the narrative and the story shifts focus away from this initial relationship. Following multiple tangents, including a history of the school's founder and a tale about an animated, perhaps even haunted, puppet, 'is your blood as red of this' ends up far beyond the territory of a tale of young love. The resolution to the story is startlingly different to the one its opening might have suggested, as it closes with an ambiguous and troubling performance by a puppeteer at the students' end of year show, which reveals the antagonistic and even damaging nature of the interrelationships the story has charted.

The rhizomatic nature of Oyeyemi's work resists a monumentalising account that might seek to put the meaning of the work into the service of a totalising critical reading or ideology. As a map of the book, the rhizome produces multiple meanings so that no one reading, or line of thought, dominates. Deleuze and Guattari explain the rhizome through the image of a puppet's strings, 'tied not to the supposed will of an artist or puppeteer but to a multiplicity of nerve fibers [sic], which form another puppet in other dimensions connected to the first' (1987: 8). In this description, as in Roland Barthes's theory of intertextuality explored in the introduction to this volume, the will or intentions of an artist are not the driving force of meaning in a work. Rather, the multiple strings of the puppet produce multiple directional movements. Fittingly, puppetry provides the theme of 'is your blood as red as this', in which the student puppeteer Radha gives over narration of the story to Gepetta, her puppet (named after Pinocchio's father and master in Carlo Collodi's 1881 novel *Le avventure di Pinocchio*). This shift in narrative perspective suggests that authorial or artistic control is relinquished, as the artistic work, or story, gains a life of its own. Later on, another student observes that she puts on puppet shows to '*see what we'd be like if we were actually in control of anything*', voicing an anxiety this collection has traced throughout Oyeyemi's fiction over how much control individuals exert over their subjectivities and identities when faced with forces beyond their control (2016: 132).

Oyeyemi develops puppetry as a theme not only to give expression to theoretical questions of artistic production, but also to explore anxieties over the fragility of subjectivity. In 'is your blood as red as this', the human characters become absent as the puppets gain motion and voice, the 'currency with which personhood is earned', drawing attention to the fragile and unfathomable nature of human subjectivity (Oyeyemi 2016: 129). Kenneth Gross's scholarly account of puppetry, which Oyeyemi references in the acknowledgements for the collection, suggests that the puppet embodies diverse and often contradictory identities at once, offering not a unified image of character, but an ability to move quickly from one identity to another 'always ready for metamorphosis' (2011: 24). Gross describes the art of puppetry as a partially violent, destructive act, as well as one of creative production, in the way puppets are dismembered and remade, asking 'is this a fracturing or expanding of the self?' (2011: 35). Oyeyemi's puppets echo this anxious question as they refigure tensions explored in her earlier works about fractured or otherwise fragile identities.

Though these anxieties about subjectivity continue to be voiced, Oyeyemi's short stories combine to increase the territory in which identity formation might take place. This expansion of territory is produced in the increasingly interconnected cast of characters, as well as in the variety of settings in which the story takes place, which incorporate real geographical locations as well as unreal, fairy tale spaces. Most of all, though, Oyeyemi expands the territory for the exploration of subjectivity through the nomadic, shifting nature of her narratives. To this end, *what is not yours is not yours* insists explicitly upon writing that is '*bigarrure*', the style requested by members of Cambridge's 'Homely Wench Society' in the sixth story of the collection. The narrator notes that '*bigarrure*' means 'a discourse running oddly and fantastically from one matter to another' (Oyeyemi 2016: 226). In this story, Dayang Sharif's contribution to the Homely Wench society is to suggest expanding the very concept of the 'homely wench' to someone who 'is not just content to accept an invitation but who wants more people to join the party, more and more and more' (Oyeyemi 2016: 238). As the rhizome 'acts on desire by external, productive outgrowths', the plot of the short story charts an expansive and inclusive movement outwards, one that seeks to increase its dimensions and expand its connections (Deleuze and Guattari 1987: 14, 8). Indeed, Day initiates a positive political and social function for the book itself when she suggests that the all-female society breaks into the building occupied by an exclusive male dining society, not to vandalize the building, but to swap the warring societies' collections of books, finding that their collection contained 'Plenty of stimulating-looking books, less than 10 percent of which were authored by women' (Oyeyemi 2016: 251). During the guerrilla book swap, Day, makes haphazard exchanges 'based on thought the titles or authors' names set in motion' (Oyeyemi 2016: 251). The book swap is explicitly modelled on her own rhizomatic thought processes, the odd connections she makes in her mind and 'the way she tried to tend them so that they thrived [. . .] a gardener growing thoughts' (Oyeyemi 2016: 249). In the story's optimistic conclusion, the book swap leads to a reconciliation between the members of the elite Bettencourt society and the Homely Wenches on the latter's terms, bringing together not only male and female students, but a multiplicity of identities, including gay characters, British Muslims, a self-identified 'Yorkshire Filipino', Greek students, the upper classes, and the economically less privileged. As Day asserts, 'when it comes to books and who can put things in them and get things out of them, it's all ours. And all theirs too' (Oyeyemi 2016: 247). Reading one of the exchanged books, Bettencourter Hercules describes the process as being smashed to pieces, then 'put back together in a wholly different order', a process that signifies the possibility of a 'new order', however painful the process (Oyeyemi, 2016: 254). This signifies the potential power of reading and writing for changing attitudes and remaking society anew.

In resisting structures of domination through her rhizomatic and anti-hierarchical writing style, Oyeyemi's work also continues to elude biographical criticism that might seek to fix the 'roots' of her fiction. In a recent interview, Oyeyemi explicitly disavows the influence of Nigeria on her work, despite the Yoruba elements in novels such as *The Icarus Girl* and *White Is for Witching*, possibly in response to biographical readings of her fiction that might label and, thus limit, the works as the product of a British Nigerian writer (Goodreads, 2016: n.p.). Explicitly rhizomatic, *what is not yours is not yours* maps multiple locations: From the Montserrat Sanctuary in Barcelona to a secret, locked library; from the village of Bezin, Iran to the 'House of Locks' in Ipswich; from Cambridge's Homely Wench Society to Cheshire's Hotel Glissando; from the Radhost mountain in the Czech Republic to less readily identifiable faery locations, this map has 'multiple entryways' depending on who is narrating whose story (Deleuze and Guattari 1987: 12). As in previous works like *Boy, Snow, Bird* and *Mr Fox*, Oyeyemi relocates and rewrites the European fairy tale tradition. Here, the fairy tale world mingles with recognisable, modern social spaces. Often, these spaces are explicitly located in a 'real' social world, as towns, counties and countries are named. However, these 'real' places also exist on the intersections of an interconnected global map, becoming liminal as they are shaped by the characters' migrant histories. Many of Oyeyemi's characters hail from or identify with places other than that in which the story plays out.

The sense of dislocation often experienced by her characters is reflected in Oyeyemi's eclectic selection of literary sources and styles. *what is not yours is not yours* draws on lesser known folk and fairy tales from Eastern Europe such as the literary folk tales of Czech writer Karel Jaromir Erben in 'dornička, and the st martin's day goose.' It also makes reference to canonical literary characters, like Goethe's Faust in 'books and roses' and the Italian puppet theatre in 'is your blood as red as this?' None of these sources are the roots of the fiction, and none provide a definitive meaning. As Deleuze and Guattari note, 'to be rhizomorphous is to produce stems and filaments that seem to be roots [. . .] but put them to strange new uses' (1987: 15). This definition offers an apt description of Oyeyemi's works, which may point to Nigeria as one potential 'root', but quickly offer trajectories and lines that lead off to other locations and imaginative spaces. Many of these stories seem to map a potential future space, too. 'freddy barandov checks . . . in?' hints at a dystopian Britain through references to an authoritarian government, which punishes the protagonist's father for repairing clock towers without authorisation as a potentially seditious political act and who controls artistic production through non-democratic literary awards that the recipients have no choice but to accept. In this way, Oyeyemi tangentially maps 'even realms that are yet to come' (Deleuze and Guattari 1987: 5).

Indeed, many of the spaces Oyeyemi maps in *what is not yours is not yours* are heterotopic in the sense suggested by Michel Foucault, as they simultaneously represent, contest and distort contemporary social worlds (1997: 333). Mapping diverse heterotopic fictional spaces, this latest work continues the project of Oyeyemi's previous novels to deterritorialize and defamiliarise readers. Deleuze and Guattari insist that writing is a political act in precisely this sense, since it forms a rhizome and so 'increase[s] your territory by deterritorialisation' (1987: 11). In *what is not yours is not yours* Oyeyemi's rhizomatic stories continue to expand the space that her fiction produces and imagines, beyond those that we explore in this volume. And yet, these heterotopic spaces are not only metaphorical or imaginative, nor are they straighforwardly utopian. Oyeyemi continues to remind the reader of the legacies of British colonialism (and its roots in the growth of capitalism), here focusing on communities and larger networks of relationships that serve to foreground contemporary global flows of capital and power. Whilst the tales shift around Europe (predominantly), characters that reappear on multiple occasions signify the interconnectedness of the world that the author creates, which reflects on the interconnectedness of the real world that her stories refract and critique.

By foregrounding real-world power relationships and the material basis of relationships, Oyeyemi's works resist the kind of criticism identified by Neil Lazarus in *The Postcolonial Unconscious*, in which he bemoans the narrowing of the discipline of postcolonial studies, due to an overemphasis on 'a discrete culture tendency' (pomo-postcolonialism) coupled with a severing of capitalism from the concepts of colonialism and imperialism (2011: 34–36). Oyeyemi's writing calls upon us as critics to resist this tendency, as postmodern narrative techniques and representations of subjectivity are perennially related to real-world politics in her work. In *White Is for Witching* for example – a novel concerned with the negotiation of borders in a highly metaphorical sense – the local refugee asylum is centralised, serving as a reminder that the ludic negotiation of borders is not possible for those forced to abandon homes and nations as a result of conflict or disaster. Noting this concern in Oyeyemi's work for both the symbolic potential of language as a force for change and hope alongside the embeddedness of her characters and locales in real-world politics, this collection has been sensitive to the material, political and economic systems that lead to disenfranchisement, as well as to the effects of cultural and epistemological subjugation, highlighting their interconnectedness. So, though Ilott's chapter on female appetite and voice focuses primarily on the symbolic richness of hunger as a motif in Oyeyemi's work, it also recognises that the realities of hunger due to malnutrition haunt the texts.

A concern with capitalism as the basis of unequal power relations past and present, as well as the classist economic politics evident in austerity measures operating across Europe and beyond since the global financial crisis of 2007–8, are increasingly apparent in *what is not yours is not yours*. In this manner, Oyeyemi's collection serves as a timely reminder and corrective to scholarship of postcolonial literature that has overlooked the material, capitalist basis of colonialism, a trend rightly identified by Lazarus (2011). Though phrased in the tautological language of the fairy tale, the title of Oyeyemi's short story collection – *what is not yours is not yours* – is an overt reference to ownership that plays out through both the mythical places summoned by the tales' imagery and their real-world referents. Weaving throughout each of the stories are references to the literal and metaphorical locks and keys that are used to maintain ownership, highlighting the power relations between those who have access and those who are locked out, or disenfranchised. Oyeyemi's locks and keys implicitly recall traditional fairy tales such as 'Bluebeard'

(Perrault 1697) and 'Rapunzel' (Brothers Grimm 1812), in which locks and keys maintain control. Symbolically rich and structurally difficult, the tales nevertheless offer a lucid appraisal of the inequalities created and exacerbated by contemporary economics. In the more fairy tale-like 'drownings', the narrator notes that 'every day there was news that made you say "Oh really." Some new tax that only people with no money had to pay' (Oyeyemi 2016: 57). This political upfrontness can leave readers with no doubt as to the contemporary relevance of the story.

Indeed, 'drownings' encapsulates Oyeyemi's literal and metaphorical engagement with ownership particularly well, and lends itself to be read as a cutting satire on a contemporary world in which the growing number of impoverished people are demonised and increasingly atomised, whilst the wealthy minority exert power in a self-serving and ruthless manner. The tale concerns a man named Arkady, who hatches a plan born of desperation. First, he must throw into a fire a key to an apartment from which he has been evicted after failing to pay the rent, in order to 'put an end to the longing' (Oyeyemi 2016: 166). Then, he intends to kidnap the daughter of the tyrant ruler of the country in order to petition said tyrant to 'take his damn foot off the nation's neck and let everybody breathe' (Oyeyemi 2016: 167). However, Arkady's plan is foiled when he is arrested and imprisoned for setting fire to the building from which he had been evicted – a crime for which there is scant evidence and that he cannot remember having committed. Arkady's economic position, which leads to the feverish behaviour that triggers the events of the plot, is foregrounded clearly at the outset:

> He probably wouldn't have done it if he'd had his head on straight, but it's not easy to think clearly when rent is due and there isn't enough money to pay it, and one who relies on you falls ill for want of nourishment but you have to leave him to walk around looking for work to do. (Oyeyemi 2016: 153)

The multiple 'buts' and 'ands' point to the mounting pressure exerted on Arkady, whilst the inclusion of the second person 'you' generalises his situation and implicates readers. The tale effectively offers an insight into the sense of powerlessness and alienation contingent with poverty, as Arkady finds himself confronted with powers and structures beyond his control, leading him increasingly to 'wish[] misfortune upon everyone he saw' (Oyeyemi 2016: 155).

This poverty-induced alienation is also reflected in the atomisation of the apartment block's residents, signified by their lack of realisation that one key opens every door in the building. The insidious structures that reinforce patterns of impoverishment are referenced through the story's title: 'drowning.' Whilst this is an overt reference to the tyrant's preferred method of punishment, it is also aligned with the structural means that ensure that Arkady 'could hardly keep afloat' (Oyeyemi 2016: 164). These structural causes of drowning in debt point to institutionalised modes of disenfranchisement that (the double meaning of the tale's title implies) are no less damaging than the overt violence of the actual drownings inflicted by the tyrant.

Another continuing concern of Oyeyemi's fiction relating to real-world politics is referenced at the end of 'drownings'; this is the focus on the damage inflicted on women by other women that is a key feature of the fairy tale tradition (discussed in Ormond's and Cousins' chapters in this collection). The story finishes as the tyrant's daughter, Eirini the Fair, sets out to rescue Arkady from his prison cell. As she leaves, she sees her mother, who 'wistfully rocked an invisible baby, motions easily interpretable as an appeal for grandchildren' – a gesture that Eirini the Fair pretends 'she hadn't seen' (Oyeyemi 2016: 178). This light-hearted reference to the centralisation of the romantic plot to stories involving women and the unfair expectations placed by mothers upon daughters is taken up in a number of the short stories. Though many of these tales could be considered contemporary fairy tale rewritings, Oyeyemi does not create a narrative of the progress of feminism. As with much of Oyeyemi's previous fiction, there is a tension between affection and antagonism that defines the female friendships and relationships portrayed therein, whilst the ever-present effects of patriarchy – albeit in ever-changing forms – are frequently referenced. These factors combine to ensure that in employing and transforming a fairy tale tradition steeped in misogyny through its depiction of women as passive objects of exchange, Oyeyemi does not create a utopian vision of female progress that would imply in the manner of post-feminism that the struggle has been won.

Many of the chapters in this collection have been concerned with Oyeyemi's representation of the physical and emotional abuse of women alongside the structures and ideologies that support sexism, through explorations of beauty, eating disorders, psychological breakdown, and intersections with racism. *what is not yours is not yours* continues in this vein with tales that revolve around current concerns affecting women, including abuse, violence, consent, and online bullying. '"sorry" doesn't sweeten her tea' sees teenage Aisha grieving for a popstar, Matyas Füst, who stands accused of physically assaulting a woman whom he has paid for sex. Starting from the premise so often adopted when a famous man is accused of a violent or sexual crime, Aisha's immediate response is to suggest to her sister 'Maybe it isn't true, Day? It probably isn't true' (Oyeyemi 2016: 70). Indicative of contemporary trolling of women on the internet, the woman who has made the accusation – along with the few who stand in solidarity – are treated with a misogynist cocktail of scepticism and scorn, ranging from assumptions that the woman is lying, to suggestions that '*she should count herself lucky: men probably treat broken down old whores worse than that in her own country*', to death threats (Oyeyemi 2016: 74).[1] Refusing to paint the internet as a heterotopia of possibility, Oyeyemi portrays it as a new avenue for violence against women.

The systemic violence of the objectification of women is also taken up in 'is your blood as red as this?' in which Radha's brother insists on 'marking girls' physical appearance out of ten' and 'a brief history of the homely wench society', in which the eponymous society is composed of women listed as potential muses for a Bettencourter searching for 'a girl whose very name conjured up the idea of ugliness the same way invoking Helen of Troy did for beauty' (Oyeyemi 2016: 105; 221). Equally, the short story collection references the lingering sexism that sees sons as heirs before their female counterparts, as despite the fact that his 'younger sister Odette is much handier', the male protagonist of 'freddy barrandov checks . . . in?' is required to take on the family trade (Oyeyemi 2016: 282). By focalising this tale through the male protagonist, Oyeyemi is also able to show the damage that sexist structures can do to men, in a manner that has not previously come to the forefront of her work.

Reflecting Oyeyemi's own antipathy for definitive conclusions, there is no tidy way of conclusively summarising this collection. Resolutely rhizomatic in its networks of characters, places and intertexts, questioning of totalising systems and structures, and blurring the lines of the richly symbolic and the depressingly mundane, these works at once offer new possibilities for knowing and being and confront characters and readers with political realities that cannot be imagined out of existence. To attempt to make greater claims for Oyeyemi's literature would be disingenuous, and as such this collection has been contained to opening up a variety of readings that exist simultaneously, and sometimes in tension. The intention of this work has been to raise the profile of Oyeyemi's oeuvre by indicating avenues for exploring this rich, complex, and important body of work. In turn, we hope that this will open the field of study up to new and varied approaches.

Notes

1 See, for example, Caroline Criado-Perez's account of online threats received by herself and other feminist activists in *Do It Like a Woman . . . and Change the World* (2015: 116–27).

Works Cited

Clark, J. C. 2015: The Ever-Expanding World of David Mitchell. *Literary Hub.* http://lithub.com/the-ever-expanding-world-of-david-mitchell/

Criado-Perez, C. 2016: *Do It Like a Woman . . . and Change the World.* London: Portobello.

Deleuze, G. and Guattari, F. 1987 [1980]: *A Thousand Plateaus.* Translated by Brian Massumi. Minneapolis: University of Minnesota Press.

Foucault, M. 1997: Of Other Spaces: Utopias and Heterotopias. Translated by Jay Miskowiec. In N. Leach (ed.) *Rethinking Architecture: A Reader in Cultural Theory.* New York: Routledge, 330–36.

Goodreads, 2016: Interview with Helen Oyeyemi. *Goodreads.* https://www.goodreads.com/interviews/show/1111.Helen_Oyeyemi?utm_medium=email&utm_source=newsletter&utm_campaign=2016-03&utm_content=oyeyemi.

Gross, K. 2011: *Puppet. An Essay on Uncanny Life.* Chicago: University of Chicago Press.

Lazarus, N. 2011: *The Postcolonial Unconscious.* Cambridge: Cambridge University Press.

Oyeyemi, H. 2016: *what is not yours is not yours.* New York: Riverhead Books.

The Editors and Contributors

Nicola Abram

Nicola is Lecturer in Literatures in English at the University of Reading, UK. Her research interests centre on postcolonial, black British and feminist writing, and she has recently published on contemporary playwrights debbie tucker green and Winsome Pinnock. Nicola is Vice-Chair for the international and interdisciplinary Postcolonial Studies Association. She also works to widen participation in the study of literature and languages.

Chloé Buckley

Chloé is a Senior Lecturer at Manchester Metropolitan University. She researches children's gothic fiction and gothic fantastika. Recent publications include a chapter on 'Remaking the Weird in contemporary Children's Fiction' in *New Directions: Gothic Children's Fiction* (Routledge 2017) and 'Gothic and the Child Reader, 1850–Present', in *The Gothic World* (Routledge 2014). Recent journal articles include 'How monsters are made: "No remorse, no pity" in Shelley, Dickens and Priestley's *Mister Creecher*' (*Horror Studies* 2016) and, with Sarah Ilott, 'Supplementary twins and abject bodies in Helen Oyeyemi's *The Icarus Girl*' (*The Journal of Commonwealth Literature* 2015).

Katie Burton

Katie is an MA student in English Studies at Teesside University, UK. She has previously presented papers on female voice and the negotiation of national identity in the work of Helen Oyeyemi. Her main research interests include postcolonial writing, queer theory and Neo-Victorianism.

Helen Cousins

Helen Cousins is a Reader in Postcolonial Literature at Newman University, Birmingham, UK. She researches in African women's writing and contemporary black British literature. Recent publications on Oyeyemi include a chapter in *Blackness in Britain* (Routledge, 2016). She is an editor for *The Literary Encyclopaedia (African cultures and literatures desk)* and is on the Advisory Board of

Postcolonial Interventions: An Interdisciplinary Journal of Postcolonial Studies.

Natalya Din-Kariuki
Natalya is a Stipendiary Lecturer in English Literature at Worcester College, Oxford. Her research interests include the literary and intellectual history of the sixteenth and seventeenth centuries, rhetoric and hermeneutics, contemporary African literature, and various strands of critical theory. She is currently completing a DPhil at Hertford College, Oxford, where she is a Drapers' Senior Scholar. Her doctoral thesis reconstructs the theory and practice of early modern rhetorical invention, the discovery of arguments and proofs, using travel writing as a case study.

Anita Harris Satkunananthan
Anita is a Senior Lecturer at the National University of Malaysia. She holds a PhD in Postcolonial Literature from the University of Queensland. Her grant-funded research looks at the significance of textual 'ghosts' in the Gothic fictions of cosmopolitan women writers from the African diaspora.

Sarah Ilott
Sarah Ilott is a Research Lecturer in English Studies at Teesside University, UK. Her main research and teaching interests are in postcolonial literature and genre fiction, particularly comedy and the gothic. Her first monograph is entitled *New Postcolonial British Genres: Shifting the Boundaries* (Palgrave, 2015). Sarah is the membership secretary for the Postcolonial Studies Association, interviews editor for *Postcolonial Text*, and is on the Advisory Board of *Postcolonial Interventions: An Interdisciplinary Journal of Postcolonial Studies.*

Jo Ormond
Jo is a research student in the Department of English and Creative Writing at Lancaster University. She is interested in representations of femininity in contemporary retellings of fairy tales and combines feminist readings of the texts with current debates about the relation between young women and society as represented in the media and popular culture.

David Punter
David Punter is a critic, poet and writer, currently Professor of Poetry at the University of Bristol and Co-Director of the Bristol Poetry

Institute. He has published extensively on the Gothic; on romantic writing; on the contemporary and modern novel; on literary theory, metaphor and modernity. A CD of his poems, *Flashes in the Dark*, became available in 2014.

Index

Literary and critical works can be found under authors' names.